Other Kaplan Books Relating to Business School Admissions:

GMAT CAT

GMAT CAT with CD-ROM

GRE/GMAT Workbook

Guide to Distance Learning

Yale Daily News Guide to Fellowships and Grants

M.B.A. Part-Time:
An Insider's Guide

by Robyn Frank-Pedersen

Simon & Schuster

NEW YORK · LONDON · SINGAPORE · SYDNEY · TORONTO

Kaplan Publishing
Published by Simon & Schuster
1230 Avenue of the Americas
New York, NY 10020

For bulk sales to schools, colleges, and universities, please contact Order Department, Simon & Schuster, 100 Front Street, Riverside, NJ 08075. Phone: (800) 223-2336. Fax: (800) 943-9831.

Project Editor: Megan Duffy

Contributing Editors: Trent Anderson, Albert Chen, and Ben Baron

Cover Design: Cheung Tai

Interior Page Layout: Laraine Giordano

Production Editor: Maude Spekes

Production Manager: Michael Shevlin

Executive Editor: Del Franz

Special thanks to: Rebecca Argyle, Doreen Beauregard, Jude Bond, Shari Holmer Lewis, Alison May, Kiernan McGuire, Alice Murphey, Jobim Rose, Julie Schmidt, James W. Schmotter, Joyce Smith, and Linda Volpano.

Manufactured in the United States of America

Published simultaneously in Canada

January 2001

10 9 8 7 6 5 4 3 2 1

ISBN: 0-7432-0188-4

Table of Contents

Preface vii

A Special Note for International Students xi

Part One: GETTING DOWN TO BUSINESS

    Chapter 1: The ABC's of the M.B.A. 3

    Chapter 2: What Are Your Options? 9

    Chapter 3: Should You Get Your M.B.A. Part Time? 21

    Chapter 4: What You Can Expect 39

Part Two: SELECTING THE RIGHT SCHOOL AND PROGRAM

    Chapter 5: Evaluating Business Schools 49

    Chapter 6: Finding the Program for You 59

Part Three: ADMISSIONS

    Chapter 7: How Do Schools Evaluate Applicants? .77

    Chapter 8: Preparing Your Application 97

    Chapter 9: Recommendations 103

    Chapter 10: Interviewing Successfully 109

    Chapter 11: Writing Your Essay 121

Part Four: FINANCING YOUR M.B.A.

Chapter 12: Planning Your Investment 145

Chapter 13: Financial Aid, Scholarships, and Loans 149

Part Five: THE PART-TIME EXPERIENCE

Chapter 14: Opening-Night Jitters 169

Chapter 15: What the Experts Say 173

Chapter 16: What the Students Say 191

Chapter 17: The M.B.A. at Work 205

Appendix A: FOR YOUR INFORMATION

Frequently Asked Questions 221

Useful Resources 227

Appendix B: DIRECTORY OF U.S. BUSINESS SCHOOLS

The Business School Directory 237

Alphabetical Index of Business Schools 239

Business Schools with Part-Time M.B.A. Programs 253

Distance Learning M.B.A. Programs 277

Preface

When I was in college, I had no clue what I wanted to do with the rest of my life. In fact, for someone who grew up in the "big city," I was surprisingly naïve. One thing was certain; I knew that attending a good university would ensure at least a few open doors. Or so I thought. After all, isn't life like the movies? You work hard, obtain your degree, and magically land the perfect job complete with fame, fortune, and satisfaction, and everyone lives happily ever after, "The End"? Okay, so I was a little green— just bear with me.

So there I was, graduating from Brandeis University, my whole life ahead of me, but unsure of where I was headed. Armed with a psychology degree, I was ready to . . . I had no clue! Back in New York City, I used my connections to land several jobs: assistant to the fashion editor at a woman's magazine, travel agent, gofer at my father's office. All in all, nothing particularly meaningful or permanent.

To my surprise, the degree that I thought would open so many doors essentially led me to: "How many words per minute can you type?" Using my language skills, I settled on the first administrative position that I was offered. Landing in a French commercial bank appeared arbitrary at first, but things started falling into place and I realized that I was beginning to find my niche.

Convincing people that I could type and actually doing it were two very separate things. In time I figured it out, but I seemed more adept with figures than words and was soon transferred to the accounting area. One thing led to another; one year flowed into the second and the third and the fifth. My direct supervisor at the time was pursuing her M.B.A. at night. When her husband was transferred to South America and she left the bank, I was alone, trying to fill her very large shoes. Maybe it was my family background (as the youngest of three girls, I was always trying to please and make things right) or my competitive nature (conquer the next obstacle), but I really needed, at that juncture, to prove myself. My bosses felt that I was not ready to take over the vice president position that was recently vacated. They did permit me, however, to do all the work and put in the hours that that position entailed. The lesson I learned was the following: my soft skills needed fine-tuning and I was not experienced enough to take on the management position of a vice president. Time would take care of the latter, but I needed something else to cure the former.

Many, many months of long hours and increasing responsibilities with small promotions and little salary increases led me to another decision. All the kudos and pats on my back at work were not going to get me that big promotion. What would guarantee it is that little square piece of paper called a diploma. My decision was made, and off I went to B-school. The decision of where to go was easy: I followed in the footsteps of my predecessor and attended Fordham University. Going at night would ensure that I would be next in line for the big promotion. The big joke was that in my situation, after taking two or three classes per trimester, I was still getting home earlier than I used to from the office! My office was footing the bill and I was a hero.

However, at 30 years old, I was unmarried, working late each night, going to school after work and spending my entire weekends in the stacks at the Fordham library. These were the few concessions I made, yet I never doubted my decisions. My one wish was that I had had a better idea of everything that I was getting into—a guide. Attending school while maintaining a full workload is an extremely challenging and ultimately rewarding endeavor. Being prepared for what lies ahead is a student's best weapon, which is why I was determined to impart some "insider info" to future part-timers.

* * *

Having recently returned to Fordham University to talk with some administrators as part of the research for this book, I was so surprised—and impressed—by the variety of programs now offered. Some were available almost 10 years ago when I started my M.B.A., unbeknownst to me, and I seriously regret not having involved or immersed myself further in the program. I did not do the one thing I advise all of you to do: adequate research. I followed in my boss' footsteps and in the process did a disservice to myself. Had I investigated the various available programs, I may have benefited more from my degree and the M.B.A. experience in general. It was my mistake; don't let it be yours. (Since graduation, I have gone back to Fordham University and audited several courses for a very nominal fee—a wonderful benefit awarded to alumni.)

In the next chapters, I will share with you some of my experiences as well as suggestions from your peers, colleagues, employers and educators. I hope to share with you some of my insights—things I wish someone had told me when I was going through the process.

Let's start off with my first piece advice: You can obtain only one M.B.A. Don't rush into it—do your homework carefully and select or create the program that is right for you.

A Special Note for International Students

The M.B.A. (Master of Business Administration) has become a degree of choice for businesspersons around the globe. Variations of U.S.-style M.B.A. programs exist in Asia, Europe, and the Americas. In recent years, hundreds of thousands of international students have studied business and management in the United States.

As the United States increases its participation in the global economy, U.S. business schools are reaching out to attract exceptional international candidates into their graduate programs. However, competition for admission to prestigious programs is heavy, and international students need to plan carefully if they wish to enter a top U.S. graduate management program.

If you are not from the United States, but are considering attending a graduate management program at a university in the United States, here is what you'll need to get started.

If English is not your first language, start there. You will probably need to take the Test of English as a Foreign Language (TOEFL) or show some other evidence that your proficient in English prior to gaining admission to a graduate program in business. Some graduate business schools now require a minimum TOEFL score of 550 (213 on the computer-based TOEFL), while others will require a minimum of 600 (250 on the computer-based TOEFL). The ability to communicate in English, both verbally and in writing, is extremely important to your success in a U.S. M.B.A. program.

You may also need to take the GMAT (Graduate Management Admissions Test). Some graduate business programs may require you to take the GRE (Graduate Record Examination) as well.

Since admission to many graduate business programs is quite competitive, you may wish to select three or four programs you would like to attend and complete applications for each program.

Select a program that meets your current or future employment needs, rather than simply a program with a big name. For example, if you hope to work in the hotel and tourism industry, make sure the program you choose specializes in that distinct area.

You need to begin the application process at least a year in advance. Be aware that many programs only offer August or September start dates. Find out application deadlines and plan accordingly.

Finally, you will need to obtain an 1-20 Certificate of Eligibility from the school you plan to attend if you intend to apply for an F-1 Student Visa to study in the United States.

KAPLAN INTERNATIONAL PROGRAMS

If you need more help with the complex process of business school admissions, assistance preparing for the TOEFL or GMAT, or help improving your English skills in general, you may be interested in Kaplan's programs for international students.

Kaplan International Programs were designed to help students and professionals from outside the United States meet their educational and career goals. At locations throughout the United States, international students take advantage of Kaplan's programs to help them improve their academic and conversational English skills, raise their scores on the TOEFL, GMAT, and other standardized exams, and gain admission to the schools of their choice. Our staff and instructors give international students the individualized instruction they need to succeed. Here is a brief description of some of Kaplan's programs for International Students:

General Intensive English

Kaplan's General Intensive English classes are designed to help you improve your skills in all areas of English and to increase your fluency in spoken and written

English. Classes are available for beginning to advanced students, and the average class size is 12 students.

English for TOEFL and University Preparation

This course provides you with the skills you need to improve your TOEFL score and succeed in an American university or graduate program. It includes advanced reading, writing, listening, grammar, and conversational English, plus university admissions counseling. You will also receive training for the TOEFL using Kaplan's exclusive computer-based practice materials.

English and GMAT

This course includes a combination of English instruction and GMAT test preparation. Our English and GMAT course is for students who need to boost their English skills while preparing for the GMAT and graduate business school.

GMAT Test Preparation Course

The Graduate Management Admissions Test (GMAT) is required for admission to many graduate programs in business in the United States. Hundreds of thousands of American students have taken this course to prepare for the GMAT. This course includes the skills you need to succeed on each section of the GMAT, as well as giving you access to Kaplan's exclusive computer-based practice materials.

Other Kaplan Programs

Since 1938, more than 3 million students have come to Kaplan to advance their studies, prepare for entry to American universities, and further their careers. In addition to the above programs, Kaplan offers courses to prepare for the SAT, GRE, LSAT, MCAT, DAT, USMLE, NCLEX, and other standardized exams at locations throughout the United States.

APPLYING TO KAPLAN INTERNATIONAL PROGRAMS

To get more information, or to apply for admission to any of Kaplan's programs for international students and professionals, contact us at:

Kaplan International Programs
370 Seventh Avenue
New York, NY 10001 USA
Telephone: (212) 492-5990
Fax: (917) 339-7505
E-mail: world@kaplan.com
Web: www.kaptest.com
Kaplan is authorized under federal law to enroll nonimmigrant alien students.
Kaplan is authorized to issue Form IAP-66 needed for a J-1 (Exchange Visitor) visa.
Kaplan is accredited by ACCET (Accrediting Council for Continuing Education and Training).
Test names are registered trademarks of their respective owners.

PART ONE

Getting Down to Business

CHAPTER 1

The ABC's of the M.B.A.

Over the past few decades, the Master of Business Administration—otherwise known as the M.B.A.—has become the most visible and popular of graduate degrees. With it comes a certain amount of clout and prestige that is unparalleled. More than 90,000 M.B.A. degrees are awarded annually in the United States alone, and the numbers of programs and graduates are proliferating all around the world. In both the business press and more popular media, the behavior and career prospects of M.B.A.'s are repeatedly described, analyzed, and stereotyped. The global selection process for admission to the M.B.A. programs has developed a life of its own, producing hundreds of thousands of GMAT examinations every year, numerous guides and publications, a worldwide recruiting network of admissions forums, and sophisticated ranking systems designed to provide information to prospective consumers of M.B.A. education.

Yet all this media hype has also produced negative publicity. As far back as 1980, a cover story in *Time*, "The Golden Ticket," described in unflattering terms "what M.B.A.'s have done to us." This theme continued throughout the decade of the 1980s, when soaring Wall Street salaries, greed, and M.B.A.'s became synonymous. In the '90s, M.B.A.'s—with their command of quantitative financial analysis and the latest management theories—were often held responsible for corporate downsizing, shifting of manufacturing overseas, and other scary aspects of 1990s capitalism. The most recent threat to the M.B.A. comes on the heels of the "dot-com" craze, as more and more B-school candidates are turning to Internet companies, with their promise of fast fortunes and generous stock options, in lieu of the traditional—and more time-intensive—education route.

So what does this all mean for you, someone who's considering whether or not an M.B.A. is worth the time, effort, and money it will require?

It's necessary to cut through the marketing and media hype to understand a few things about the multifaceted, evolving phenomenon we call M.B.A. education. The fact is that the M.B.A. remains a very good investment for most business careers. For some careers—for example, investment banking or management consulting—it is virtually a prerequisite. Business schools strive to meet the practical needs of business leaders, and it is certainly still the case that those who wish to attain the highest positions in the world of business would do well to get their M.B.A.'s.

The obvious fact about M.B.A. programs is that—like anything else worthwhile—one gets out of them what one puts into them. Usually the enthusiasm and dedication of the student will be more important to his or her eventual success than the "reputation" or "ranking" of any one program.

WHAT'S IN A NAME?

All graduate management degrees are not necessarily termed M.B.A.; some might be referred to as Master of Business Studies (M.B.S.) or Graduate Business Administration (G.B.A.), to name a couple. Just because the degree is not called "M.B.A." does not necessarily mean it's not what you are looking for. The M.B.A. is a professional degree intended for those who want to pursue a degree in business, management, and administration in order to succeed at an executive level. The M.B.A. compresses all the skills needed to succeed in business, and it permits you to do so in a short period of time. It represents the knowledge and the skills an employee may obtain over the course of many years if he or she is fortunate enough to have interdisciplinary exposure (i.e., accounting, finance, management, information sys-

An M.B.A. Program by Any Other Name . . .

Although the M.B.A. is the common name for a graduate management degree, many institutions offer substantially the same program with another name—Master of Management (M.M.), Master of Public and Private Management (M.M.P.M.), Master of Administrative Science (M.A.S.), and Master of Science in Business Administration (M.S.B.A.), to name a few.

KAPLAN

tems, etcetera). The degree is pervasive amongst all industries spanning the medical, governmental, academic, and financial worlds. Since its inception, there has been no standard uniformity to the degree—there are many different types of M.B.A. programs, which vary in length, curriculum, and ideology.

If you are looking for a degree that will focus on one specific field, perhaps the M.B.A. is not the right certificate for you. Many new master's programs are being developed in specialized fields such as International Business, Business Economics, Information Systems, and others. These are usually one-year, full-time degrees that do necessarily have the same standing as an M.B.A. degree. More traditional master's programs, such as those in economics or finance, may be well suited for the candidate looking for access into very specialized technical or academic fields. To date, though, the M.B.A. is the most renowned and accepted degree for those looking to acquire a well-rounded management background. Later, we will discuss different M.B.A. program concentrations available that allow students to gain additional depth in their specific area of interest (such as marketing, finance, e-commerce, and international business).

THE HISTORY OF THE M.B.A.

The idea for a Master's of Business Administration degree was first considered in the United States in the 1950s. From its inception, the M.B.A. designation was intended to provide practical "hands on" skills and theoretical experience for the up-and-coming management elite. The degree caught on rapidly, and history has proven the M.B.A. as an excellent long-term investment for students as well as their employers.

The degree is now so pervasive that currently hundreds of thousands of candidates apply to programs each year. As new programs are being introduced to facilitate attaining the degree, such as Internet degrees

Born in the USA

The M.B.A. degree still remains a predominantly American degree—and the one that sets the standard. But there are international alternatives. In the UK, postgraduate degree-level management education was jump-started in the late 1960s with the opening of both Manchester Business School and the London School of Economics.

Accredited programs are now popping up all over the world at universities as well as cyber-universities, which are "located" solely on the Internet. Some of these programs are following the U.S. lead (emphasizing team projects and process management), whereas others develop their own focus. For example, the European Institute of Business Administration—INSEAD in Paris, France—is highly analytical in nature.

and shortened programs, this number is on the rise. Although more and more people are able to reap the benefits and status of an M.B.A., the competition is getting steeper as more candidates apply for a limited number of spots.

The late 1980s revolutionized the M.B.A. degree with the birth of Internet-based programs. The acceptance of such a degree is now widespread—many programs have earned regional accreditation and recognition amongst employers who not only approve tuition reimbursement but also value the initiative and maturity of candidates able to demonstrate the motivation to pursue such a program.

RECENT TRENDS IN B-SCHOOLS

In *Gravy Training: Inside the Business of Business Schools* (Jossey-Bass Books, 1999), authors Stuart Crainer and Des Dearlove take at critical look at the past, present, and future of B-schools. The authors identify the many challenges that schools are faced with as a result of a changing environment. Some new trends and suggestions for future improvements include:

- The U.S. business school model should get international and learn from other cultures.
- Business schools should move beyond case studies and focus their attention on people management.
- B-schools should recruit from a broader base, end faculty moonlighting, and involve alumni in teaching.
- Business schools should increase the number of women in their programs, as they largely remain a male-dominated environment. This is not an accurate reflection of business reality, and until this changes, schools cannot claim to be "developing tomorrow's leaders."
- Business schools need to make their programs more user-friendly; for example, they need to cater more to students' busy schedules, particularly those who work full time.

F.Y.I.: The "B" Stands for Business

"When the *Business Week* list of the best B-schools came out, I was surprised when the administrators at my school were so excited about making the list. After all, who wants to be a 'B' school when you can be an 'A' school! Little did I know there was no such thing."

— *B-school student*

Business schools are attempting to meet new demands by:

- Emphasizing practice rather than preaching
- Internationalizing their programs (student body, faculty, content)
- Expanding their concentrations to meet the needs of the new business environment
- Accentuating leadership, management, and communication skills
- Starting to offer shorter programs
- Re-evaluating the way things are done. For instance, in many institutions, students can register for classes or reserve library books on the phone or via the Internet.

WWW 101

Business schools are expanding their scope. Many of the schools that offer the M.B.A. are revising their programs as well as their course offerings on a more frequent basis. New classes in e-commerce, entrepreneurship, and global management and communications are no longer the exception on the roster of elective course offerings. Web offerings are now commonplace, and some schools even give students the option of taking all core courses in the Internet domain.

Students entering B-school at this exciting time are able to witness many of these changes taking effect. Most schools are concentrating their efforts on increasing the *flexibility* of their programs, and they are achieving this primarily by:

- Designing new, improved, and shorter programs
- Creating new concentrations, including custommade degrees
- Developing new Internet-based online courses to allow students to complete the core requirements from home or the office

THE VARIOUS SEGMENTS OF THE M.B.A. MARKET

As a prospective M.B.A. student, it is important for you to realize that the M.B.A. degree is becoming stratified and differentiated as time goes on. There is no one uniform M.B.A. program. We will discuss later in this book some examples of the basic M.B.A. curriculum—but each school is different. As a result, it is very difficult to define who "an M.B.A. candidate" is. There are programs that require one year of studies, and there are those that require more. Some schools are now emphasizing language skills (apart from computer languages) while others concentrate their academics on quantitative skills such as statistics and process management. Many programs, including part-time programs, now require their students to spend some time abroad to study or work.

One thing is certain: Business schools are among the most vibrant and successful components of universities all around the world. By practicing what they preach, they have continued to adjust to economic and market change, and they still provide arguably the best preparation for the challenging careers of business in the 21st century. Schools continuously attempt to individualize their programs to meet the needs of the student. In today's environment, the clients (i.e., you, the student, as well as prospective employers) are savvier than ever. You know what you want out of a program and are less likely to settle on a school or program just to have the piece of paper or the initials after your name. As a result, the pressure is on the schools to offer a unique and valuable product.

You must do your part as well. Approach this endeavor with the seriousness and dedication that any important venture in life requires. And that starts with a careful and systematic examination of what individual schools offer and a candid self-assessment of your priorities, strengths, weaknesses, and goals. You'll find help in the pages ahead. Best of luck!

CHAPTER 2

What Are Your Options?

Woody Allen once said, "Eighty percent of success is showing up." This is no longer a requirement to complete an M.B.A. program. Today, the options for pursuing a higher diploma are as varied as the programs themselves. This chapter will cover your alternatives, as well as the pros and cons of each option.

THE TRADITIONAL M.B.A.–ATTENDING FULL TIME

The experience of attending the M.B.A. program on a full-time basis can be the most rewarding part of enrollment in graduate school. Since most of your time will be spent on location, which school you choose to attend is crucial. When selecting a graduate school, you may want to consider the following important criteria: enrollment, ratio of professors to students, facilities and programs offered (M.B.A. concentrations), reputation of the school and faculty, statistics on job placement following graduation, and the location of the university. Try to collect as much information as possible on the faculty (academicians vs. practitioners) and the student body (average age and years of business experience). Keep in mind that a significant part of the M.B.A. experience will not be learned in textbooks but from your professors and fellow classmates.

Full-Time M.B.A.–Pros:

- The fully integrated system may provide you with the opportunity to develop close ties with the school, other students, and the faculty.
- You will be eligible for financial aid and scholarships; more options, such as graduate assistantships, will be available to you.
- As a full-time student, it's much easier to participate in clubs and networking events offered at the school.
- At some schools, you may have the option of studying abroad.
- A full-timer can take on various internships in different fields. This will give you a taste of the many options that are available after graduation.
- The degree can be obtained in one or two years.

Full-Time M.B.A.–Cons:

- You will be undertaking a large financial investment that could put your earnings on hold for a few years.
- If you decide to attend the full-time program right out of undergraduate school, employers may frown upon your lack of experience.
- It is more difficult to apply recently learned knowledge if you're not currently employed.
- Many school admissions boards require some work experience; also, fellow full-time students may have limited exposure and, as a result, bring less to the classroom.
- The degree requires a career break of one or two years.

Shared Learning

Many full-time students take their elective courses at night with the part-time students in order to benefit from their current workplace experiences.

THE PART-TIME PROGRAM

As more and more workplaces are deciding to subsidize their employees through the M.B.A. process, the part-time alternative is becoming very commonplace. Even for those not sponsored by their company, the part-time option is a viable one, since the student has a continuous income flow to help finance the degree. One of many advantages of a part-time program is certainly the on-the-job application of classroom skills.

Semester Hours Required to Complete the M.B.A. Degree

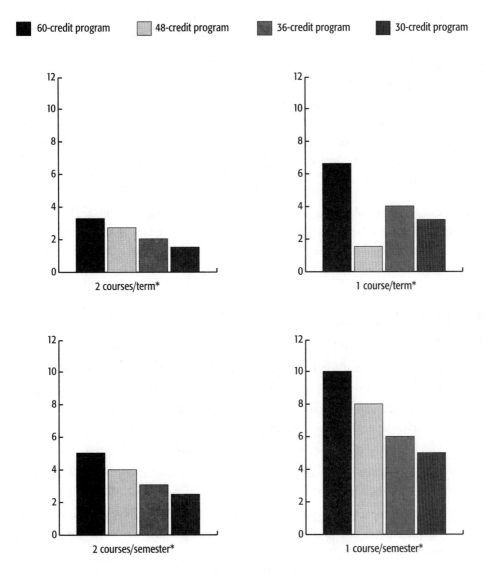

■ 60-credit program   ▨ 48-credit program   ▨ 36-credit program   ▨ 30-credit program

2 courses/term*

1 course/term*

2 courses/semester*

1 course/semester*

*3 terms per year and 2 semesters per year

There are many factors to consider when deciding which school and part-time program to attend. Convenience to your work and home are primary considerations in order to minimize on your commuting time. As you can see by the graphic on the previous page, time is a major factor in the part-time program. The part-timer needs to be extremely organized and patient, as well as being a meticulous planner.

Remember also that just because your employer is reimbursing your tuition, you must be prepared to *prepay* all expenses. By the time your reimbursement check comes in, it may be time to pay for your next trimester of school. Another frequently overlooked expense is the cost of books. Refer to your company's human resources specialist for the complete procedure on tuition reimbursement and speak to other employees who have completed similar programs. Learn from others. This will turn out to be your most valuable resource.

Those of you contemplating a part-time program (including the online, E.M.B.A., or flextime alternatives) are to be applauded. It is a daunting task that, once completed, will speak very highly of your time management skills, your discipline, and your motivation, as well as your maturity.

Part-Time M.B.A.–Pros:

- As a part-time student, you will continue to earn your full salary.
- Oftentimes, the student is sponsored by his or her employer. If this applies to you, your investment in time and money is felt to a lesser degree.
- You will be exposed to other seasoned professionals who will share work experiences and outlooks in their particular field of expertise.
- You will have the ability to apply what you learn as you learn it.
- Going to school part time will permit you to simultaneously move ahead in your current employment as you advance your studies.
- If you, as a part-time graduate, decide to change jobs or occupations, potential employers like to see experienced hires who have demonstrated the ability to multitask.
- Potential employers may place less weight on the prestige of the school you attend (for example, choosing to go to a local school for convenience's sake rather than a more reputed school in a neighboring town).

- Since most part-time graduates remain with their current employers—in new jobs or with additional responsibilities—they reap the benefits of a new position without the stress and costs related to researching a new employer.

- No relocation is necessary.

- Many schools do not differentiate between the part-time and full-time programs. The professors are the same, and the schools fully endow both programs and empower both student bodies.

> **New Development**
>
> This year, Boston University is launching a new program for part-timers called the Professional Evening M.B.A. (P.E.-M.B.A.). This program will give the part-timers a cohort experience similar to those of their full-time and E.M.B.A. students.

Part-Time M.B.A.–Cons:

- Going to school part time requires a high demand on your personal and professional lives. It's hard to do everything well—something is bound to suffer!

- There is no guarantee you will get a promotion after graduation.

- It is difficult to maintain the intensity and enthusiasm about school over a longer period of time (see above for an estimated breakdown of the number of hours you'll need to complete your degree part time).

- Not all employers finance the degree. Additionally, some company policies will cover only certain schools or programs.

- You may have difficulty breaking into a new field, since on-campus recruiters are more likely to cater to full-time students.

- It lacks internationalism—part-time programs do not generally include a study abroad. (Also, admissions statistics show that fewer international students are enrolled in part-time programs than in full-time programs.)

THE EXECUTIVE M.B.A. (E.M.B.A.)

For years, the University of Chicago was the only school to offer the E.M.B.A. But that's all changed now: Many schools have jumped to offer students this unique program, and new, expanded curriculums are continually being explored. The E.M.B.A. requires the greatest support from your employer. Not all schools offer such programs, which usually consist of Friday and Saturday classes and/or full-time study during the summers. There are more stringent admissions requirements, including a minimum number of years of professional experience. One of the program's greatest strengths is its participants: You will be exposed to a wealth of real-life business experiences, and your network possibilities are envious. If your company does not offer this benefit, be prepared to negotiate—organizations that do not wish to lose good employees are now more willing to agree to time off for educational ventures.

E.M.B.A.–Pros:

- Since students are required to be fully sponsored by their employers, there is less of a personal investment than with a regular part-time program.
- The Executive M.B.A. degree is generally completed in a shorter period of time.
- As these programs require students to have a minimum number of years of work experience, you will be surrounded by very skilled professionals.
- You will have the ability to apply as you learn.
- Going to school part-time permits you to move ahead in your current employment as you are advancing your studies.
- You will be exposed to great networking opportunities.
- Because the E.M.B.A. program is so lucrative for the schools (since businesses pay, no financial aid is necessary), it tends to recruit the best faculty.
- You will reap many of the benefits of full-time status in a part-time program. Some programs even have study-abroad requirements.

E.M.B.A.–Cons:

- There is usually a set curriculum with limited choice of courses.
- The E.M.B.A. is a very intensive program: It can be very difficult to juggle work, family, and school responsibilities.

- Students need to time this degree very carefully—many schools require at least ten years of work experience, and you may not want to wait that long to further your education.

- Some E.M.B.A. programs require the student to participate in annual study-abroad sessions. This can be difficult if you have a hectic work schedule as well as family responsibilities.

DISTANCE LEARNING M.B.A.

The growth of the Internet and the marriage of technology and higher education have expanded the opportunities available to the prospective M.B.A. student. Although online programs are geared towards convenience and ease, a significant part of the educational experience may be lost from not having direct contact with professors and a classroom of other students. Interactions are limited to chat rooms, e-mails, and phone calls between students and professors. However, in this way, the student can benefit from the insights of other "classmates" from around the world, while gaining firsthand insight into how the World Wide Web is changing the way we do things. All in all, the prospective Distance Learning M.B.A. student must be organized and disciplined, and will have to excel at online presentations and Internet research.

> **The Name Game**
>
> Since distance learning is still a relatively new phenomenon (within the last 20 years) many names have been used, essentially as synonyms. Some terms you may hear include Computer-Based Programs, Electronic Programs, Online Programs . . . and these are just a few!

Jones International University (JIU) offered the first regionally accredited online M.B.A. program. Dr. Pam Pease, president of this virtual university, says that those students who opt for this type of degree program are highly motivated and self-directed. Since GMAT (Graduate Management Admissions Test) scores are not required and interviews are not granted, admission to the program weighs heavily on a requisite writing sample. Some students do not take the writing sample seriously, and this is a big mistake: It's the university's predominant means of ensuring the quality of the student body. Typical of all online degree students, JIU M.B.A.'s are required to be very technologically savvy. (Obviously, they must be very comfortable with e-mail, the Internet, and computers in general.)

This type of program might be ideal for students who cannot be pinned down for scheduled classes, or, say, who do a great deal of business traveling. Distance learning programs assume that students can relate what they learn within their organizations—an attribute which makes it very attractive for companies who decide to sponsor their employees. IBM, for example, was reported to have sponsored as many as 700 students for the Open University's M.B.A., and has switched financial support from full-time M.B.A.'s to distance learning ones.

Distance Learning M.B.A.–Pros:

- The program will enhance your cyber skills (Internet, e-mail, video conferencing, etcetera).

- It is a cheaper alternative to the traditional M.B.A. programs.

- Location is not an issue.

- Students may receive excellent support from most schools. (Also, it is ideal if your employer is making an exception by financing your degree, as it is transparent to other colleagues.)

- You will have the freedom to work at your own pace; you can take your time to finish the degree and attend lectures at any time of day or night.

- You will gain exposure to students from all over the world.

- The program is a solution whose time has come: Many prospective employers will value the motivation and innovation of the distance learning graduate.

Distance Learning M.B.A.–Cons:

- There is a very high dropout rate—it's hard to stay self-motivated.

- Few companies will sponsor this degree.

- You will have no physical interaction with other students and faculty; it can be difficult to network.

- There are few fully accredited programs; therefore, there is not much prestige in this degree.

Distance Learning Technologies

As a distance learning M.B.A., you may see some of the following features offered in the program. All these technologies are continuing to become more user-friendly and are often used in combination with one another.

Audioconferencing
Audiographics
Broadcast or Cable Television
Computer Courses
Satellite Courses
Video Conferencing
Videotape Delivery

— Adapted from Newsweek/Kaplan's How to Use the Internet to Choose or Change Careers, *2000*

FLEXIBLE M.B.A.

A derivative of the Distance Learning M.B.A. is the Flexible M.B.A., which combines classroom and online courses. New programs are developing that permit students to supplement their online work with classroom attendance during select weekends and vacations. Over 50 business schools have such programs in place where students can complete most of their M.B.A. degree with minimal time on campus. In 1997, the Ohio University College of Business initiated a course in which students can earn an M.B.A. in only two years and are required to be on campus for just two weeks during the entire program. Another cyber-university program is offered at the University of Florida. Here, the university's Internet-based Flexible Program offers the student the opportunity to download courses and then attend a class for one weekend at the end of each month.

Flexible M.B.A.–Pros:

- It offers many of the same advantages as a Distance Learning M.B.A. program.
- Many fully accredited programs are including some online courses.
- You will have the ability to meet with colleagues and faculty.
- The Flexible M.B.A. has more structure than a distance program: the onus is less on the student.
- Students have the ability to speed up the degree.

Flexible M.B.A.–Cons:

- You will need to factor in the expense and time required to travel to school if it is not nearby.
- You must take vacation time from work to attend courses on campus.

U.S. VS. EUROPEAN M.B.A. PROGRAMS

Throughout Europe, many schools since the mid-20th century have offered the M.B.A. degree. The programs differ from U.S. M.B.A.'s on several distinct planes:

- **Duration**: The European full-time programs usually take one year to complete.
- **Emphasis**: The European programs focus predominantly on analytical and quantitative skills, with less weight on group projects and other "soft skills."
- **Variety of degrees available**

Remember: Selecting the right school and program requires a great deal of research. Treat this project as a your first homework assignment—it may be the most crucial assignment of your graduate academic career. Part 2, Selecting the Right School and Program, will help you take this first step to a challenging and rewarding experience.

Program	Available in the U.S.?	Available in Europe?	Comments
Full-Time M.B.A.	Yes	Yes	U.S./European programs vary in length. Some European companies will sponsor the F/T M.B.A.
Part-Time M.B.A.	Yes	Yes	
Executive M.B.A.	Yes	Yes	A growing development in Europe.
Modular	No	Yes	Employer-sponsored program that is project based.
Consortium	No	Yes	Employee-sponsored program within a company.
Distance Learning	Yes	Yes	Global degree

THE RISKS AND REWARDS OF THE M.B.A. PROGRAM: IS IT WORTH THE PRICE OF ADMISSION?

When weighing the pros and cons of each M.B.A. program, you shouldn't discount the various costs involved. If, for example, you have determined that a flexible or distance-learning M.B.A. program is better suited to your lifestyle, you may find that the costs associated with this type of degree are significantly less than attending full or part time.

With the decision to attend on the part-time basis often comes the security of some financial backing from your employer. But what if your employer does not pay? And even if they do sponsor you, that may not always entail full tuition reimbursement.

You may have a general idea of the total financial outlay necessary to complete a part-time program. The timing of payments is up to you. You can determine how many classes you will take over a given semester—choosing to take two classes or one will obviously affect your expenses for the term. Additionally, it is important to remember that the per-credit costs are not static; in fact, they often increase over the course of study. If you choose to attend part time over a longer span of time, you may find that your classes down the road are significantly more expensive than your first.

So how do you weigh if this degree is worth the cost and the sacrifice that you will put into it? The simple fact that you are reading this book indicates that you have already given this question some thought and that you are seriously considering pursuing an M.B.A. degree. Be forewarned: The M.B.A. is a major personal investment of time and money. Although the degree has become widely popular in recent years, it may not be the appropriate choice for meeting your career goals. You need to consider whether you can do what you want to do in your career without the M.B.A., or whether another degree or nondegree study would serve you just as well or better, perhaps for a smaller investment of time and money.

Your education may be the second largest investment you make in your life—after, say, the purchase of a house—because it demands much of your time and, often, much of your money. Remember, to complete the M.B.A. degree on a part-time basis will take you a minimum of two years. And most people will agree that buying a home should not be done on the spur of the moment. Rather, the decision should be preceded by an examination of many financial

> ## Well Worth It
>
> "As a student, I have experienced changes in both my professional and personal growth. On a professional level, I'm able to directly apply my learnings to my daily job. School has also taught me new concepts and a vocabulary for business. I'm less intimidated with the senior folks when they start talking about things like what discount rate to use, because, while I would not profess to be a pro, school has given me a solid foundation to work from. I've noticed around the office and in many other environments that people really admire someone who is willing to make the sacrifices of going to school part time while working full time."
>
> *– Kimberly, M.B.A. candidate, Boston University*

aspects, such as the home's location, projected resale value, and quality. The same is true of your investment in an M.B.A. education. The value of your degree will be greatly enhanced if you approach this decision with as much care as you would the decision to buy a house—and perhaps even more. Many people will own more than one house in the course of a lifetime, but no one ever earns more than one M.B.A. degree.

The steps below provide a short guideline to assist you in determining whether the M.B.A. program is worth the financial investment for you.

Step 1

Figure the total cost to graduation. Be sure to include: application fee, total cost for all credits at the current price, cost of books (it is usually safe to estimate $75 for books per class), travel, and other incidentals.

Step 2

Calculate the opportunity cost of your money. If you estimate the total cost to graduation to be $60,000 over three years, figure out how much this money could yield you over that same period of time.

Step 3

The last step can be very difficult: You need to estimate the benefits you will receive from your degree. Some employers may indicate to you what to expect once you have graduated. You can also learn quite a bit from other employees who have chosen to obtain a graduate degree. How have they succeeded?

If you're able to quantify step 3, then it should be quite easy to determine if a graduate degree is for you. Yet, there are so many other factors involved that cannot be quantified. For example, the prestige, the confidence, and the discipline that you obtain from going through this process are immeasurable. The next chapter will help you determine if you have the right profile to obtain an M.B.A., and how to decide which program is for you.

CHAPTER 3

Should You Get Your M.B.A. Part Time?

Now that you have a general idea of the options available to you, it may be helpful to understand what makes people take the plunge and invest in the commitment of getting their M.B.A. part-time. You may have purchased this book because:

- Your employers think you have "potential," but at annual review time it's not reflected in your salary increase or bonus; or

- You know deep down inside that you are much smarter than your boss and if you can add those three little initials after your name (M.B.A.) then others will find out as well; or

- You have told yourself that you want to branch out and this is the last (the very, very last) year you are going to put in all your hard work for someone else's bank account.

Whatever your reasons, you're not alone. There is a general consensus of why people go for an M.B.A. on a part-time basis.

It costs a lot to go for an M.B.A. . . . in time and money. So why do people go? And why should you? There are many reasons, which can be broken down into three general categories: the emotional, the financial, and the ambitious decisions.

> **Part-Time Popularity**
>
> The AACSB currently estimates that two-thirds of all M.B.A. students are now attending on a part-time basis.

THE EMOTIONAL DECISION: "SO I CAN PROVE I COULD DO IT"

Some students go for their M.B.A. for the prestige that accompanies the degree, or just to be able to say that they have achieved it. With this accomplishment, you can parlay the degree into something worthwhile at the office and increase your confidence. There are other emotional factors at play here, including:

Because you'd like to meet new and diverse people.

Although attending school part time does limit some of your opportunities to network (there just are not enough hours in a day!), you will be exposed to many different people and industries, and have abundant opportunities for making new friends and workplace allies.

Because your friends, family, or work colleagues recommend it— and you can't let them down.

Believe it or not, this is actually a pretty good reason for attending school part time. Why?

Your friends recommend it to you. If your friends suggest that you obtain an M.B.A. on a part-time basis, chances are they themselves have done it and have a positive opinion about their experience and can guide you through your decisions. Or perhaps they know your personality well and think you are capable of the challenge. (Although, maybe they are not really that good a friend and would just like to see you suffer!)

Your family recommends it to you. Well, if your family recommends that you go for an M.B.A. part time, you can rest assured that they will cut you some slack during the tough times. When you have to miss the Sunday barbecues in order to meet with your group, when you can't go to your cousin's wedding because it conflicts with finals—for these reasons, and a myriad of other events that you will need to forgo, it will be helpful to have your family behind you in your decision to return to school.

Keep Your Spouse Happy

Your spouse's mental state may have an effect on how successful you are at B-school. Make sure that he or she will be happy with the program you choose.

Your company has suggested it for you. If your colleagues suggest that you attend school on a part-time basis, this means that your company will most likely sponsor you. If your boss in particular recommends you for a part-time M.B.A. program, it really is in your best interest to consider fulfilling his or her request. If not, it may be perceived as a lack of ambition or interest in your job or company. If you choose not to accept the company's suggestion/sponsorship, be prepared to give valid reasons why you have made that choice.

In any case, one thing is sure: If you are encouraged to take the plunge, you should seriously think it over. If it is something you are considering and would like your employers to take note, try introducing the subject during an annual review.

Because you like challenges and have a thirst for knowledge.

Some people just like continuously testing the boundaries of their limits. Take, for example, an M.B.A. student at Fordham University, who was around 30 years old and already working towards his third master's degree. Did his executive job at CBS require him to get an M.B.A.? Not really—he just wanted the challenge.

THE FINANCIAL DECISION: "SO I CAN MAKE MORE MONEY"

The 1990s were the golden age of the M.B.A. Unemployment reached record lows and the opportunities were bountiful for the recent graduate. With the advent of the new millennium, directions may be shifting. By attending part time, the student does not have to forsake income during the one or two years it takes to complete the degree full time.

The investment in an M.B.A. and can range between $20,000 and over $150,000. To invest that kind of money, one certainly must expect great returns. Although the financial rewards may not come immediately, your status as an M.B.A. will increase your earning potential and greatly improve your marketability. If salary is the primary motivation, you should be aware that the better reputation of the school, the more its graduates usually earn.

Try to get a clear reading from your current employer if the firm plans to sponsor you both financially (tuition reimbursement) and emotionally (when you need to use the conference room for a group meeting) through the M.B.A. process. Additionally, you should try to get an understanding from them about their expectations during and after you finish your degree. How long will you need to stay employed with them? Will you need to wait until the completion of your degree for a promotion or significant raise?

THE AMBITIOUS DECISION: "TO MOVE UP THE CORPORATE LADDER"

Perhaps money is not your primary motivator; perhaps you are just simply ambitious in your career. Whether you want to give your career the little boost it needs, or get yourself noticed by the "powers that be" at the office, or just try your hand at something new, the M.B.A. degree is a great vehicle to get you going!

Jump Start Your Career

If you have decided to pursue the M.B.A. degree because you feel that this decision is the natural progression of your career path, you are not alone. When you feel stagnant in your job, the degree can be the jump-start you are looking for. Perhaps you have not been promoted in many years, or you aren't getting the type of salary adjustment that you feel your hours and dedication warrant. Obtaining an M.B.A. can be the wake-up call your employers need to remind them that you are on the fast track.

> ### Night and Day
>
> "I've always found the combination of class work and real life effective. One tends to reinforce the other. What I learned Monday night, I can apply Tuesday morning."
>
> – *M.B.A., Fordham University*

Advancing in your current career/field.

Most M.B.A. part-time students stay on in their current field—in fact, many continue with their same company.

Shifting your current work responsibilities and learning to manage others.

A part-time program is perfectly suited for you if you are looking to gain more experience at managing people and teams. There are two main reasons for this:

- You will a lot of practice with team projects in B-school. Also, when you attend on a part-time basis, you need to develop your time-management skills very quickly and acutely. If you can juggle all this, you are learning far more than what is in your textbook or in your class notes.

- You will be able to apply what you are learning over a longer period of time. Team-management and leadership skills are not only taught in business school, they are implemented. As time goes on, these skills are drummed into the students who truly learn how to apply them as they are learning. This is very different from attending a one- or two-year full-time program without applying your knowledge as you are learning it—and potential employers realize this!

> **Moving Up**
>
> Many part-time students receive at least one promotion as they proceed through the M.B.A. program.

Switch Gears Completely

Unless you have signed agreements with your employer that bind you to your job for several years,* your new degree can be a wonderful opportunity to shift careers by changing industries. This may give you the door-opening opportunities (and credibility) to translate your new skills into your field of interest. While in school, you will likely be amazed at the wonderful diversity of your fellow students' backgrounds. You may be in classes with accountants, doctors, nurses, administrators, and architects: Every sector requires experts in management. Take advantage of this time to network with your fellow students.

For those of you considering an M.B.A. in order to change careers, be advised that a part-time program may not be the best solution for you. Why not?

---

* Try to remember, without being threatening, that you are in the driver's seat. With unemployment rates so low, employers are taking all the necessary measures to keep good employees. Signing long contracts without very favorable conditions should therefore be avoided.

• It will take you longer to complete the part-time M.B.A. You may think that you can wait three years or more to change careers, but those three years (on average) is a long time to put your life's ambition on hold. If you decide that the program is taking too long on a part-time basis and consider switching to full-time status, be advised that not all schools will allow students to switch from one program to another.

Playing the Field

Most part-time students do not seek to change fields. They have a distinct disadvantage over full-time students, who have the opportunity to test-drive new occupations with internships before taking the plunge.

• If financing the degree is an issue and going part time is the best way for you to proceed, make sure that you carefully read your company's policies and procedures regarding tuition reimbursement. You want to make sure that you have not implicitly agreed to stay on with your firm for a given period of time during (and after) the completion of your program in exchange for the financing of your degree.

• As a part-timer, you may not have the same access to career placement services as the full-time student. It's advisable to make an appointment directly with the Career Development Office and develop a good rapport before you begin your M.B.A. program.

• Networking options may be more limited in a part-time program. You will be juggling many different tasks simultaneously: work, school, family, social obligations, and so forth. It will be very difficult to devote the time and effort necessary to develop strong ties with your fellow classmates, professors, peers, etcetera.

• Time: As mentioned above, you will not be able to dedicate the proper amount of time it takes to research and apply to the industry you are interested in moving to if you are juggling too many things at once. It is hard enough to do one thing at a time properly, and practically impossible to do everything well at once. A career change is too important to take lightly, and you should really devote the proper amount of time to this venture.

If, on the other hand, you are looking to broaden your skill set in order to start your own business, a part-time program may be ideal solution for you. In the time it will take for you earn your degree, you will have the opportunity to:

- Let your company pay tuition;
- Learn how to put together an effective business plan;
- Save money for your new venture; and
- Meet interesting people and forge good contacts.

Whether you have already decided to attend part time or are still deciding the right path for you, consider this: If you are unhappy in your current employment and are looking to obtain an M.B.A. as an out, beware! Be sure to have a clear sight of your goals and what you plan to do with your degree once you have it. As GMAC suggests, "The strongest candidates competing to gain admission into grad school are very focused on their career paths."

Reasons	Full-Time Program	E.M.B.A. Program	Part-Time Program	Distance Learning Program
Others recommend it	X	X	X	X
Career advancement		X	X	X
Professional improvement		X	X	X
Career switch	X			
Increase earning potential	X	X	X	X
Increase knowledge	X	X	X	X
In between jobs	X			

WHY GO PART TIME?

Each M.B.A. candidate and alumnus will give you a unique answer to the question of why he or she returned to school part time. Herewith are two students' responses, as well as my own:

"Why did I pursue my M.B.A. part time? Well, I was interested in maintaining a continuous salary stream, I understood how to manage potential work and graduate school time conflicts, and I like my present company. In my situation, there was no need to pursue my studies full time. Even though going full-time may save you a year and a half, and you may have occasional free time during the day, I believe when you add up the benefits of the part-time M.B.A. program—having a steady income, possible tuition reimbursement, and frequent company support with regard to various course-specific data—you'll see it far outweighs the pluses of the full-time program."

— *Michael, Fairfield University M.B.A.*

Working and Learning Moms

"As a mid-career, mid-life working mother, I view my sabbatical to do an Executive M.B.A. as the best way to achieve work/life balance in the longer term. The E.M.B.A. program is designed for individuals with full-time positions. Over the course of the 20-month program, I will consider my full-time position to be that of mother to my children, but I know I am working towards future professional growth as well. Seeing Mom go to school should also illustrate the importance of education to my kids."

– *Diane Turek Pire, M.B.A. candidate*

"As a working mother, I was able to use my time wisely. I could use the day and evening for my job and my family, and when the kids went to bed, I went online."

– *M.B.A., University of Phoenix Online*

"I attend school part time for two reasons. First, I have a great job with a great company. I'm challenged and engaged so I didn't want to leave, but I did want to gain a greater understanding of business principles . . . which leads me to my second reason. I wanted to be able to apply my knowledge immediately. I'm not necessarily a student—in fact, I'd say, along with many of the people I work with, I've got a slight touch of Attention Deficit Disorder. Give me a never-been-done-before challenge and I'll accomplish it; lecture at me and I'll fall asleep. I knew that in order to be successful in going back to school, I needed to apply my learning immediately—to make it stick in my mind and to see the results."

— *Maureen, Boston University M.B.A.*

Those of you considering an M.B.A. on a part-time basis, be prepared: It is not like college! In the late 1980s when I was a part-time student, my decision to pursue a M.B.A. was driven by four motivating factors:

Reason #1: "I'll have shorter hours."

I was working very long hours, and since my company was willing to sponsor me—why not go? My thought process was that at least I would get something tangible out of the long workday. I did not realize at the time that even if I was getting home from school around the same time as I had from work, my weekends were exhausted doing assignments for school or catching up on my work from the office (forget about my social life and home life, let alone the laundry piling up!).

Reason #2: "I'll meet new people."

College was a blast, I thought, and what a great opportunity to meet people and network. B-school should be even more so! Well, there was a flaw in this reasoning as well. What I did not realize was that other students were not there to have a good time. Everyone has his or her own personal mission. For some (I should say most), the five free minutes before the start of classes is the only free time in the day—without the phones ringing, the boss or client monopolizing the day, or the kids crying for attention—to read *The Wall Street Journal*. Although my initial reaction was disappointment, I did not let this discourage me. Before long, I had met very interesting people who I still try to keep in contact with today.

Reason #3: "I don't have to pay for it."

My company was paying for my M.B.A., so I thought it would not cost me anything: another semifallacy. Just because your company is paying for the M.B.A. doesn't mean it's free for you. Consider the float of your money. In most cases, you will be required to pay up front. Your reimbursement may be pegged to your results (for example, 100 percent reimbursement for an "A" or equivalent, 80 percent reimburse-

> **It's not free!**
>
> Regardless of company sponsorship, your expenses will include:
>
> Payment up front
> Books/Supplies
> Laptop/Computer
> Activities
> Travel
> Insurance

ment for a "B," etcetera). Whether or not this is the case, do not expect to see your money back for several months. Another (nonreimbursable) expense, which can be significant, is the cost of books. I remember spending approximately $300 per trimester on books.

Reason #4: "I want to say I did it."

You need an M.B.A. to get ahead in today's business environment, and my company had me on the fast track. Well, I figured, it certainly can't hurt to have the degree (especially since a colleague of mine had recently finished hers). First, though, make sure that you really want the degree, and most important, that you have a clear idea why you want it, what your focus will be, and what you plan to do with it after obtaining the degree.

I erred in all four reasons I had given myself for going back to school. Try to benefit from my misjudgments. Getting an M.B.A. part time can be a rewarding and challenging experience. I do not regret for one day my experiences and the diploma that is prominently displayed in my home office. But do not make the same mistakes I made. Before embarking on this pursuit, make sure you are prepared. One way of preparing yourself is to carefully evaluate whether the timing is right and whether you have the right personality and demeanor to take on the challenge. Then and only then can you judge for yourself if you have what it takes to go for the part-time degree.

TIMING ISSUES

Believe it or not, your age may help you determine which program is the right one for you. If you have just completed your undergraduate degree within the last few years and are eager to return for a higher degree, you should realize that the executive programs are not designed for you. In addition, perhaps you should reconsider the part-time option as well. The average age of part-time students is around 27 years old. Your classmates on average will have over four years of professional experience. If you do not fall within this category, and you do not want to postpone your degree, you may want to ask yourself why you can't wait. Fewer schools are accepting students right out of undergraduate studies.

When Is the Right Time?

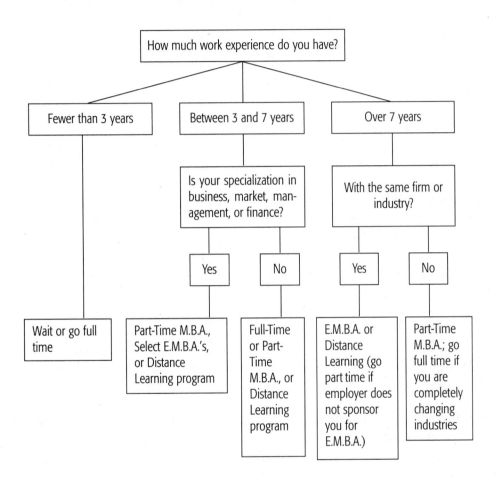

When considering the right time to go back to school, you should also consider where you are in your life stage. Take the example of a stay-at-home father or mother who is anxious to return to the working world but fears his or her skills may have atrophied. For this candidate, now is the perfect time to apply to a part-time M.B.A. program. In the next few years the children will be more autonomous; classes can be scheduled at night, on weekends, online, or all taken one day a week when a baby-sitter can be hired. What a productive use of time!

ANALYZE YOURSELF

To assist you in determining if B-school will make a good fit into your life at this time, we have developed the following self-assessment for you to work through. It is always important to take a long look at your attributes and realize what your strengths and weaknesses are. Identify the tasks you enjoy and those that you always drag your feet on. In addition to helping you determine if an M.B.A. is indeed for you, taking inventory of your characteristics will help in all facets of your life. If you have never done a self-assessment, this is a good time to start. It will help you focus your attention on the types of things that interest you and decide where you want to be in five or ten years.

Additionally, if you do decide that an M.B.A. is for you, with this section complete, and with careful introspection, you will have all the tools in place to successfully complete an application for admission as well—and be better prepared for an interview!

Although you needn't respond to every question in one sitting, you should realize that this exercise should be taken seriously. Think of this as one of your first school assignments. Be clear and detailed in your responses.

Lastly, run through the questions more than once and at different times—you may be surprised at the variance in some of your answers from one week to another.

SELF-ASSESSMENT

List the ten characteristics that best describe you.

1._____ 2._____

3._____ 4._____

5._____ 6._____

7._____ 8._____

9._____ 10._____

What do these characteristics say about you? Give an example of each—now what does this say about you?

_____

_____

_____

_____

What are your life goals?

_____

What are your career goals?

_____

What do you hope to achieve from furthering your educational degree?

_____

What are the top five things you excel at (and enjoy)? Give examples of how you apply these skills, and identify what they say about you.

WHAT YOU EXCEL AT	HOW YOU APPLY IT	WHAT THIS SAYS ABOUT YOU
Ex: Good with children	Coach Little League	Organizer, leader, guide, enthusiastic, good at dealing with others.

What would you say are your five greatest weaknesses? Identify how they are manifested in your behavior/how they have hindered your performance (at work, home, etcetera).

WEAKNESS	HOW HAS THIS MANIFESTED / HINDERED YOUR PERFORMANCE?
Ex: Perfectionist	I tend to take too long on projects by focusing on the small details (i.e., formatting).
Ex: Impatience	I tend to cut people off in midsentence (a lack of respect to others).

What would others who know you well list as your greatest weaknesses?

_____

If you decide against obtaining an M.B.A., how will this change your career objectives? (By answering this question, you should be able to tell what you plan to achieve from the M.B.A. degree.)

_____

_____

What primary obstacles do you foresee if you become a part-time student and full-time employee?

_____

List your three greatest accomplishments and explain why they make you proud.

1. _____

2. _____

3. _____

What is the toughest obstacle you have ever overcome? How did you react? In retrospect, what would you do differently? What did you learn about yourself from this experience?

_____

_____

Review your answers as if you were reading about a total stranger. Pretend you are an admissions officer—or employer—reviewing one of thousands of applicants. What is your impression of the answers?

Have a close friend or relative read through your answers. Ask them the following questions: "Does this sound like me? Do any of the responses surprise you as coming from me?" Then ask them why.

Here is a list of some of the skills you will need in order to succeed as a part-time student. How do you match up?

- **Focus**: Keep your sights set on the future and on your goals. Try not to get led off the path you have created for yourself.

- **Discipline**: This is probably one of the skills many people lack the most prior to applying to graduate school—and the skill they learn the quickest! Just don't be too hard on yourself.

- **Perseverance and motivation**: Obtaining a degree on a part-time basis will take several years. Try not to get discouraged; the time will fly by before you know it. Some students decide to take a term or semester off (usually during the summer) while attending the M.B.A. on a part-time basis. This is an example of the importance of perseverance. Unless there are personal reasons for needing the time off, you should be discouraged from doing so, because it is very hard to get remotivated after having a long break.

- **Flexibility:** Be determined enough to achieve your goals but flexible enough to change direction if necessary. An example: A group assignment is due in two days and your fellow classmate is called out of town on business—you will need to finish his or her part of the project and make the presentation on your own. Learn to adapt. You will be experiencing many changes if and when you decide to attend graduate school, so stay open minded and flexible.

- **Patience with yourself and with others:** You may notice that tempers tend to flare when your time is short and you have a million things to do. Try to be patient, and most importantly, try not to take things out on the ones you care about.

- **Tolerance and acceptance towards others and yourself:** You are human, and it is virtually impossible for you to be able to do everything well. Take it one day at a time. Some things will suffer—don't let it be you!

> ### Do You Have what It Takes?
>
> When asked what characteristics a Part-Time M.B.A. student would possess, Amy Drill, Chief Marketing Officer and Senior Vice President of Development at nano.com and adjunct professor at NYU says: "They are hard-working, driven, strong analytical and communications skills, ability to work under pressure, ambitious, highly motivated, and self-confident."

- **Time-management skills:** In today's multitask society, even without attending school, time management is one of the most revered skills. As we have mentioned several times, as a part-time student you will face the very difficult challenge of trying to do everything in a day when there are only so many hours available to you.

- **Ability to prioritize:** This skill goes hand in hand with time-management skills. You will have a limited amount of time to get many things accomplished—so learn how to identify which items are the most crucial. Keep lists!

- **Organization:** This is an invaluable tool that will help you save a great amount of time. Develop and keep a personal filing system. For example: Color-code your class notes (i.e., yellow notebook and yellow file folder—even yellow computer icons—for finance). This may seem very simplistic, but everyone has experienced anxieties and stress due to lost or misplaced documents, phone numbers, and so on. Spend ten minutes a day getting yourself structured.

- **Independence**: No one is going to stand over you reminding you of class assignments, work projects due, or family responsibilities. The ball is in your court and you must have a strong sense of independence and responsibility in order to succeed.

- **Self-motivation**: You will need to be extremely intrinsically motivated (especially if you are considering the Distance Learning (online) M.B.A. option).

- **Self-knowledge**: Most important, know and accept yourself for who you really are rather than who you think you should be. Do what you expect of yourself and not what others expect of you. In the long run, you will be much happier.

- **Optimism**: Be able to handle little setbacks—you will encounter them. Just stay focused, confident, and optimistic.

Have Direction

"Potential M.B.A.'s should have a pretty good idea of what career direction they're looking to take before starting the application process. Unlike with undergraduate programs, you tend to start taking classes within your focused area and specialty by your first or second semester."

– M.B.A., Stern School of Business,
New York University

Now you should have a pretty good idea if you have what it takes to attend the M.B.A. program part time. Do think carefully about bringing up the idea (at home and at the office) of obtaining the degree. Once you start talking a great deal about it, people will expect you to actually do it. So make sure you are ready and have what it takes to complete the task.

CHAPTER 4

What You Can Expect

Applying for an M.B.A. involves the same commitment and consideration as applying for a job. You wouldn't just apply to any company; you would probably research it and ask around. Is it a good place to work? What will the commute be like? What kind of hours will it require, and what type of commitment is involved? These are some of the questions you would consider before applying for—or accepting—a new position. Once you have targeted a job, you would probably need to discuss the decision with your family and give notice at work. Well, applying and accepting admission to an M.B.A. program is really very similar.

MAKING TIME FOR EVERYTHING

As a part-time student, you will probably be able to handle about two classes per term. Typically, part-time M.B.A. students wish to complete their degree in two to four years.

The amount of time necessary to complete your degree will depend on the following variables:

- The number of courses you are eligible to waive.*

---

* Remember that most schools will permit you to waive a course if you have taken it within the last 5 years and have received a "B" or better. This is not a universal rule, but a general guideline. Check with your school.

- The number of courses you register for each term.
- The number of terms your school offers per year. (Do they operate on a trimester or semester basis?)
- The availability of summer sessions.
- The flexibility of your work responsibilities. If you are required to start traveling, this will certainly affect your study and school time and finally
- Your schedule—some students may need a break between terms to spend time with family or for vacations or work responsibilities. Although this usually should be discouraged because the student tends to lose steam, sometimes this is unavoidable.

Juggling Act: A Student's Sample Week

Although everyone's schedule will be different, the chart on the following pages should give you a general idea of the commitment you would undertake as a part-time M.B.A. student. Whether you are single, married, a parent, or travel for your job—or any combination thereof—the part-time M.B.A. will significantly change your life.

Of course, every week will not be the same. Some days there will be special mandatory lectures in addition to your class time; other times you may need to go to the computer lab to sign on to a computer simulated program. If you are like most students, you will be a bit more enthusiastic about your class time and assignment during the first year. As time goes on, you may learn where you can cut a few corners.

DAY	SINGLE/MARRIED WORKING STUDENT	PARENT & WORKING STUDENT	WORKING STUDENT WHO TRAVELS
Monday	7:00 A.M.: Wake up 8:00–5:15 P.M.: Work 6:00–9:00 P.M.: Class 9:00–9:30 P.M.: Discuss project w/classmates 10:00 P.M.–12 A.M.: Dinner and Homework 12:30 A.M.: Sleep	6:00 A.M.: Wake up 6:30–7:30 A.M.: Kid time 8:00–5:15 P.M.: Work 6:00–9:00 P.M.: Class 9:00–9:30 P.M.: Discuss project w/classmates 10:00 P.M.–12 A.M.: Dinner and homework 12:30 A.M.: Sleep	Now, imagine Column 1 and Column 2 coupled with a very demanding job that required you to travel! This process is too difficult even to chart out!
Tuesday	7:00 A.M.: Wake up 8:00 A.M.–7:00 P.M.: Work 8:00–9:00 P.M.: Dinner and relax 10:00 P.M.–12 A.M.: Homework (reading assignment)	6:00 A.M.: Wake up 6:30–7:30 A.M.: Kid time 8:00 A.M.–6:00 P.M.: Work 6:30–9:00 P.M.: Dinner w/kids and relax 10:00 P.M.–12 A.M.: Homework (reading)	
Wednesday	7:00 A.M.: Wake up 8:00 A.M.–5:15 P.M.: Work 6:00–9:00 P.M.: Class 9:00–11:30 P.M.: Discuss project/have dinner w/classmates 12 A.M.: Home and to bed (maybe a little TV?)	6:00 A.M.: Wake up 6:30–7:30 A.M.: Kid time 8:00 A.M.–5:15 P.M.: Work 6:00–9:00 P.M.: Class 9:00–11:30 P.M.: Have dinner w/classmates 12 A.M.: Home and to bed (maybe a little TV?)	

Thursday	7:00 A.M.: Wake up 8:00 A.M.–6:30 P.M.: Work 7:00–8:00 P.M.: Gym 9:00–10:30 P.M.: Dinner 10:00 P.M.–12 A.M.: I know I should do work, but . . .	7:30 A.M.: Overslept! 8:00 A.M.–6:30 P.M.: Work 7:00–8:00 P.M.: Gym 9:00–10:00 P.M.: Dinner (kids already asleep) 10:00 P.M.–12 A.M.: Homework (reading)	
Friday	7:00 A.M.: Wake up 8:00 A.M.–6:15 P.M.: Work 7:00–8:00 P.M.: Gym 8:30–9:30 P.M.: Dinner 10:00 P.M.–12 A.M.: Homework (reading)	6:00 A.M.: Wake Up 6:30–7:30 A.M.: Kid time 8:00 A.M.–6:15 P.M.: Work 7:00–9:30 P.M.: Dinner w/kids 10:00 P.M.–12 A.M.: Homework (reading)	
Saturday	10:00 A.M.: Slept late 1:00–6:00 P.M.: Library to research Business Law cases 7:00 P.M.–on: Time off for good behavior!	7:30 A.M.: Wake up 7:45 A.M.–12:00 P.M.: Family time 1:00–6:00 P.M.: Library to research Business Law cases 7 P.M.–on: Time off for good behavior!	

Sunday	8:00 A.M.: Wake up	7:00 A.M.: Wake up	
	8:00–9:30 A.M.: Gym	8:00–9:30 A.M.: Gym	
	11:00 A.M.–3:00 P.M.: Meeting and lunch w/ classmates Re: project	11:00 A.M.–3:00 P.M.: Meeting and lunch w/ classmates Re: project	
	5:00–8:00 P.M.: Regroup information from today's meeting	5:00–8:00 P.M.: Regroup information from today's meeting	
	9:00 P.M.–on: Dinner and sleep	9:00 P.M.–on: Dinner and sleep	

You may find that with two classes per term, you can easily complete your M.B.A. degree in two years. Of course, as the above chart demonstrates, your kids will start walking and utter their first words without you, your spouse will forget what you look like, and you probably will have put on ten pounds because you really never do get to go to the gym . . . but you *will* have your degree! So, if you can live with this schedule, fine, but first make sure that you have your loved ones' full support and that they are aware of the time constraints that will be placed on you for the next few years.

Okay, you've broached the subject on the home front. But you're not done yet: The next step is discussing your M.B.A. plans at the office.

WILL YOUR EMPLOYER SUPPORT YOUR EDUCATION?

Although a graduate management education can contribute to your career advancement, you should know that part-time M.B.A. graduates are in a very different situation than full-time graduates. Let us explain.

Employers who hire graduates from full-time M.B.A. programs know that they are getting an M.B.A. In addition, some companies have programs in which they hire holders of baccalaureate degrees with the requirement that they earn an M.B.A. within a certain time frame. Most part-time students, though, are in positions in which there has been no expectation that they will earn the graduate degree. This distinction makes it important for you to investigate your company's policy regarding the value of the M.B.A. and what their stance on tuition reimbursement is. Use this to your advantage; show your firm that you are motivated and the go-getter that they want on their team.

While some companies strongly encourage their employees to obtain graduate management education, others are not that supportive. Often, unsupportive companies are concerned about the job marketability that employees attain along with their degrees. In part, they may be worried that current employees will form expectations about their future with the company as a result of the M.B.A. degree, and, if these expectations are not met, will promptly depart for greener fields elsewhere. This climate makes degree completion more difficult. Under these circumstances, if your firm will not financially or emotionally support your decision, leaving your job for another firm or for full-time study may be a preferable alternative.

Will They Work with You?

"Because our jobs are so demanding, most managers are looking for full-time employees, not part-time employees. However, there are some exceptions. If an individual who has worked full-time is requesting a part-time schedule, the firm usually works with them to try and accommodate their schedule if they have a good track record. All regular full-time employees at my company are eligible for a tuition reimbursement program of $1,000 per year for tuition and books."

— Manager of employment at a multinational firm in Seattle, WA.

To Pay or Not to Pay: Tuition Reimbursement

Some companies clearly recognize the value of further education for their employees, but have turned away from financial support of a full degree. Do not take this personally. If the company policy is not to reimburse tuition, they will have difficulty changing their position.

There are so many factors involved in addressing the "Will they pay for it?" question, including the size of the company, your role within the organization, and the amount of time you've been working there.

How big is your company?

If you are employed at a small company that does not have a tuition reimbursement policy, size can work to your benefit. Perhaps they can be more flexible with their rules, make an exception in your case. Or, they may be willing to give you an additional "bonus" to assist in the payment of your expenses. Remember that any nonreimbursed work-related expenses can be claimed on your income taxes. Ask your tax accountant for more information.

Where do you fit in within the company?

Does your job require a great deal of interaction and group projects, or are you a "solo" worker? If you have constant contact with others, ask around and see if anyone has obtained a degree on a part-time basis. How did they go about asking at work? Depending on your work environment, you may want to discuss these matters outside the office (at lunch or over a drink, say). Your colleague may be more comfortable and receptive to helping you and giving you insight if you're at an offsite location.

How long have you been employed?

If you are a recent hire, it may be premature to discuss whether or not the company would financially support your M.B.A. pursuit. Even if this issue was discussed in your interview, don't be surprised if your boss is taken aback if you suggest that you are ready to start your application process when the first paycheck hasn't cleared yet!

No one is indispensable, but . . .

Maybe you are lucky enough to be in a bargaining position at work. If this is the case, even if your firm does not offer tuition reimbursement, they may be willing to make an exception—just this once.

Once you have evaluated your employment situation, consider doing the following:

- Read your policy and procedure manual or human resources booklet that describes your benefits. Is their mention of a tuition reimbursement program? Are you eligible?
- Informally talk to colleagues and casually broach the subject.
- Talk to friends and family who are currently employed in similar industries. What is their company's policy?

- Prepare a formal letter of request to your boss, with a copy for human resources. In this letter, explain why you wish to obtain an M.B.A. degree, detail the program(s) you are interested in pursuing, and identify the timeline for admission and completion of the degree.

- If you have a close relationship with your boss, go to him or her first. Show that you have done your research, and explain your timeframe and game plan. Remember, it is much easier to shoot down a proposal when it is not well thought out. Ask for his or her advice regarding the next step. Have your written request on hand should it be requested.

- If you do not feel comfortable approaching your boss, ask for a confidential appointment with your personnel director. A word of caution: If your company does not offer a tuition reimbursement plan, do not expect any flexibility on behalf of the human resources team. They are required to enforce the rules of the company. If you are requesting an exception to be made on your behalf, go directly to the people empowered to change the rule or exempt you from the policy.

Whew! Your family, friends, colleagues, and boss are behind you as you embark on your pursuit of the M.B.A. degree. Now you must start your search for the perfect fit. The next section will help you choose the right school and program for you and help guide you through the brochures and literature you will need to filter through. If you do your research properly, the desirable program is out there for you. The lesson to be learned is that there are as many programs as there are schools.

KAPLAN

PART TWO

Selecting the Right School and Program

CHAPTER 5

Evaluating Business Schools

Now that you are quite determined to take the plunge into B-school, it's time to start thinking about the most effective ways of finding the right school and program for you.

HOW TO FIND OUT ABOUT SCHOOLS

Since you are applying to a part-time M.B.A. program, your selection of schools to attend will be limited by your location and current job restrictions. But how is the best way to start your research?

Friends, Family, or Work

It's possible that a family member or friend has already been through the process. If this is the case, pick their brain; ask what helped them determine which school to attend. Keep an open mind, and remember: What works for others—even your sibling or best friend—doesn't necessarily work for you.

As far as work is concerned, unless you are setting a precedent, someone must have led the way before you. Perhaps your employers have a listing of schools for which they authorize tuition reimbursement. Check your human resources manual or ask to speak confidentially with someone in the personnel office. If you are the first in your office to break this new ground, congratulations—you've achieved quite a bit already! Be sure to check out the next two points, as your B-school investigation will most likely be based on reputation and/or pure research.

Reputation/Word of Mouth

Depending on where you live, you may have only a few options. Unless you reside in a vacuum, you are most likely aware of the universities in your city or town. Which ones are perceived as the best?

Internet Info

Check out www.mbainfo.com, a global M.B.A. Program Information Site where you can get the e-mail address to correspond with schools and obtain feedback on more than 2,280 M.B.A. programs from current students and graduates.

Research

In the back of this book, you'll find a geographical listing of all schools offering Part-Time M.B.A., Executive M.B.A., and Distance Learning programs. This is a great place to kick off your B-school search. Also, you can do a little browsing on the Internet. There are several sites out there (for example, www.gmat.org) that list neighboring schools with M.B.A. programs. Request brochures and read through them carefully—but don't judge a book by its cover. The school with the nicest brochure and the snazziest Web site is not always the best selection for you!

HOW TO SELECT THE RIGHT SCHOOL

As a part-time B-school candidate, who, more likely than not, will continue to work on a full-time basis, you will be limited in your options. When selecting which schools to apply to, your decision will probably be based on several factors, including institutional and professional accreditation, location, programs offered, ranking, faculty, and facilities offered.

Accreditation

An important determination in the selecting a program and school is whether or not the institution is accredited. Currently, there are so many different agencies that accredit colleges and universities—12 in all!—that the pertinent question to ask is whether the Council on Postsecondary Education (COPA), the authorized entity that recognizes the accreditation agencies, accredits them. Though the nature of their organization remains the same, COPA has since been dissolved in lieu of the Commission on Recognition of Postsecondary Accreditation (CORPA), which, in turn, has been replaced by a new agency called the Council for Higher Education Accreditation (CHEA).

COPA had originally approved six regional accreditation agencies: the New England Association of Schools and Colleges (NEASC), the Middle States Association of Schools and Colleges (MSASC), the Northwest Association of Schools and Colleges (NASC), the North Central Association of Schools and Colleges (NCASC), the Southern Association of Schools and Colleges (SASC), and the Western Association of Schools and Colleges (WASC).

> ## What Matters
>
> Greg Gomez, Director of Admissions at Southern Illinois University–Edwardsville, identifies the most important criteria to consider when selecting a school:
>
> - Travel and location
> - Schedule of classes
> - Transferability of undergraduate courses
> - Company tuition reimbursement
> - Career services and job placement
> - Evening or weekend options
> - Size of class and teaching methodologies
> - Accessibility of the faculty
> - Admissions requirements
> - Accreditation of program

Although the six regional agencies are separate and distinct, they retain essentially the same standards. A prospective student should understand that the regional accreditation bodies sanction the whole institution and not just some individual parts of the university. What this means is, the university as a *whole* is accredited, and not the M.B.A. program specifically.

The Professional World Chimes In

In addition to this regional accreditation bestowed upon an entire institution, professional accreditations exist that look solely at the quality within a particular discipline. There are two organizations in the United States that accredit business schools. One is the American Assembly of Collegiate Schools of Business (AACSB). This not-for-profit membership company, established in 1916 and located in St. Louis, is the organization originally sanctioned by COPA to accredit bachelor's, master's, and doctoral degree programs in business administration and management. As of September 2000, there are 391 accredited programs: 379 in North America, six in Europe, three in Asia, two in South America, and one in Central America. The AACSB membership consists of over 660 U.S. educational institutions, over 140 international educational institutions, and approximately 50 business, government, and nonprofit organizations. AACSB has bestowed accreditation to only a small percentage of those members seeking inclusion. Standards for AACSB professional accreditation include faculty quality, student quality, curriculum, and program resources, including support staff, library holdings, and computer facilities. For more information regarding AACSB accreditation, refer to their Website at http://www.aacsb.edu.

A second accrediting organization is the Association of Collegiate Business Schools and Programs (ACBSP). This membership organization was established in 1988 to meet the needs of the smaller schools. Its mission is to promote and improve the quality of education for business schools and programs. In 1992, ACBSP received national recognition by the U.S. Department of Education. The ACBSP has now applied for initial eligibility for recognition from the Council for Higher Education Accreditation (CHEA). You may want to check out their Website at http://www.acbsp.org.

Although regional accreditation is necessary for an institution to participate in the federal student aid programs and thus may be very important for you, professional accreditation may not be. More specialized programs may not even be able to obtain such accreditation because of the unorthodoxy of their curricula, even if they are of very high quality.

Location

It's a fact: Unless you are opting for the Distance Learning programs, you will regularly be shuttling from work to school to home and back again. Therefore, you'll need to carefully consider how much time and effort you want to expend on this commute.

Do you want a school close to your office or close to your home? If you will be commuting by car, what will traffic be like during rush hour? Is parking available? Even if you will be taking advantage of public transportation, you must take into account rush-hour congestion.

If you're like everyone else, chances are, nine times out of ten you will leave yourself too little time to get to class on time. Of course, you won't plan for this to happen, but sometimes meetings can't be avoided and the telephone doesn't know to stop ringing at 5 P.M. You want to arrive at school in a calm and composed frame of mind so that you are able to concentrate on the subject at hand (instead of sweating and stressing over commuting issues). This may sound minor to you right now, but remember, on average you will be commuting to school two or three times per week.

Available Programs

Since you have opted to stay employed, you must contend with finding a school in your vicinity that offers either:

- Traditional Part-Time M.B.A. programs,
- Executive M.B.A. programs (if your company will sponsor you), or
- Distance Learning M.B.A. programs.

Not all schools do. Just because a school offers an M.B.A. program does not guarantee that there is a part-time option available. Although more and more programs are being developed that emphasize flexibility, make sure that the schools you are contemplating are very invested in their part-time

---

Don't Feel Like Commuting after Work?

Santa Clara University in Santa Clara, California, has launched a new weekend M.B.A. program to commence in 2000–2001. The weekend M.B.A. is designed for working professionals who are unable to attend evening classes or who would prefer a Saturday meeting time. It is particularly appropriate for individuals who must travel during the week, or who live and work in locations that make it difficult to reach the Santa Clara campus during weekday evening hours.

Highlights:

- Classes meet on Saturdays, approximately twice a month.
- Intensive residential sessions punctuate the program.
- Online components supplement the Saturday sessions.
- Students move through the program as the cohort—everyone takes the same classes in the same sequence.
- The degree is completed in 2 1/2 years (the combination of extended Saturday sessions, intensive residential sessions, and the online component, together with the cohort model, enable the accelerated progress to the degree).

For more information, visit their Website at http://business.scu.edu/weekendmba/.

Are the Classes Limited in Size?

You want to make sure that you are not "shut out"—especially if the class you want is a prerequisite for another one you have planned to register for in the following semester.

programs. Consider the following questions: Can full-time students register for evening courses? Will you be competing with these full-time students for a seat in an evening or weekend class? How many sections of the class are offered (i.e., is the same class offered on different nights)?

Ranking/Reputation

Narrowing down the available part-time B-schools in your commutable area has probably already whittled down your list. But which schools will make the final cut? Rankings are a rough guide to the reputation and quality of the schools and their programs. It is not an exact science, though. When you read "The 10 Best B-Schools in the Northeast," you probably can't help but wonder what the operational definition of "best" is. Best social life? Best placement statistics? Best library (most volumes)? Best applicants (highest GMAT scores)? Best food on campus? Read the fine print when you are perusing some of these surveys and be advised that there is no single accepted ranking system founded on the quality of business schools. Sifting through the recent rankings in *U.S. News and World Report, Business Week,* and others, it's hard to ignore that the same schools do indeed keep popping up, so look for a consensus.

Who Does the Ranking?

In U.S. newsstands you will find rankings in the following publications:

- *Business Week* (includes E.M.B.A. ranking)
- *U.S. News and World Report* (including Part-Time M.B.A. ranking)
- *Which M.B.A.?* (includes Part-Time M.B.A. and E.M.B.A. ranking, as well as some international rankings)
- *The Insiders Guide to the Top 10 M.B.A.'s*
- *The M.B.A. Advantage*

Other rankings:

- Association of M.B.A.'s (a British association founded in 1967)
- *Capital*

You are not alone in reading these articles—your employers (or future employers) look at these statistics as well. Rankings and reputation are appropriate guidelines if your employer is considering these opinions when recommending you for a tuition reimbursement program. So if the prestige, reputation, and marketing of the schools are important to you and your employer, then by all means, take these rankings seriously.

Another important statistic to factor in is the school's placement record, especially if you are considering a career change once you have obtained your degree. Most schools will provide you with a listing of employers who recruit on campus.

Value of Your Degree

The return on investment of your M.B.A. education should be taken into account when selecting a school and program. Most schools will identify the average starting salary ranges for their graduates—look on their Website or brochure. With this information, you can figure out how many years it will take to you recoup your investment.

Numbers Can Be Deceiving

Here's your first accounting lesson: Understand how to read a number. For example, "ten" can be a very small number or a very large amount. Ten cents can be immaterial when you are rounding to the nearest dollar, and ten cents can keep you at your desk for hours on end when your balance sheet is out of balance. The lesson is this: Be very wary in how you interpret the numbers you are reading.

Quality of the Faculty

The quality of a school's faculty is important and is reflected in each program's reputation. Nonetheless, there are several important questions to ask. Since faculty reputation is typically based on research output, how adept are the faculty members at translating research and theory to usable information? Indeed, how much emphasis is given to teaching? Is teaching an activity in which all the faculty members engage, or is it something left to those who no longer are succeeding researchers? What proportion of the classes is taught by full-time faculty members, and what proportion is assigned to adjunct part-time instructors who may not have equivalent credentials? Will you get to take classes with the school's marquis professors? With a proliferation of executive education programs, teachers at many well-known schools are sometimes assigned to teach executive education students instead of the M.B.A.'s. If one of your prime motivations in attending a certain program is to take classes from specific professors, make sure you'll have that opportunity.

School Facilities

Apart from classroom time and study-group session, you probably will not spend too much time on campus. Despite this, you should consider what additional facilities are available to the part-time students.

Specific questions you should ask include:

- What are the library resources and hours of operation?
- When is the bookstore open?
- Is there a computer lab available for part-time students, and what are its hours of operations?
- Is there an area available for you to meet with your group or study in silence? Again, check on the hours of operation.
- Do part-time students have access to the dean's and registrar's office? Is financial aid available to part-time students? If school offices close at 5:00, what other access to information does the student have (such as call-in registration, e-mail, etcetera)?

Try Out a Course

Some schools may allow you to take a course as a nondegree student before applying to the degree program. If the program requires certain prerequisites that you do not have, consider taking them at the school at which you are planning to study for the M.B.A. This will give you the opportunity to personally experience conditions at the school before committing yourself to it.

Part-time students are combining school with the often-hectic demand of work and family, and as a result, they need access to information as effectively as possible. Some schools will handle routine administrative business electronically; for example, allowing students to register and pay for classes over the telephone.

There once was a time when all students needed to register for classes in person or by mail via "registration cards"—drop them in a slot and pray. Fortunately, these days are long gone.

To give yourself a preview of what to expect, ask to take a tour of the campus one evening after work or on a weekend. Peer into the classrooms and library facilities (are they new or antiquated?) and see if you can imagine spending the next few years of your life there. If courses are offered at more than one site, check to ensure that the facilities and services are equivalent at each location. If you will be required to travel to various locales in order to take advantage of all the facilities, you should be aware of this up front, and be forewarned: This information probably will not be volunteered.

Now that you know what kinds of options are available and what you are looking for, how do you choose the specific programs to which you want to apply? The next chapter will deal with the process of narrowing down the field.

Some Nice Extras

Rollins College Crummer Graduate School of Business in Winter Park, FL provides each student with a notebook computer upon enrollment. The computer is loaded with Windows™-based software and used extensively in and out of the classrooms for spreadsheet analysis, online research, slide-show presentations, and electronic communications.

CHAPTER 6

Finding the Program for You

For each school to which you've chosen to apply, you may have to select from several different M.B.A. programs—different specializations and/or joint degrees. As a result, you may be faced with hundreds of options. When you sit back and imagine your ideal M.B.A. program, what issues come into play? You need to decide what is important to you. Do you need a program with a flexible schedule? How big a workload do you think you can handle? In what sort of learning environment do you thrive best? You will need to take a number of factors into account when assessing which M.B.A. programs fit your wants and needs, ranging from curriculum to cost.

CURRICULUM

Although all M.B.A. programs differ, there exists a general core curriculum that all students must follow. To complement the core courses, students usually have the option of selecting a "concentration"—similar to a major in undergraduate studies. The selection of concentrations in the M.B.A. program focuses on major business disciplines, such as finance, management, marketing, accounting and taxation, organizational behavior, communications, and now, e-business. This selection is gradually broadening as the business field's demand for a more well-rounded student increases.

No Travel Required

Depending on where you live, you may not have a very expansive selection of schools left. If this is the case, you should also consider Distance Learning programs. In the back of this book, we have provided a listing of all available M.B.A. programs.

For the student who has been out of undergraduate school for many years, some programs require a foundation, leveling, or prerequisite coursework to be completed in order to obtain the M.B.A. degree. A sampling of some of these courses includes:

- Mathematics or calculus for business
- Statistics
- Marketing
- Accounting
- Business law
- Economics

These types of courses cover the common body of business knowledge that would normally be included in an undergraduate business curriculum. Depending on the student's background, many of the courses listed above can be waived. Although each school has their own policy, credit for leveling-type courses taken at the undergraduate level are generally applied towards the M.B.A. degree only if the student received a B or better and if the course was taken within the last five years. Check with the admissions office of the prospective B-school and inquire as to their policy regarding waivers. Some schools may require you to pass a placement exam to judge whether or not you have the competency to waive a certain course.

One piece of advice: Don't make this your first question. There's nothing worse than starting off a program by asking which courses you can waive. It may come across as though you are not serious about putting your all into getting your M.B.A., which is a very serious and time-consuming endeavor indeed. However, this is obviously an important question to ask when determining which program is right for you, so voice this concern to the admissions department without stressing the urgency of the request. Try to think about your discussions with the university personnel in the

---

Is the School Web-Savvy?

"E-Commerce" combines telecommunications, information technology, and computer technology to support and record business transactions without human intervention. It is vital for tomorrow's managers to understand how the Internet is changing the way business is conducted, and be comfortable with emergent technologies. Rutgers Graduate School of Management, for one, provides a comprehensive look at this rapidly growing field. Some topics covered in the curriculum include Web publishing, network security, legal issues, understanding buyer behavior on the Web, and growing new business ventures.

same light as talking with a future employer. Imagine that the first question you pose at an interview is how much vacation time you would be entitled to. Doesn't sound quite right, does it? Show respect to the admissions office—there are *thousands* of applicants who request admission to M.B.A. programs but only a few spots available. Even though you are the customer, there is a shortage of supply, so be advised.

Cohort Programs

Some M.B.A. programs, mainly full-time and executive M.B.A.'s, are cohorted, which means that all students are required to follow the same curriculum at the same pace. In this program, students usually do not have the option of skipping a class unless they agree to take off a full year and resume studies with the incumbent class. While the scheduling procedures can be very frustrating, the cohort programs are wonderful in that the student has a terrific opportunity to bond with other classmates and learn a great deal from them as well as from the faculty.

Other M.B.A. programs will permit the student to take classes in the order that most suits the student's schedule. Although there is some flexibility in the scheduling of your classes, registration for a particular course may require a prerequisite. For example, Corporate Finance may be your area of interest, but most institutions will require that you take Financial Accounting first.

As mentioned above, for the student looking to attend part-time, cohort programs have historically been available only for the Executive M.B.A. candidate. However, to allow more part-time students to take advantage of this type of curriculum, new cohorted weekend M.B.A. programs are surfacing nationwide. Although very taxing on your time, these programs allow part-timers to get the flavor of a full-time degree.

> **Important Questions to Ask Yourself**
>
> "Is the program AACSB accredited? Are the faculty and administration fully linked with top companies in business? Is the organization made up of students, faculty, and administration who are active and open to change, or is the situation bureaucratic? What are the faculty credentials, and is there a sense of pride and excitement about what they are doing?"
>
> — *Pamela Curry, Assistant Director of Graduate Programs, Dolan School of Business, Fairfield University*

Sample Curriculum

(Some schools may require proficiency in Calculus, Statistics, and Economics prior to matriculation.)

Management Courses (6 credits)

Overview & Major Paradigms of Business	Managing Diversity
Managing in a Global Setting	Managing Total Quality
Problem Solving & Critical Thinking	Ethics

Personal Skills Courses (2 credits)

Leadership & Change	Executive Communications
Managing Conflict	Team Work

Core Courses (31 credits)

Financial Accounting	Budgeting & Planning
Economics	Principles of Finance
Statistical Models and Process Management	Math for Managers
Marketing Management	Business Policy
Business Law	Managing Human Resources
Development & Management of Information Systems	International Business Environment
Formulating & Implementing Strategy	Operations Management

Elective/Concentration Courses (21 credits)

Accounting/Taxation	Marketing Management
General Management	Finance/Banking
Global Management/Entrepreneurship	MIS
Supply Chain Management	Human Resources Management

Total   60 credits

Back to Basics

Many business schools have expanded the requirements of their core curriculum to include courses that will better equip the student in today's management environment by focusing on the quality of their "soft skills" (refer to the end of this chapter for a complete definition of this term). For some of the more experienced professionals going back to school to obtain their M.B.A., this may be a source of great frustration. Effective communications, managing conflict, managing human resources, and computer proficiency are skills used daily by top-level management. Management seminars and conferences dealing with these subjects are commonplace for today's managers, yet they usually do not count, credit-wise.

> **You Do the Math**
>
> "When I was in grad school, I was exempt from Statistics (I had received a B or better in college and had taken it within five years). Math, on the other hand, I had not taken since high school! I was always a whiz at Algebra, and did not feel the need to take it again. I was informed that I was required take Algebra. What I don't understand is how I was waived from Statistics, whose prerequisite is math, and still required to take math!"
>
> – *M.B.A., Fordham University*

Keep in mind that although you may think you know it all, you will be surprised at what you can learn. Soft skills always need fine-tuning, and you will soon come to realize that these courses are not waste of time or money.

Once again, there are practically as many M.B.A. programs as there are students. The sample curriculum on the previous page is for reference only and can provide you with an understanding of the types of courses you will be expected to complete (and in what order) prior to graduating with an M.B.A. Depending on your undergraduate results and your experience, you may be entitled to waive certain classes. (Each school has its own policy for waivers.)

YOUR AREA OF INTEREST

Many schools will offer programs with a specialization that matches your area of interest. You should ask whether the program is very structured (i.e., all the classes are preselected for the student) or if it permits you to select from an array of electives. How diverse are the electives? Are new courses being added?

"I travel too much for work now, but that will change soon."

If you want to attend a traditional Part-Time M.B.A. program but for now are required to travel too much, you can either postpone enrollment or consider programs that permit you to take core courses on the Internet. That will buy you a little time!

YOUR SCHEDULE

The demanding nature of your current work and home schedules should not be minimized. If your job requires you to do a lot of traveling, you should consider a Flexible M.B.A. program, which permit the student to take some classes online, or a Weekend M.B.A. program, now being developed at schools all over the nation.

ENTRY BARRIERS

Do you have the right profile to gain admission? Most M.B.A. programs will require you to have an undergraduate degree from an accredited school; there will also be GMAT standards and perhaps a requirement for the number of years of professional experience. Do you make the cut?

TEACHING METHODOLOGIES

Most M.B.A. programs will use a mix of the four major varieties of teaching methods: case studies, lectures, group assignments, and individual assignments.

Case Studies

In the case method environment, the professor doesn't lecture but rather facilitates the open dialogue with the students by asking probing questions, expecting the students to fill most of the class time with their observations, insights, and analysis. Each class revolves around actual business situations, and students are cast in the role of decision makers. For example, the class is given the facts about a struggling business, and must develop a plan to improve its performance.

There are a few schools where the case method is the primary teaching tool, but you'll find cases in general management courses at even the most analytical programs. The objective of the case method is to stimulate a real-world environment. Students must

KAPLAN

analyze each case and develop a plan of action—i.e., what they're going to do and how they plan to do it—with limited information and time at their disposal. Occasionally, individuals whose experience is the basis for a case may sit in on the class to share their insights. In some instances, you may have the opportunity to do advanced planning for case studies. The details are assigned as homework to be carefully considered and prepared by the next class.

Lectures by Faculty and Staff

A lecture-based classroom is, in all likelihood, what you experienced as an undergraduate. The professor provides information, and interaction between students and the professor, or between students, is controlled and generally limited. Students need to sit and take notes, and not necessarily participate in any of the discussions, although participation is often expected, and sometimes graded. Many schools invite guest lecturers to speak. Look for a listing of recent lecturers—the high quality of guest speakers reflects positively on the school.

Group Projects and Presentations

Project-oriented classes have resulted from student demand that classes be closely related to real-world business situations. They are akin to the case method approach in the role in which they cast the student. In project courses, a student—or, more often, a team of students—works as a consultant with the client company on a project or problem facing that company. While in a case discussion the facts of the case are assembled beforehand, the team working on a project often has to start from scratch, determining what information is needed, reviewing company documents, and interviewing company employees. Regular class meetings with the professor provide an opportunity to learn more about the subject and to discuss the particular problems and applications arising from the projects themselves. The course may end with each team presenting the project recommendations and actions to the class and to the actual clients of the company. Project courses tend to be extremely time-consuming, because of the need to consult with the clients and

> **Work That Counts Twice**
>
> "As a part-time student, I was able to apply what I learned immediately, and, as a bonus, get credit on both the school and office fronts. On many occasions my professors allowed me to use a work-related project as basis for a homework assignment. The double duty paid off—with an M.B.A. degree and a promotion!"
>
> — *M.B.A. graduate*

with the other members of the team, but are effective at bridging the gap between classroom and the workplace. Some groups may be chosen by the students themselves, others by the professors—presumably to promote a cross-disciplinary team approach.

The Right Atmosphere?

"Everyone wanted to do well. The atmosphere was competitive, but not cutthroat. That may be because the team structure sort of forces students to help each other."

– *M.B.A., Stern School of Business, New York University*

Individual Assignments and Presentations

This teaching method most closely resembles undergraduate assignments. Most core curriculum is a mixture of lecture and individual assignments or presentations (such as statistics, math, economics, etcetera).

Everyone learns differently, so select a program with the teaching environment that will allow you to thrive. Another issue to keep in mind is how well your learning style fits with the course expectations of the programs you are considering. For example in case method classrooms, as much as half of your grade will be based on class participation. If you think you may be less than eager to participate in this kind of forum, or you believe that your business travel schedule may force you to be absent during some of the classrooms discussions, you should ask yourself seriously if a case school is appropriate environment for you.

COST OF THE PROGRAM

If your employer is paying for your program, finances will probably not be weighed too heavily in your decision. Even so, remember that you will probably need to:

- Make the payments up front (you may not be reimbursed until your grades are official)
- Pay for a percentage of the tuition if you don't get all A's
- Cover the expense of books and incidentals
- Pay for school fees (such as registration, insurance, and so forth)

If your employer is not paying for your degree, there are a few options to consider, such as:

- School loans
- Scholarships
- Government aid
- Your savings
- Family loan

In part 4 we will review these and other possible funding sources in the event that your company does not have a tuition reimbursement policy in place.

LENGTH OF THE PROGRAM

More and more M.B.A. programs are streamlining the number of credits required to complete the degree. Cognizant of your personal schedule, how long will the degree take you to complete? What is the school's policy on waiving courses? And most importantly: Is the program start date consistent with when you want to begin the program? If this is not the case, and there are no rolling admissions, you may find yourself missing a deadline and waiting a full year before entering a program.

WORKLOAD

Think about how hard you are prepared to work. It is generally true that the more effort you put into your program, the more you will gain from it, but some programs demand an extraordinary amount of work.

If the program uses teams for projects and cases, the time required can rise rapidly. Even without group or team meetings, you may need to spend six or more hours per week outside the classroom for each course.

> **How Many Credits?**
>
> In general, the M.B.A. student is expected to earn around 60 credits in order to graduate. That translates to about 20 classes!

FLEXIBILITY OF THE PROGRAM

Obviously, you need to weigh the importance of various aspects of the program are and see where you need the most flexibility. Some areas you should consider include:

- Can you transfer from part-time to full-time programs (or vice-versa)?
- Can you transfer credits from other schools?
- Can you take time off during your program?
- Is there any traveling required?
- When are the classes taught: evenings only? weekends?
- How diverse is the student body?

PARETO CHART

One of the tools you will learn to use in your M.B.A. program is the Pareto Chart. The Pareto Chart is a special form of vertical bar graph that helps determine which problems to solve in which order. When you need to display the relative importance of all the problems and conditions in order to choose the starting point for problem solving, monitor success, or identify the basic cause of a problem, use the Pareto.

Let's try one to determine which M.B.A. program is right for you!

Step 1
Identify which items need to be compared and rank-order them. Since this is a very subjective exercise, you may want to brainstorm with your friends, family, and colleagues to determine which criteria should be weighed more heavily than others.

Step 2
Select the standard for comparison unit of measurement, for example, the items that came up most frequently in discussion (i.e., location or reputation of school).

Step 3

List the categories from left to right on the horizontal axis in order of decreasing occurrence. Categories with the fewest items can be combined, listed as "Other," and placed to the right of the last bar.

Step 4

Above each classification of category, draw a rectangle to represent the frequency of that classification.

Here is a very simplified example:

- Proximity to home: very important.
- Availability to take core courses online: somewhat important.
- Availability of broadband concentration: crucial.
- Depth of the part-time program course offerings (a wide selection of courses offered on each day with availability to take a prerequisite several days per week): most important.

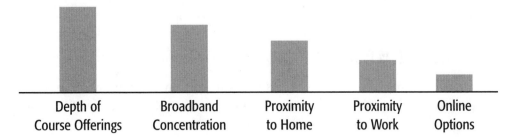

| Depth of Course Offerings | Broadband Concentration | Proximity to Home | Proximity to Work | Online Options |

Now remember, this is an example. You can do the same: Fill in the table below and see if you can create a Pareto Chart too.

You can rank the importance on a scale of 1–10 or rank it by percent. Those with low importance can be grouped together in an "Other" category.

Category/Criteria	Importance
Proximity of school to home	
Proximity of school to work	
Availability of concentration in _____	
Flexibility of the program	
Start time of the program	
Reputation of the school/program	
Cost (tuition reimbursement?)	
Quality of faculty	
Quality of life issues (workload, etcetera)	
School facilities (library, computer lab, gym, etcetera)	
Length of the program	

Now chart your responses (you can add categories) and see which programs at which schools match your criteria.

LEARNING THE M.B.A. LANGUAGE

Before reading through school brochures or setting off on the application process described in the next section, you should familiarize yourself with the M.B.A. language. The definitions below will assist you and acclimate you to the world of M.B.A.!

M.B.A. Lexicon

AACSB: The International Association for Management Education. This is the main accrediting agency for American B.A. programs. For further information, refer to their Website at http://www.aacsb.edu.

Accreditation: The validation or acceptance of a program and/or school by an independent organization that determines the standards for the degree. The accrediting body for U.S. M.B.A.'s is the AACSB.

ACBSP: The Association of Collegiate Business Schools and Programs. Founded in 1988, ACBSP is an accrediting agency that operates mainly in the United States. It aims to establish, promote, and recognize educational standards that contribute to the continuous improvement of business education and to recognize those schools and programs which adhere to these standards. ACBSP has become a principal creditor for small to midsize graduate degree programs. For additional information, go to their Website: http://www.acbsp.org.

AMA: The American Management Association. The AMA is a nonprofit organization that assists individuals and corporate members worldwide through regional chapters. AMA services include publishing "best practices," conducting seminars and conferences, and publishing business-related books and CD-ROMs. The AMA is one of the world's largest management associations with locations worldwide. Visit their Website at http://www.amanet.org.

Case Study Method: A teaching method that involves the study of actual business cases.

Cohort Programs: A group program in which all students follow the same course of study together and graduate together.

Company (or Corporate) Program or Consortium Program: M.B.A. degrees run exclusively for the executives of a single company; these programs are not available to the public. Consortium programs have gained a great amount of popularity abroad; however, they have yet to catch on in the United States.

Computer-Based Program: See **Electronic Program**

Concentration, Focus, or Specialization: Although the majority of M.B.A. programs focus on general management skills, most require the student to select from a range of business sectors, such as marketing, finance, management, and information management. A recent trend at M.B.A. schools is the expanded selection of specialization offered to the students (i.e., e-commerce, entrepreneurship, broadband, etcetera).

Core: Central curriculum of a program representing the required courses. Students must complete these courses prior to any concentration courses or electives.

CV (Curriculum Vitae): Latin wording for résumé, although a CV tends to be longer and more detailed. Basically, it's a summary of one's personal history and professional qualifications. An admissions packet may require this document. Ensure that your CV is neat and up to date.

Distance Learning Program: This term was originally used for mail correspondence-type programs but has evolved to include other media besides print. Distance learning now encapsulates computer and video conferencing, Internet classes, and other sophisticated tools used to simulate a virtual classroom.

Elective: Not core courses; courses unrelated to a one's area of specialization or concentration. Most M.B.A. programs will allow students to select from a number of electives. For example: An M.B.A. student concentrating in marketing can opt to take a finance elective in Futures and Options.

Electronic Program: This usually related to the method of communication for non-classroom courses (such as Distance Learning programs or courses offered over the Internet). An electronic program can be considered the Internet, video conferencing, e-mail delivery of material and submission of assignments, and so forth.

Executive M.B.A. (E.M.B.A.): A type of Part-Time M.B.A. program that is completely sponsored by an employer. This program is designed for executives with several years of management experience. Students of the E.M.B.A. will usually be required to attend classes on Fridays and Saturdays throughout the year.

FAFSA: Free Application for Federal Student Aid. This form is required in your application packet if you wish to apply for financial assistance. Visit FAFSA's Website at http://www.fafsa.ed.gov/.

Faculty: Although each school is different, the teaching staff of a university usually is ranked based on years of experience and accomplishment. Assistant professors, associate professors, and full professors are examples of faculty titles.

Functional Areas: The basic disciplines of business.

GMAT: Graduate Management Admissions Test, the exam which measures a candidate's language, quantitative skills, and writing ability. The test is administered as computer-adaptive test, or GMAT CAT. Scores range from 200 to 800.

M.B.A.: Masters of Business Administration. This is the generic term for a graduate degree in business administration, although some schools opt to use their own nomenclature. Just because a program is not called "M.B.A." does not mean it is not a graduate degree in business administration (refer to chapter 1).

Modular Programs: Very similar to part-time programs. While part-time programs usually require attendance at the school on a frequent basis for short periods of time, modular programs normally demand less frequent but longer periods of attendance—ranging from a few days to a few weeks. Some schools refer to this type of program as a **Flexible Program.** These programs have not caught on yet in the U.S. but are quite popular overseas.

TOEFL: Test of English as a Foreign Language. This is a test of English Language ability for those whose first language is not English; for nonnative speakers, taking the TOEFL is usually a requirement.

Pre-Enrollment Courses: Some schools may require a certain proficiency in basic quantitative skills prior to starting the M.B.A. program. These skills need to be fine tuned prior to debuting the M.B.A. program.

Rolling Admissions: Schools using rolling admissions evaluate the student's application as they are submitted. Applicants usually learn of the school's decision within a month's time. Many part-time programs operate on a rolling admissions basis.

Rounds Admissions: Schools using rounds admissions will group together all applications and evaluate all candidates together. Therefore, a student who applies to a school using rounds admissions can apply in September but not find out until December if they have been accepted to the program.

Sallie Mae: Student Loan Marketing Association, Inc. It's a company that provides funds for educational loans, primarily, federally guaranteed student loans originated under the Federal Family Education Loan Program (FFELP). For more information, check out their Web site at http://www.salliemae.com.

Soft Courses: Less quantitative core and elective classes. Management, Human Resource, Organizational Behavior, Leadership, and Communication are examples soft courses. Recently, these courses are being emphasized in M.B.A. programs.

Soft Skills: Skills taught in **Soft Courses.** These include oral and written communication, conflict resolution, negotiation, teamwork, and leadership.

Study Abroad: Carrying out some portion of M.B.A. study at another (international) location. Once available only to full-time students, study abroad programs have been introduced at M.B.A. schools nationwide. At Syracuse University, part-time M.B.A.'s can now experience a one-week study abroad residency program.

Web Application: A means of applying to school online. Schools may promote this function by waiving or discounting the standard application fee. Check with the school's Website prior to mailing in your application.

So there you have it, a few terms and acronyms to know. Hopefully they will help you through the application process and detangle some of the jargon you may come across on a school Website or in a brochure. Good luck!

PART THREE

Admissions

CHAPTER 7

How Do Schools Evaluate Applicants?

Each business school has its own admissions policies and practices, but most programs evaluate applications using a range of objective and subjective criteria. Regardless of which schools you are pursuing, understanding how admissions officers judge your candidacy can give you a leg up on the competition, enhancing your prospects for being admitted to the school of your choice.

Generally, admissions officers use the application process to measure your intellectual abilities, management skills, and personal characteristics. When you submit your application, admissions officers will evaluate the total package. Most admissions officers look for reasons to admit candidates, not for reasons to reject them. Your challenge, therefore, is to distinguish yourself positively from the other candidates in a variety of arenas.

ACADEMIC RECORD

Admissions officers are likely to start their review by looking at your prior academic record. They want to see evidence of your ability to handle the academic rigors of their program. Also, your academic record enables admissions officers to compare you to other students, albeit imperfectly.

This is why your admissions application must include official copies of your academic transcripts from every postsecondary school you attended, whether or not you received a degree. You must request that these transcripts be sent to you in sealed envelopes for you to include in your self-managed application. Even if you have an official copy of your college transcript, the B-school requires that you submit an official copy in an envelope sealed by the registrar of your college. Colleges usually charge a fee for copies of your transcript, so contact the college registrar's office to find out the costs and request the transcripts.

Ask Yourself . . .

- Do my grades show an upward trend?
- Did I perform well in my major?
- Did I fare well in calculus and other quantitative courses?

If the answer to any of these questions is no, you may have to take action to improve your transcript.

Your grade point average (GPA) is important, but it's just part of the picture. Admissions officers will consider the reputation of your undergraduate institution and the difficulty of your courses. Admissions officers are well aware that comparing GPAs from different schools and even different majors from the same school is like comparing apples and oranges. So they'll look closely at your transcript.

Calculus, statistics, and other quantitative courses may be prerequisites for your intended program. Quantitative skills are considered essential in completing M.B.A. coursework, and your record in these areas will be carefully scrutinized for difficulty, currency, and overall quality by admissions committees. If your transcript does not show any evidence of quantitative skills, you should consider taking courses in accounting and statistics to demonstrate your aptitude and to reinforce your commitment to pursuing a business degree.

A strong performance in your advanced courses and major is interpreted as an indication that you can handle difficult work and that you can excel in your field of choice. An admissions officer may pay particularly close attention to your GPA in your last two years of undergraduate study, since most students complete work in their major as college juniors and seniors. But don't think an attempt to raise your GPA by taking introductory level courses your last term will not be recognized for what it is.

The weight that is given to your undergraduate grades in the admission decision is affected in part by the length of time you have been out of school. If you have been out of school for some time, the passage of years makes it easier to argue that low grades can be attributed to youthful inexperience, now replaced by maturity. Unfortunately, it also raises the question of maintenance over time of skills that once brought impressive grades but that may now be rusty, if not in total disrepair. Admissions officers will look for evidence in other parts of your application to support their reading of a transcript earned years earlier.

> **Brush up on Your Skills**
>
> "Since I had been out of school for more than 20 years, I took an algebra course at a local community college before starting my GMAT preparation. This not only started me thinking mathematically, but also helped me do well on the GMAT."
>
> – E.M.B.A. candidate, Stern School of Business, New York University

For more recent graduates, meanwhile, the transcript is seen as a likely predictor of current skills and performance. This implies that strong grades may help offset weakness in other areas, but weak grades are much harder to dismiss or counter.

Admissions officers focus primarily on your undergraduate performance, but they will consider graduate studies and nondegree coursework that you have completed. If you have a weak undergraduate record, you may want to take additional courses to demonstrate your ability to succeed in the classroom. You may be inclined to enroll for nondegree courses in an M.B.A. program rather than in a community college or four-year undergraduate program to show your ability to handle this type of work. Be aware, though, that some top-tier programs will not accept students who have substantially completed another M.B.A. program, even from a nonaccredited program, and that admissions officers will examine these transcripts with as much care as they will use for transcripts of your undergraduate degree.

If you have a poor academic record, it will be tougher to get into a top school, but by no means impossible. Your challenge is to find other ways to demonstrate your intellectual horsepower. A high GMAT score, intelligently written essays, and recommendations that highlight your analytical abilities will help. Your work experience may show a record of promotion and success in meeting new intellectual challenges.

GMAT

The second criterion that admissions officers use to measure your intellectual ability is the Graduate Management Admission Test (GMAT). An integral part of the admissions process at virtually all schools, the GMAT measures verbal, quantitative, and analytical writing skills that are developed over your educational career. It does not test business competence or specific subject knowledge beyond general mathematics and English usage. The GMAT is designed to predict academic success in the first year of a graduate business school program.

Unlike undergraduate grades, which vary in their meaning from institution to institution and from discipline to discipline, GMAT scores use a consistent standard for all test takers. Thus the GMAT can be a useful guide in comparing the credentials of candidates from widely different backgrounds. Used by itself, the GMAT may not be a highly reliable predictor of academic performance, but it is the single best one available. Many schools routinely perform studies to gauge the effectiveness of the GMAT and other admission criteria in predicting performance in their program, and use this information to help them interpret the scores applicants present.

Description of the GMAT

Since October 1997, the GMAT has been administered exclusively in a computerized format in North American and in many other parts of the world. This new type of test is called the Computer Adaptive Test (CAT), and is more than just a computerized version of a traditional paper-and-pencil test. The CAT allows you to see only one question at a time; you must answer that question to continue the test. Each question is chosen from a large pool of questions of varying degrees of difficulty. The first question is of medium difficulty. The selection of each subsequent question is determined by your response to all previous questions. If you keep answering questions correctly, the test will increase in difficulty; if you slip and make some mistakes, the test will adjust and start giving you easier problems. If you answer the easier questions correctly, the CAT will return to the harder ones.

One of the major differences between the CAT and a traditional paper-and-pencil test is that the CAT doesn't permit you to skip around within a section and do questions in any order. You also cannot go back and change your answer. Instead, you have to do your best to get a question right the first time you see it.

Work systematically at the beginning of a GMAT CAT section. Use scratch paper to help you organize your thinking. The first 10–15 questions of a section are crucial in determining your ability estimate, so invest the necessary time to try and answer these questions correctly. You must, however, pace yourself so that you have time to answer every question in the section. You will be penalized for questions you don't reach.

The purpose of the CAT is to give you a score based on the level at which you answer questions correctly about half the time. Hence the overall number you get right is not as important as the level at which you start getting about half the questions wrong. In spite of all these differences, computer-based test scores are considered comparable to paper scores.

There are a number of advantages to the new testing format. Among these are:

Convenience

Unlike the paper-and-pencil GMAT, which was administered only four times a year, the CAT is available throughout the year on an appointment basis. You can take it at hundreds of computer centers around the country.

Additional Time Per Question

The CAT allows you more time per question than the traditional test did.

Immediate Scoring

Once you have completed the computer-adaptive GMAT, you can choose to see your scores for the multiple-choice sections of the test at the test center. If you are not happy with your performance, you may cancel your scores before you see them.

Faster Score Reporting

An official score report, including scores for the Analytical Writing Assessment, will be mailed to you and your designated institutions about two weeks after testing. Scores for the paper-based GMAT used to be reported four to ten weeks after the testing date.

Individualized Environment

When you take the CAT, you are alone with a computer in the quiet and privacy of a separate testing station, not elbow to elbow with many other people in a large room. This no-distractions environment is very beneficial to some people.

Test Your Best on the GMAT

Kaplan's GMAT course teaches you the content and strategies you'll need to maximize your GMAT score and provides you with the opportunity to practice on authentic computer-adaptive tests. Call (800) KAP-TEST or visit kaptest.com to find out more details. You can also find Kaplan/Simon & Schuster's test-prep guide, *GMAT CAT*, in most bookstores.

You do not need to be computer-literate to take the CAT. Before beginning the test, you'll complete a tutorial to ensure that you are comfortable at the keyboard. It covers such areas as using a computer mouse, entering a response, using the word processor, accessing the help function, and moving on to the next question. The help function will be available throughout the actual test.

The GMAT CAT includes verbal, quantitative, and analytical writing questions that you answer on the computer. You will have 75 minutes to complete 37 quantitative questions, 75 minutes for 41 verbal questions, and 30 minutes for each of the two analytical writing topics. The types of questions are the same as in the paper-based test, but the multiple choice questions are not grouped into sections by specific question types. Instead, Data Sufficiency and Problem Solving questions are interspersed throughout the quantitative section, and Sentence Correction, Reading Comprehension, and Critical Reasoning questions can be found throughout the verbal section.

Analytical Writing Assessment

The GMAT contains an essay section, the Analytical Writing Assessment (AWA), that asks you to write two essays—one, an analysis of an issue and the other, an analysis of an argument. The AWA is designed to provide schools with information about your communications skills that is not otherwise captured by the GMAT.

Essentially, the AWA is another tool that schools can use to evaluate you. Although it won't reduce the importance of the essays on your applications, it does provide you with an opportunity to demonstrate your ability to think critically and communicate complex ideas in a very limited time period. For that reason, admissions officers may be as interested in reading your writing samples as they are in relying on your overall GMAT score.

> **AWA Prep**
>
> Look through a dictionary of quotations and memorize some useful sayings. Even if you wind up not including them in your essay, you can impress friends and colleagues by quoting famous people at your next cocktail party.

On the other hand, admissions officers at top-tier schools already struggle to get through all their applications. That will limit the time they can spend reviewing these handwritten essays. Remember also that some applicants are still submitting old GMAT scores that do not include writing samples. Admissions officers are careful not to discriminate for or against candidates based on which GMAT they've taken.

Even though the AWA is scored separately from the multiple-choice sections, you should prepare for it with the same intensity that you put into preparing for the rest of the GMAT. Outstanding writing samples can help you stand out from the crowd. Conversely, seriously flawed essays can reduce your admissions chances.

What Your GMAT Scores Mean

You will receive a total of four scores on the GMAT: one each for the verbal, quantitative, and analytical writing sections and an overall score. It is this overall score that is used when programs report an "average GMAT score" for candidates accepted to the program, and the overall score that receives the most attention when admissions officers review your application. If you've taken the GMAT more than once, schools will generally credit you with your highest score, though some may average the scores or take the most recent one.

The total score is reported an a 200 to 800 scale, with an average score of 500. Each standard deviation from the mean (average) equals 100 points. According to this scale, a score of 700 is two standard deviations above the mean, indicating that approximately 97 percent of all scores fall below this mark.

In addition to the actual score you receive on the 200 to 800 scale, you will get a "percentile ranking" that tells you what percentage of test takers had scores below yours. You will also receive a percentile ranking for your performance on the verbal portion of the test and a second percentile ranking for the quantitative section. Although these scores typically do not receive as much attention from schools as your overall score, they can be very helpful in corroborating impressions from other parts of your application or filling in gaps in the information. For example, if you have never taken a college-level quantitative course, your score on the quantitative section of the GMAT may provide evidence of your current skills in that area.

The score on the Analytical Writing Assessment is reported separately from the score on the multiple choice sections of the GMAT. Reported on a scale of zero to six in half-point increments, a score of six is defined as "outstanding," whereas a four is considered "adequate," and a score of one is "fundamentally deficient." A zero score is given if the essay is off-topic, in a foreign language, or merely attempts to copy the topic. The average score is about 3.5. As with the scores on the verbal and quantitative sections, the AWA score provides additional information about this important skill. It will be reviewed more closely if there are questions about your critical thinking and writing skills than if you have clearly demonstrated expertise in these areas from your credentials.

Registering for the GMAT

In the United States, U.S. territories, Puerto Rico, and Canada, you can register for the GMAT by phone using a credit card. If you don't have a credit card, you can submit a registration form by mail and receive a voucher that will then allow you to schedule your GMAT CAT appointment by phone. Phone registration is available at (800) GMAT-NOW ((800) 462-8669) or at a local Sylvan Technology Center. Phone registration is available through regional registration centers located around the world.

Although the computer adaptive test is given on many days during the month and it is typically possible to get a testing time within 30 days of your request, the most popular times are filled quickly. Advance booking will allow you to get the time and place you want. Moreover, since you can take the GMAT CAT only once per calendar month, taking it early will allow you to repeat it, if necessary, and still have scores before the end of the admission season.

Score reports are mailed weekly to the schools that you indicate on your registration form should receive your test results. Additional information on GMAT registration, both in the United States and internationally, is available through the Graduate Management Admission Council's Web site at http://www.gmat.org.

Repeating the GMAT

Although some people repeat the GMAT because a management school requests more recent scores than currently on record, the most common reason for repeating the test is to attempt to improve test scores. Although mere familiarity with the test may push scores slightly higher the second time, scores can also drop. Unless your scores seem unusually low compared with other indicators of your ability to succeed in an M.B.A. program or there are other reasons to believe you have not performed your best, such as illness or lack of preparation, taking the GMAT more than once may not be helpful.

If you choose to repeat the test, your scores from the latest test date and the two most recent administrations in the past five years will be reported to the institutions you designate as score recipients.

MANAGEMENT SKILLS

To evaluate your management skills, admissions officers look at work experience and other relevant activities. They generally believe that the best way to measure your management potential is to look at what you've actually done. Many graduate business programs expect candidates to have several years of work experience prior to entrance. If your credentials fall outside the typical range of work experience for the program, you may need to compensate with the quality of your experience in other arenas.

You can communicate some of your management abilities through the straightforward "data" part of your application. Be sure to describe your job responsibilities. Don't just list your title and assume that an admissions officer knows what you do or the level of your responsibilities. This is especially important if your job is nontraditional for an aspiring M.B.A.

Many M.B.A. candidates come from the traditional areas of consumer goods, financial institutions, consulting, and accounting. This background is good training ground for management education, especially since there is demand in these industries for M.B.A. graduates. However, applicants from one of these fields will be competing with many others with similar backgrounds, and will need to distinguish themselves through their achievements and the presentation of their other qualities.

Although major companies are a natural path into a graduate management program, they are by no means the only route. If you have experience in a not-for-profit organization, government agency, small- or medium-sized enterprise, or some other institution, your application will already stand out in contrast to those from candidates with large company experience. However, you still face the challenge of translating your experience for the admissions officer and showing why you are a good candidate for an M.B.A. degree.

Admissions officers will look at your overall career record. Have you been an outstanding performer? What do your recommendation writers say about your performance? Have you progressed to increasingly higher levels of responsibility? If you have limited work experience, you will not be expected to match the accomplishments of an applicant with ten years' experience, but you will be expected to demonstrate your abilities.

As you are thinking about your work experience, ask yourself the following questions:

- How can I show that I have been successful in accomplishing my job responsibilities? Additional responsibilities, promotions, salary increases, and leadership assignments might form part of your answer.

- Do I work well with people? M.B.A. programs that stress teamwork are particularly interested in your ability to work well with others, but the general tendency in business to use teams makes this attribute important in all settings.

- What have I managed? Not all jobs involve direct management of people. Perhaps you have managed projects or financial assets, or perhaps you have accomplished goals through other people, even though you have not had direct management authority over them.

- What is the range of my experience? Have I demonstrated abilities in a variety of areas? An M.B.A. is a general management degree. Both during the program and after graduation, M.B.A.'s are expected to be able to work in a variety of disciplines, using a variety of skills.

- Have I excelled in what I do and worked beyond average expectations for the position?

The essays also provide an opportunity to demonstrate your management aptitude. Many essay questions specifically ask you to discuss your professional experiences and how you handled different situations. With thoughtful, well-written essays, you can highlight your management strengths.

EXTRACURRICULAR ACTIVITIES AND COMMUNITY INVOLVEMENT

Extracurricular activities and community involvement also present opportunities for you to highlight your skills. For younger applicants, college activities play a more significant role than for more seasoned applicants. Your activities say a lot about who you are and what's important to you. Were you a campus leader? Did your activities require discipline and commitment? Did your work with a team? What did you learn from your involvement?

Active community involvement provides a way for you to demonstrate your management skills and to impress admissions officers with your personal character. In fact, many applications ask directly about community activities. Many programs like to see candidates who demonstrate concern for individuals other than themselves, who are willing and able to assume responsibility beyond their jobs, and who can function in a variety of settings. If you are contemplating getting involved in your community, here's a chance to do something worthwhile and enhance your application in the process.

A good way to organize your thinking is to compile a Personal Data Sheet (PDS) on which you can list all your extracurricular activities, relevant dates of participation, and any honors or positions of leadership you won, along with basic information such as your name, address, phone, undergraduate and graduate GPAs, and GMAT scores. Give this form to your recommenders to remind them of your accomplishments.

> ### Stand Out from the Crowd
>
> "If I had a traditional career (analyst for example), I would be sure that I had an 'unusual' experience about which to write. This means spending a summer as a volunteer building homes for Habitat for Humanity, being a mentor, getting involved with a community 'do-good' organization, etcetera."
>
> – *E.M.B.A., Stern School of Business, New York University*

PERSONAL CHARACTERISTICS

The most subjective criterion on which schools evaluate you is your personal characteristics. Admissions officers judge you in this area primarily through essays, recommendations, and your interview.

Although different schools emphasize different qualities, most seek candidates who demonstrate leadership, maturity, integrity, responsibility, and teamwork. The more competitive schools place special emphasis on these criteria because they have many qualified applicants for each available spot in the class. In fact, the top-tier programs generally require numerous essays so that they can get a complete feel for each applicant's personal qualities.

Your presentation of your personal characteristics is important in demonstrating how well you will fit into the program of your choice. If the program emphasizes teamwork, you will want to make sure you demonstrate interpersonal skills. If you are looking at an international focus, you will want to show that you can adapt to different cultures and environments. If the program is highly competitive, you will want admissions officers to see that you can thrive in that setting.

Business School Admissions Stereotypes		
Background	Perceived Strengths	Perceived Weaknesses
Engineers	Good quantitative skills; process oriented; low risk of poor academic performance	Less developed communication/ interpersonal skills; weaker writing skills
Consultants	Smart; well-grounded in fundamentals; good exposure to business situations	Limited management experience; many qualified applicants to top schools with similar experience
Financial Analysts	Good quantitative skills; solid understanding of business analysis/ research	Limited management experience; many qualified applicants to top schools with similar experience
Entrepreneurs	Hands-on understanding of how business works; high energy; proactive; not many in applicant pool	Impatient with classroom environment; limited interest in business theory
Human Resources People	Interpersonal skills and understanding of employee-related issues; strong team players	Weak quantitative skills; less competitive approach may create academic pressure at top schools
Salespeople	Great "in the trenches" experience; understanding of the customer; strong interpersonal/communication skills	Limited exposure to management; sales sometimes not viewed as training ground for management
Artists, "Poets"	Strong creative skills; unique backgrounds increase classroom diversity	Weaker quantitative skills; limited business exposure; questionable fit; academic risk
Military Personnel	Strong leadership; excellent discipline; hands-on management experience	Inflexible; may have trouble adjusting to a less hierarchical business environment
Accountants	Good numbers skills; understand "language" of business; background helpful for most classes	Quiet; may not participate much in class; not creative

Overcoming Stereotypes

Admissions officers know that all applicants are unique, each with his or her own strengths and weaknesses, and they will judge you on that basis. But after evaluating thousands of applications, stereotypes do emerge, as you can see from the table on the previous page. Understanding how admissions officers will initially perceive your experience—and what it says about you—can help you think strategically about ways to differentiate yourself from other applicants with similar backgrounds.

Increasing Classroom Diversity

Your "personal characteristics" also encompass your gender and ethnic background. Admissions officers work hard to maximize classroom diversity. Each year, they invest significant time and effort to recruit candidates from underrepresented groups. Nevertheless, women and minorities remain underrepresented at most programs. Schools will not admit students they feel are not academically qualified, but diversity goals will help some students stand out in the applicant pool.

Admissions officers encourage applications from international candidates because they add to classroom diversity and provide a fresh perspective. Because all students must be able to communicate effectively, applicants whose native language is not English may be required to take the Test of English as a Foreign Language (TOEFL), Test of Written English (TWE), and/or Test of Spoken English (TSE). Although some schools have minimum test requirements and others use the scores as a guideline, 600 on the TOEFL is generally considered a measure of adequate English skills. Some schools may require or recommend that international students who are admitted with marginal language skills take English coursework before matriculating.

Be aware that diversity extends beyond nationality, race and gender. It may encompass such factors as geography, professional experience, and college studies. The following programs, chosen by their programmatic and geographical diversity, were asked to describe their class profiles in a survey. Their responses should help you identify what the schools are looking for in M.B.A. candidates, and to consider how you can leverage various aspects of your background to your advantage.

What Top M.B.A. Programs Say: Class Profile

University of Chicago

"The typical student at the Graduate School of Business is able to combine superior intellectual skills with excellent interpersonal skills. The typical incoming class that we strive to put together is quite diverse in terms of educational and ethnic backgrounds, career paths and social experience, and country of origin. Many students say they learn as much from the diversity of the other students they meet and work with at the school as they do from their course work. Because each class represents a wide variety of undergraduate majors and backgrounds, the curriculum is wide-ranging enough to satisfy any interest. The faculty is drawn from a variety of disciplines as well, and this diversity is reflected in teaching styles.

"The school seeks candidates with strong potential for success in both an academically demanding program of study and a professional career. We accept applications from students in all fields of undergraduate study and evaluate work experience on an individual basis as well."

Indiana University

"Diversity in terms of race, gender, ethnicity, leadership ability, work experience, and evidence of management potential is important to our matrix. We look for individuals who buy into the team work concept, too. Whether they are Peace Corps volunteers or engineers, it's important for students to have a focus and vision of who they are and where they are going. A rich and diverse profile makes the educational environment beneficial.

"We seek to bring in people who fit our institution. We have a sense of who we are and we project that. We look for a mixture of those with backgrounds in liberal arts and science and engineering as well as business. That way, different approaches to problem solving can be achieved."

Unorthodox Backgrounds at Kellogg

- A Renaissance English major worked in catalog production at Sotheby's auction house in New York City before being accepted to Kellogg Graduate School of Management.

- A pastor at the Fourth Presbyterian Church of Chicago attended Kellogg in order to learn how to manage the church's finances and to rise to the top of her profession.

– Adapted from Newsweek/*Kaplan's* How to Choose a Career and Graduate School, *1999, and* Careers 2000

Fairfield University, Dolan School

"Professional experience is very important because it raises the level of dialogue about business practice in the classroom and in team meetings. A record of academic success, good GMAT scores, and drive are major considerations as well. We also look for diversity and emotional intelligence. Sincerity, intelligence, and self-knowledge are always attractive."

University of California—Los Angeles, Anderson School

"The Anderson School admission policy emphasizes academic ability, leadership, and work experience. The admissions committee evaluates applicants' prospects as effective managers and their projected ability to succeed in and profit from the M.B.A. program. Committee members carefully consider biographical and academic background information, GMAT and TOEFL (for most international applicants) scores, achievements, distinctions, awards and honors, employment history, letters of recommendation, and college and community involvement, especially when candidates have served in a leadership capacity."

THE ADMISSIONS REVIEW PROCESS

To understand the review process, you will need a basic grasp of the review committee, their procedures, and their decisions.

Admissions Committees

Knowing what kind of people are likely to review your application will help you find the appropriate tone for it. Admissions committees vary by school, but, despite common perception, they don't consist entirely of old men with long white beards. At most schools, the committee includes professional admissions officers whose primary responsibility is to select the M.B.A. class from among the applicant pool. Some schools include faculty members on the committee, but many do not. Some schools hire recent graduates to sit on the committee, believing these individuals are in a good position to judge which candidates will benefit from and contribute to the overall business school experience. And at some schools, second year students and/or alumni play a role in reviewing applications and interviewing candidates.

As with most things, knowing the right people helps. But when it comes to the admissions process, it's hard to predict how much benefit you'll receive from an inside connection. If a school's faculty member, administrator, or respected alumnus can put in a good word for you, great. Depending on how influential that person is and how heavily they'll go to bat for you, they can have an impact. But be careful. Generally, the impact is negligible, and you risk antagonizing the admissions committee if you pursue this tactic.

Admissions officers are not always representative of the group of students they admit. Many committees contain a high percentage of women and minorities, and are likely to recognize the importance of diversity in the classroom. Although some admissions officers have had management training and business experience, many have not. They tend to be people-oriented and have strong interpersonal skills. They want to get to "know" you through your application, and they are partial to well-written essays. They're dedicated to maintaining their objectivity in an inherently subjective process, but they all have their "pet" biases (sometimes related to their own academic or professional experience).

Review Procedures

Just as the composition of the admissions committee varies by school, so does the process by which decisions are made. Some schools make decisions by committee, but many use a system in which each application, or "file," is routed from one committee member to another. Here is a standard procedure:

- Application materials are received. The file is compiled by operations staff, who ensure that all components have been received.
- Based on an initial review, the application is put in categories ranging from strong to long-shot. This process varies by school and may involve calculating a weighted average of GPA, GMAT, and work experience. Alternatively, the application may be reviewed by an individual committee member.
- The application is routed to admissions officers, who carefully read it and make written evaluations and recommendations.
- The application goes to the director, who reviews committee members' comments, personally evaluates the application, and makes a final decision.

Evaluations of individual applications are typically "blind," that is, made without knowledge of any prior evaluation, shielding the reviewer from possible effects of bias from the other readers. If all the reviews recommend admission, the application may not go to the director or committee for a final review; applications with split decisions are passed to the committee or director for a decision.

Application Review Cycles

There are two primary models for admission cycles: "rolling" admissions and "rounds." Under the rolling admissions model, applications are reviewed as they are received and completed. They are processed in a stream and are not grouped for review with large numbers of other applications. In applications rounds, on the other hand, applications received and completed by the given deadline are reviewed together and decisions are announced by a specified date. Both these models provide a system for the admissions office to cope with the flood of paper and a structure for careful review of all applications.

Schools that use admission rounds typically have three or four decision periods. The deadline for the first cycle is often in early or mid-December, with decisions due three or four weeks later. If you submit your application in late October for a cycle with a December 1 deadline, you will not receive your decision until several weeks after that deadline. Under rolling admissions, however, your decision would usually reach you within a few weeks of your submission of your completed application.

It is important to remember that an application will not be reviewed until it is entirely complete. If a deadline for an admissions cycle arrives and your application is still missing one letter of recommendation, your application will be considered incomplete and held until the next decision cycle.

Review Decisions

Upon reviewing your application, the admissions committee may make any number of decisions, including:

Admit

Congratulations, you're in. But read the letter carefully. The committee may recommend or, in some cases, require you to do some preparatory coursework to ensure that your quantitative or language skills are up to speed.

Deferred Admit

This decision is reserved for situations in which the admissions committee considers you a strong candidate, but believes you would benefit from an additional year or two of work experience before attending. Because most applicants now have at least two years of experience before applying to school, deferred admission is not as common now as it once was.

Reject with Encouragement to Reapply

This isn't just a polite rejection. One step down from a deferred admit, it's a way for a school to say, "we like you, and we think that with more experience, you'll be a strong candidate."

Hold Over Until the Next Decision Period

Sometimes the admissions committee isn't comfortable making a decision by the scheduled reply date. Perhaps you are right on the borderline, and the committee wants to see how you stack up with the next group of applicants. In this case, all you can do is wait, but frequently, the end result is positive.

Waiting List

Schools use the waiting list—the educational equivalent of purgatory—to manage class size. The good news is that you wouldn't be on the list if you weren't considered a strong candidate, and schools do tend to look kindly upon wait-listed candidates

Don't Be a Pest, Be Polite

If you decide to appeal an admissions decision, do not expect the admissions staff to have your file on hand and know all about you when you call. Make an appointment to come in and talk to a dean, or ask them to call you back at their convenience.

who reapply in a subsequent year. The bad news is that there is no way to know with certainty whether you'll be accepted. Take the time to write the office a little note reaffirming your interest in the program. If you did not opt for an interview, now may be a good time to request one, if it's not too late.

Request for an Interview

Schools that do not require an interview may request that you interview with them before they make their final decision. Your application may have raised some specific issues that you can address in an interview, or perhaps the committee feels your essays did not give them a complete enough picture to render a decision. Look at this as a positive opportunity to strengthen your case. We'll talk later about how to use an interview to your best advantage.

Reject

As a full-time employee, it can be very embarrassing to be rejected by a school once you have been approved for your company's tuition reimbursement program. If you have been rejected from all of the schools to which you applied, it may be a good idea to find out why. Perhaps you do not have sufficient work experience, or your English needs improving—instances such as these may be justified to your employer. If you are lucky, a school may talk to you and attempt to work something out. You can always appeal the decision, but be advised that doing so may hurt your prospects for readmission in the future.

Want to Reapply?

If you are considering reapplying, try to find out why you were rejected and whether you have a reasonable chance of being admitted the next time around. Some schools will speak to you about your application, but you may find these conversations unsatisfying because admissions decisions are subjective and cannot be quantified.

This chapter has given you a behind-the-scenes look at the admissions process. The next chapters will discuss the secrets of successful applications.

CHAPTER 8

Preparing Your Application

A key part of getting into the business school of your choice is to develop a basic application strategy so that you can present yourself in the best possible light. In this chapter and the chapters to come, we'll show you how to make the most of every aspect of your application, ranging from timing strategies to essay-writing tips.

WHEN TO APPLY

Understanding how each school's application cycle operates can help you determine the optimum time to submit your application. The same guidelines as to when to send in your application may be used whether a school uses admissions rounds or a rolling cycle.

The Best Time

There are potential risks and rewards regardless of when you apply. However, the general rule is: It's better to apply early than late. Because so many candidates wait until the final deadline to apply, you'll be evaluated in a larger pool if you wait. Although schools are committed to judging all applicants on the same set of criteria throughout the year, they have

Apply Early

"I was not successful my first year of applying to B-school. The next time around, I applied earlier in the application cycle. For schools that had rounds, I sent in my application for the second of three rounds."

— *E.M.B.A., Stern School of Business, New York University*

no obligation to admit the same number of students from each cycle. So the prospects of being admitted from the later period may be worse than if you apply earlier.

Applying too early can work against you, however. First of all, at the start of the admissions season, admissions committees need time to "calibrate" the yardstick by which they measure candidates. As a result, they may be less consistent in their judgments. This need to get a sense of the year's applicant pool applies to smaller programs more so than to programs that consistently, year after year, have a very large number of applicants and are very selective, admitting as few as one in every ten applicants. Second, because there are fewer applicants in the early stages, you may be scrutinized more closely than you would otherwise be. Third, the first period typically contains very strong applicants. And finally, because the application season is just starting, there's no pressure to fill class slots. Overall, however, if you are a strong candidate, it does make sense to apply early, because there are plenty of open slots. If your application stands out, you'll be accepted.

If you are planning to apply for scholarships, grants, or other merit-based financial assistance, early submission of your completed application can be very important. Some of these awards have very early deadlines; you cannot even be considered for the award unless all required application materials have been received. If you are taking part in your company's tuition reimbursement program, you'll certainly need to find out if there is a specific timetable you need to follow in order to receive funds.

The Worst Strategy

Regardless of when you make your decision to go to business school, the very worst thing you can do is wait until the last minute. Your school application is made up of many different pieces, including some that need outside attention, such as transcripts and recommendations. Each piece of the application that is beyond your control is one more disaster waiting to happen. You need to be prepared for the worst, and you need plenty of time to recover if and when things go wrong.

The middle admissions periods are the "safest" times to apply. By then, the admissions committee has a good sense of what the applicant pool is like and has hit its stride in making consistent evaluations. Plus, there are still many spots available. Although the admissions office is typically awash in files at this time of year, the committee will still pay careful attention to your application.

Your chances of being admitted to your program of choice at the end of the admissions cycle are hard to predict. Programs that receive an abundance of applications typically have few spaces still available in the class at this stage. Backgrounds and credentials that stood out early in the year may not now appear so fresh and different. Still, if your background is highly unusual, it may be just what the admissions office is seeking to round out the class. On the other hand, if the office did not receive as large a flood of applications during the middle period as it expected, more seats may be available than anticipated, increasing your chances of being accepted. However, targeting the end of the application cycle is a risky move. Programs keep good records of application trends at their school so that they can plan appropriately and matriculate the best class possible; openings in the late cycle are created only when this planning has not produced the expected results.

All timing strategies aside, the best time of all to apply is whenever you can devote the time necessary to prepare your best application. This entails completing and submitting all your application materials in a careful and timely manner.

Make a Schedule

There are perfect times to begin and end the application process, and some people are able to move smoothly from step to step on the road to B-school admissions. Set time aside on a regular basis to complete the application materials. The key is to spread out the work. If the process is gradual and relaxed, it will be much less painful, and every piece of your application will get the attention that it deserves.

You should begin a year before you plan to enter school, preferably in the summer. Don't worry if the following schedule doesn't exactly meet your needs. You may just have to rush things a little more than some of your colleagues, or you may have several extra months to think and explore possibilities. Keep in mind, though, that a few dates are written in stone.

> **Request Your Application Early Because:**
>
> - The closer it gets to the application deadline, the longer it takes for the school to get an application mailed to you, and you want to familiarize yourself with the application itself so you have time to figure out exactly what the school is asking for.
>
> - Most B-schools require a self-managed application, one in which you put together the parts of the application yourself and send it to the school as one big packet. It takes time to assemble these various parts.

You should find out what they are as early as possible and incorporate them into your own personal application schedule, which should include the following dates:

- Standardized test registration deadlines
- Transcript deadlines (some schools send out transcripts only on particular dates, so check with your records office to find out when you have to make requests)
- Letters of recommendation (be sure to give your recommendation writers plenty of time!)
- Application deadlines (submit your application as early as possible to ensure that you get a fair and comprehensive review)
- Financial aid forms (federal and state programs have definite deadlines, and you should also check deadlines from individual universities and independent sources of aid)

TARGETING YOUR APPLICATION

When it comes to applying to business school, you're the product. Your application is your marketing document. Marketing yourself doesn't mean that you should lie or even embellish; it just means that you need to make a tight and coherent presentation of the facts. Everything in your application should add up and underscore the fact that you are not only qualified to be in the class—you should be in the class!

Many application forms have a certain tone, one that's comforting and accepting. "Why would you like to come to our school?" they seem to be asking. They do want an answer to that question, but what's even more important—the subtext for the whole application process—is a bigger question: "Why should we accept you?" This is the question that your application will answer. And with some effective marketing strategies, your answer will be clear, concise, coherent, and strong.

Be "Reader-Friendly"

Try to make things as easy as possible for those who are reviewing your application. Part of marketing yourself is making sure the presentation of your application is flawless. Small type fonts or narrow margins can become real irritants, especially during the long days and nights of "crunch time." Whenever you submit your application, make sure it is "reader-friendly."

So what sort of image should you project? First of all, it should fit who you are; it should be natural. Don't bother to try to sell yourself as something you're not. The strategy will just make you uncomfortable, and it probably won't work. Besides, part of what readers do when they evaluate your application is to form an image of you from the various parts of your application. Your job is to help them, not hinder them.

Assembling Your Application

Let's recap the basic elements of the business school application. Whatever school you apply to, you will probably be required to supply:

- Completed application data form
- Your most recent résumé
- The application fee
- Your GMAT test score(s)
- TOEFL scores (if required)
- Official transcripts from all postsecondary schools that you have attended (whether or not you graduated)
- Letters of recommendations
- Personal interview
- Essays

Of the documents listed above, the only one(s) that will not be in the packet you provide are your GMAT and TOEFL scores. You need to contact the Educational Testing Service in Princeton, NJ at (609) 921-9000 to have these sent to your school(s).

Each school has its own policy about accepting supplemental materials that are not requested in the application packet, such as videotapes, audiotapes, and project samples. Most schools with large applicant pools either discourage them or simply don't consider them. They believe you should be able to

Don't Be a Laughing Stock

Some of the more "entertainment-oriented" admissions committees save the videos they receive until the end of the season, cook up some popcorn, and have their own screening of B-School's Funniest Home Videos. If you decide to send in a video in support of your application, make sure it isn't unintentionally amusing.

make your case within the framework of the application. Other schools are more receptive to reviewing supplemental materials. If you have something you feel would strengthen your candidacy and you would like to submit it, call the school and ask about their policy.

The GMAT, TOEFL, college grades, and your work experience are those parts of your application that are pretty settled before you even start the important work on your application. The following chapters will examine how you should strategically approach the remaining crucial parts of your application—recommendations, your essay, and the interview.

CHAPTER 9

Recommendations

Whether a school requires one, two, or three recommendations, it will generally look to them as supporting documents that will confirm the substance of your other application materials. You should not neglect this portion of your application.

CHOOSING A RECOMMENDER

One of your tasks in preparing your application materials is to think strategically about the selection of individuals you ask to write on your behalf. Choose recommendation writers who can write meaningfully about your strengths and, whenever possible, match the perspective of the writer with your overall strategy for the particular application.

One of the most common mistakes applicants make is to sacrifice an insightful recommendation from someone who knows them well for a generic recommendation from a celebrity or an alumnus. Admissions officers are not impressed by famous names. So unless a famous individual knows you and can write convincingly on your behalf, this is not a strategy worth pursuing. Similarly, since admissions officers are looking

Easy Decision

"My immediate supervisor was an alumna of the M.B.A. program I was applying to. This made my choice of recommender a no-brainer and assured my admission."

– *M.B.A., Fordham University*

for an objective confirmation of your qualifications, you should also avoid submitting letters from relatives and family friends, unless they can clearly base their assessment on professional criteria.

Good choices for recommendation writers include current and past supervisors, professors, academic and nonacademic advisers, and people you work with in community activities. In some cases, professional peers and/or subordinates can write effective recommendations, but such approaches are reserved for special circumstances. Remember that you do not need to use the same set of letter writers for each application. You will want to have at least one recommender who can speak to your work experience, but you may choose your other writers to complement the information in your application. If you have highlighted volunteer or community involvement, you can ask someone who has worked with you in this area.

If the school is particularly interested in leadership or teamwork skills, you may want to choose a recommender who can address this side of you. Make sure, however, that the individuals you choose have recent knowledge of you and can relate it to your professional goals. Your high school basketball coach, for example, would not be a good choice as a writer, unless you have worked extensively with the coach in the last few years and this work is a good demonstration of your capabilities and skills.

If a school requests an academic recommendation but you aren't able to provide one, try to identify someone who can discuss your intellectual attributes, particularly if your academic record is not your forte. Similarly, if requesting a recommendation from your employer would create an awkward situation, look for someone else who can comment on your management skills. Your recommendations are not likely to make or break your application, but they will confirm your strengths and in some cases help you overcome perceived weaknesses in your application.

If you wish to submit an extra recommendation, it's generally not a problem. Most schools will include the letter in your file, and those that don't will not penalize you for it. You should, however, send a note explaining why you have requested an additional recommendation so it doesn't appear that you can't follow instructions.

ASKING FOR RECOMMENDATIONS

There are two fundamental rules of requesting recommendations: ask early and ask nicely. As soon as you decide to go to business school, you should start sizing up potential recommendation writers and let them know that you may ask them for a recommendation. This will given them plenty of time to think about what to say.

Once they've agreed, let them know about deadlines well in advance to avoid potential scheduling conflicts. The more time they have, the better job they'll do recommending you. As for asking nicely, you should let the person know you think highly of their opinion and you'd be happy and honored if they would consider writing you a recommendation.

> **Time Out!**
>
> If you are asking a supervisor or colleague for a recommendation, pick the right moment when you can have several minutes of uninterrupted time, such as after-hours or over lunch.

Help Them Get to Know You

It is your responsibility to make sure that your recommendations writers know enough about you to write a meaningful letter. Discuss your personal and academic goals with them; help them get to know you well enough to write excellent recommendations. It is also helpful to tell your recommenders exactly why you are applying to a specific program, so they can understand your fit with it and emphasize this in their letters. If you have selected this writer to complement a specific aspect of your application, be sure to mention this connection, particularly if the school has an interest in this aspect.

Make Things Easy for Them

Make the task of writing a letter as easy as possible for your recommenders by organizing materials and information. Be sure that have all the necessary forms and instructions and have a stamped, addressed envelope to use for each letter. If the school uses a recommendation form, find out whether a letter on letterhead may be substituted for the form. Most schools will accept a letter, but many want the recommender

> **Give Them the Highlights**
>
> "I would have ready some personal pointers/highlights that you want included in the letter of recommendation. Be sure to include examples of leadership, growth, and initiative."
>
> – E.M.B.A., Stern School of Business, New York University

to address the specific questions on the form and want to receive the form in addition to any formal letter. Some schools provide an acknowledgment card that the recommender is to include in the return envelope. Make sure that it is correctly addressed and stamped as well before you give it to the recommender. These steps will help show your appreciation for the effort being made on your behalf and will help ensure that the correct materials get sent to each school.

In addition to the required materials themselves, it is often helpful to provide your recommenders with a written summary of your background, a copy of your current résumé, and your application essays. Copies of any written feedback that they might have given you in the past can also be useful, in order to help them remember the details of your achievements. Reviewing the recommendation forms or questions yourself before sending them to the letter writer will help you determine what information may be useful. Providing your recommenders with the exact dates of employment or names of specific courses will save them from needing to research information or to rely on memories that might not be absolutely accurate.

> **Help Them Help You**
>
> Take the following actions to assist your recommenders:
>
> - Tell them about deadlines early
> - Arrange a meeting to discuss your background and goals
> - Clue them in on the marketing image you're using
>
> *— Former admissions official, Harvard Business School*

Under most self-managed application processes, your recommenders will return their letter to you, in a sealed envelope, for you to enclose when you submit the rest of your application materials. In this case, you will know when and whether the recommendation letters are complete. If an application deadline is looming and you are still missing a letter, you will need to follow up with your desired recommender—but be polite and discreet. On occasion, someone who has agreed to write will not be able to do so before your deadline, even though you have given that person adequate notice. You can inquire about submitting your application without one of your letters, but typically an application will not be reviewed until all materials have been received, including all required letters of recommendation. In some cases, you are better advised to seek a letter from someone else.

Confidentiality

One last issue with regard to recommendations is confidentiality. You'll need to decide whether or not to waive your right to read letters written about you. Many writers will only write confidential letter, and, unless you have serious reservations, you should waive this right. Some schools request confidentiality in recommendations, so pay close attention to each school's requirements.

WHAT WILL THE RECOMMENDER SAY ABOUT YOU?

In many cases, your recommenders will be asked to fill out a reference form for each B-school. The following are some of the most common questions recommenders are asked in these forms about the students they are recommending. Think about the responses the person you have chosen to recommend you might have to the following questions before you take the plunge and commit to him or her.

1. How long have you (i.e., the writer of the reference letter) known the applicant and in what capacity?

2. What are the applicant's primary strengths and weaknesses?

3. Discuss the applicant's competence in his or her area of responsibility.

4. Are the applicant's achievements thus far a true indication of his/her ability? Please explain your response.

5. How carefully has the applicant considered his or her plans for M.B.A. study and subsequent career?

6. Rate the applicant on the following abilities or traits, using a scale of below average, average, good, excellent, superior. Please indicate the reference group being used.

Common Questions

1. How long should a recommendation be?

   Short and concise; no more than two pages.

2. Should I ask to look at the recommendation?

   This is not generally advisable. If the school believes that the recommender cannot be completely honest, it will discount what is written, no matter how laudatory.

3. What if my recommender says, "Write it up and I'll sign it"?

   An absolute no-no. You will not be able to reflect the distinctive, authentic voice of the recommender, and it's unethical.

- Analytical ability and problem-solving skill
- Ability to work in a team
- Ability to work independently
- Writing skill
- Speaking skill
- Motivation
- Maturity
- Leadership potential

Don't Forget Your Manners

When you are accepted into an M.B.A. program, remember to appropriately thank the people who wrote your recommendations. They did help you get in, after all. Flowers, stationery, or a nice bottle of wine are usually appreciated!

CHAPTER 10

Interviewing Successfully

In the mid to late '80s, many top business schools began requiring their applicants to attend a personal interview before making a final decision on acceptance into their programs. Before that time, not only were interviews not required, but many schools would not even accommodate an interview request.

As the top schools began strongly recommending or requiring interviews, other schools followed suit. The rush to emulate programs that first established interview requirements was motivated by more than a desire to imitate the leaders. There was a heightened recognition that success in business is not always correlated with academic success. This was accompanied by an increased interest in attracting students who were not only qualified to perform well in a rigorous academic program, but who also possessed the personal qualities that would contribute to a successful post-M.B.A. job search and greater likelihood of rapid career advancement. The current emphasis on leadership, teamwork, communication, and interpersonal skills within M.B.A. programs is an outgrowth of the insights and goals that originally led to the admissions interview.

Most schools will say that the interview gives the admission committee a chance to evaluate aspects of the candidate that are not apparent or that cannot be judged on the basis of the written application alone. These attributes include poise, self-confidence, social skills, ability to think on one's feet, reaction to stress, maturity, and communication skills. A clear understanding of what the school expects to accomplish in an admissions interview and what you wish to gain from it will help you to prepare appropriately and gain maximum benefit from the interview experience.

INTERVIEW FORMAT

The interview format you encounter will depend on whether you requested the interview or it was recommended/required by the school. If you requested the interview, you need to go into it with a firm idea of what you want to discuss. Schools that do not routinely grant interviews will expect you to provide them with information that was not included in your application. The school may wonder why you feel the information is so important that it couldn't be written up and included as an additional essay. You'd better be prepared to do more than just chat with the interviewer.

> **Multiple Questions**
>
> Some schools conduct panel interviews, so be prepared to meet more than one person at the same time. Remember to be yourself and don't get defensive.

When the interview is recommended/required by the admissions office, on the other hand, the school is much better prepared to handle it. You had better be prepared also. Most interviews follow the same basic format: introduction, some welcoming comments and relaxed conversation, a little information about the school and how the interview will be conducted, detailed questions about your educational and work experience, future plans and goals, and so forth, followed by your chance to ask questions, and finally the wrap-up. They usually last 30 to 60 minutes. You need to make sure that you use the time wisely, that you make the points you want to convey and ask the questions you want to get answered, without seeming to take control of the interview. The only way to ensure success is to prepare.

HOW TO PREPARE FOR YOUR INTERVIEW

The very first thing you should do is review your application. What did you say and how did you present yourself? You need to remind yourself of these items before you go into to your interview so that you can give the interviewer some value-added information. Always assume that the interviewer has read your application thoroughly and reviewed it before the interview began. You can (and should) refer to details that you covered in your application, but you need to be able to discuss them in more depth if asked. If you refer back to your essay drafts, you should find that there is much more information to impart that you edited out in the name of length or simplicity. This is good information to have on hand for the interview portion of the application process.

You should also review everything that you know about the school with which you are about to interview. Nothing irritates an interviewer more than an unprepared interviewee who obviously hasn't read the catalog or done enough research to confirm that he or she has chosen the right school. It will also help you if you have read some other material about the school that will show that you were interested enough to do further research. Knowing which departments are strong or well known will allow you to discuss why you have chosen to apply to this school and why you will be a good choice as a student.

It is certainly helpful if you know something about the background and education of students who are already attending the school. You may find that you fit the mold of the accepted student quite well, or that you need to convince the interviewer that you can add something to the school.

In order to get an impression of what an interviewer might be looking for, take a look at the following interview form from Carnegie Mellon University. This form should help you identify the skills and demeanor required to impress the interviewer. Review the categories and make sure that you can express yourself in a manner that will convince your interviewer to rate you on the "5" end of the scale for each quality.

The Experts Advise . . .

Some suggestions courtesy of Karen Davis, an admissions adviser at North-western University's Kellogg Graduate School of Management:

DO:

Come prepared. Make sure that you prepare for your interview and bring a current résumé. Know that you will be asked questions like: Why have you selected the school? Why have you opted for the part-time program? Be ready to discuss your academic and professional objectives and be able to trace your career history from undergraduate school through your current position, validating the choices you made along the way.

Give thorough and complete answers. The interviewer is not privy to your complete application—he or she must provide an independent opinion, with no bias from you quantitative results.

DON'T:

Speak negative of other schools. Be positive about your decisions and your experiences with other academic institutions.

Interview Report				

Name of Applicant _____

Date of Interview _____

Name of Interviewer _____

	Inappropriate Attire; Poor Grooming			Appropriate Attire; Presents Self Attractively
APPEARANCE	1	2	3	4 5
	Abrasive or Bland			Charismatic, Likable; Participative Temperament
PERSONALITY	1	2	3	4 5
	Awkward, Threatened by Interview Situation, Excessively Reticent			At Ease, Polished, Sophisticated, Easily Able to Maintain Social Conversation
POISE	1	2	3	4 5
	Defensive; Poorly Defined or Negative Self-Image			Outgoing, Strong Sense of Self, Forthright
SELF-CONFIDENCE	1	2	3	4 5
	Inappropriate or Ill-Mannered Responses			Handshake, Eye Contact, Appropriate Display of Manners
SOCIAL SKILLS	1	2	3	4 5
	Irresponsible Attitude, Dependent, Immature			Clearly Responsible, Industrious, Conscientious, Decisive
MATURITY	1	2	3	4 5
	Passive, Withdrawn, Took No Verbal Initiative, Uninformed about Program			Persistent, Formulated Specific Questions about Program, Assertive
INITIATIVE	1	2	3	4 5
	Poor Enunciation and Grammar			Enunciates Well, Structurally Correct
SPEECH	1	2	3	4 5
	Difficulty Expressing Self, Uses Slang, Substandard Vocabulary			Articulate; Excellent Vocabulary and Word Choice
VERBAL FACILITY	1	2	3	4 5

Interview Report continued				
Not Cohesive, Erratic Thought Patterns			Precise, Logical Continuity of Ideas	
LOGICAL PRESENTATION 1	2	3	4	5
Inattentive, Does Not Comprehend Questions Easily, No Clear Thought Development			Attentive, Alert, Perceptive, Skilled Comprehension of Questions, Emphatic Listener	
LISTENING SKILLS 1	2	3	4	5
Confused, Unplanned, Displays Little Need for Achievement			Realistic, Clearly Defined Goals; Shows Need for Clear Ascendency	
PROFESSIONAL AMBITIONS 1	2	3	4	5
Vaguely Defined, Naive			Qualified by Experience and Future Goals, Formulated Thoughtfully	
REASONS FOR APPLYING 1	2	3	4	5
Unrealistic, No Sense of Strong Commitment			Determined, Realistic Appraisal of Time and Discipline Involved	
COMMITMENT TO GRADUATE STUDIES 1	2	3	4	5
Self-Restrained, Pessimistic, Lethargic			Involved, Optimistic, Vibrant, Alert, Enterprising	
ENERGY/ENTHUSIASM 1	2	3	4	5

Work on your body language—don't fidget or present barriers between yourself and the interviewer (such as leaning back and crossing your legs). Maintain eye contact. Good, nondistracting body language will help you come across as confident, poised, and mature.

If you are concerned about your presentation, you may want to practice your interviewing skills before the actual event. You should select someone to practice with who will give you good feedback and understands what is involved in this type of interview. The best choice would be an M.B.A. grad who has gone through this process himself, or someone who is also applying to B-school and understands the importance of this exercise. You may also want to give a copy of the form to your interview partner. Ask him or her to give you both positive and negative feedback so that you can work on the weak portions of your presentation.

WHAT ABOUT THE INTERVIEWER?

How you present yourself is very important, but how you are perceived will depend on the interviewer. You may find yourself being interviewed by a permanent member of the admissions staff, a faculty member, another administrator, an alumni, a part-time admissions person, or even a student.

Ask Questions

The interview is as much an opportunity for you to learn about the school as for the school to learn about you. Good questions demonstrate your knowledge of a particular program and your thoughtfulness about the entire process.

Many B-schools, especially those who conduct numerous interviews, have extensive training sessions for their interviewers and may even require that questions be asked in a certain order. Other schools are more flexible, allowing their interviewers to conduct the interview in whatever way is comfortable for them. It's important to keep in mind that different types of interviewers may have different approaches to the interview and different sets of primary interests. For example, a student may assess you as a potential fellow member of a group for a class project and feel free to ask pointed questions that admission staff, who are also recruiters, would not. Similarly, current students and alumni may provide you with insights about the program that you won't get from the admissions office.

Although students and alumni may be able to spend more time with you than admissions staff charged with conducting hundreds of interviews each, be just as respectful of their time as you are of everyone else's. Business schools want these volunteers to feel good about the time and effort they spend interviewing applicants and will take any complaint about demeanor or behavior very seriously.

WHAT QUESTIONS WILL YOU BE ASKED?

Some general areas are often covered by interviewers. Here are a range of questions that they might ask:

- **College Career**

   How did you plan your course of study in college?

   How did you decided which college to attend?

   If you had it to do again, would you make the same choice and why?

   What extracurricular activities did you participate in?

- **Motivation**

   Tell me about an instance/incident in which you were particularly motivated.

   What are your career goals?

   What do you plan to do to achieve these goals?

- **Management Potential**

   Have you developed a managerial style? If so, what is it?

   How would the people who report to you describe you?

   What are your weaknesses as a manager?

- **Intellectual Capacity**

   What courses did you do best in?

   Do your grades reflect your capacity to succeed in this program?

- **Work Experience**

   What are your current job responsibilities?

   Describe your changes in responsibilities since you started the job.

   How have you handled the changes in responsibilities?

   What have your major successes been?

> **The "Right" Answers**
>
> Don't struggle to think of "right" answers to the questions you're asked in the interview. The only right answers are those that are right for you. By responding openly and honestly, you'll find the interview less stressful, and you'll come across as a more genuine, attractive candidate.

- **Interpersonal Relations**

  What kind of people do you find it most difficult to work with?

  What is it about them that you would like to change?

  What do you normally do about such people?

  How would your co-workers describe you?

- **Perseverance**

  In your first job, what were the drawbacks in pursuing it as a career?

  What were some of the problems you ran into in doing your job?

  Which one frustrates you the most?

  What do you usually do about it?

- **Communication Skills**

  Tell me about an instance when you had to persuade someone to do something he did not want to do. How did you do it? What were the results? Were you successful?

It's Not Just Luck

"Some of what happens in the interview is luck, but you can prepare for it to a certain extent. I would suggest that you call each school that suggests an interview early for an appointment. Usually you are asked why now and why this particular school, what you can contribute to the school, and how you plan to use the degree, so you should know how to respond to those questions before you go in."

— E.M.B.A., Stern School of Business, New York University

Remember that this is just a general description of some of the types of questions that you may be asked. You can't prepare for every possibility, but as long as you feel confident about your background and application, you should do fine. You do not need to "script" or overrehearse your responses, but you should go into the interview confident that you can field any question.

Some interviewers won't ask you any of these questions. Instead, some experienced interviewers feel that they can carry on a general conversation with you, drawing you out to talk about yourself and your interests, and get enough information to make an admissions decision. Professionally trained interviewers are more likely to ask you about specific situations than they are to ask broad open-ended questions. They can learn more by asking what you've done in situations than by asking what you think you would do. Be prepared to discuss specifics—what you did and why you did it that way.

If you experience this type of interview, you may walk away wondering what just happened! Don't worry. Even if the interview seems somewhat unconventional, it doesn't mean that it was unfair or incomplete. Just be glad that you were given the opportunity to express yourself.

> **Special to the International Student**
>
> As an international student, you are faced with additional challenges and pressures when interviewing in a language that is not your native tongue. Practice with a friend or colleague beforehand, arrive at your interview early, speak slowly, and stay calm.

What the Top M.B.A. Programs Say: Interviews

Southern Illinois University—Edwardsville

"Applicants should understand how the interview will be used in admissions process. Applicants should be prepared to put their best foot forward; don't show up like you just arrived from the beach. This is just like a job interview; make an impression. An interview allows applicants to amplify more about their application. They should be ready to give examples about their work or school experiences that are related to their intended degree interest. Applicants should be prepared to sell themselves by stating how they can contribute to the overall classroom climate and environment."

Tulane University, Freeman School

"The Freeman School requires interviews of all applicants living in the United States or Canada, and encourages interviews for international applicants as well. All interviews are conducted by a member of the admissions staff. The interview may be completed on campus, by phone, or off campus, if admissions representatives will be in the applicant's area. The candidate's application is not reviewed prior to the interview; therefore, the interview can be conducted at any time during the admission process.

"The advantages and disadvantages of each interview option greatly depend on the preferences of the candidates. I feel most candidates believe they can make a stronger impression in person and prefer the on-campus or off-campus interview. However, the admissions committee has no preference as to how the interview requirement is satisfied."

Indiana University

"We encourage interviews prior to admission—either on- or off-campus—at forums and receptions. On-campus interviews are preferable, because the applicant can get a feel for who we are, learn our culture, and sit in on classes. The interview process is a two-way street. We're each looking for a good fit."

University of California/Berkeley, Haas School of Business

"Interviews are strongly recommended. Both on-campus and off-campus alumni interviews are available. On the east coast, alumni interviews are available in Washington, D.C., New York, and Boston. As regards assessment value, no particular advantage or disadvantage applies to either type of interview. However, because a campus visit is highly recommended, applicants who are able to visit the school, meet with students, and attend classes are at a distinct advantage in making an informed decision about the school that best meets their requirements and expectations."

The Complete Picture

"The best advantage of an on-campus interview is that it allows the candidate to see the school, meet with students, sit in on classes, and explore the city. This complete picture of the school is not possible with other interview options."

— Admissions officer, Tulane University

Emory University, Roberto C. Goizueta Business School

"Interviews are strongly encouraged. The majority of interviews are conducted on campus, but admissions officers conduct interviews (by appointment) in selected U.S. cities in the spring. Phone interviews are available upon request. Trained alumni also conduct off-campus interviews. Face-to-face interviews (be they with admissions officers on campus or with officers or alumni off campus) are preferred because they provide the most interactive, and therefore, typically, the most fruitful discussions."

Columbia University

"While not required, we encourage face-to-face interviews. While the majority of interviews take place on campus, should an applicant not be able to visit the campus, we will arrange, through Project Interview, an interview with an alum located in close proximity to the applicant. Phone interviews may be conducted if there are no other alternatives."

Northwestern University, J. L. Kellogg Graduate School of Management

"All applicants are required to interview as a part of the admissions process. Applicants may interview on campus with a staff member or student or in their area with a member of the 1,200-member alumni admissions organization. All interviews are given equal consideration."

FINAL THOUGHTS ABOUT ADMISSIONS INTERVIEWS

The most important thing to remember is to be yourself. Present yourself in as positive and professional a manner as you are able, but don't try to make yourself into someone that you are not. The interviewer will pick up on that and try to pin you down or catch you in an untruth. Be as relaxed as possible.

Don't ramble through your answers. Be as concise as you can be without shortchanging yourself in providing the information. Try to listen to the questions you are asked so that you answer appropriately.

Finally, dress as you would for any job interview. Be courteous to the support staff. Be on time for the interview. Follow up with thank-you letters.

> **Don't Forget**
>
> A well-worded thank you letter speaks highly of the candidate, and is usually retained in your file and considered when the admissions decisions are made. Don't e-mail! If you decide to handwrite your note, make sure your writing is legible.

Remember that this is one of the areas of your application over which you have control, so do everything in your power to make the interview a positive experience for both you and the interviewer.

CHAPTER 11

Writing Your Essay

One of the most crucial components of your admissions application is your essays. Admissions officers use these essays to get to know more about you than can be seen through your work experience, your undergraduate grades, and your GMAT scores.

Many B-school applicants look upon the essay requirement as a part of the admissions application to be gotten through as quickly as possible. They throw together something that may or may not answer the questions asked and send it in, assuming that the rest of their credentials will be more important than the essays. They couldn't be more wrong. You can make or break an admissions application by writing outstanding or awful essays. Taking the time to compose an impressive essay can only help your chances of getting into the B-school of your choice.

Before you begin crafting your essays for any application, take a look at the big picture.

- What are your competitive strengths?
- Are there any weaknesses you'll have to overcome?
- How do your grades, scores, and experience stack up against the overall class profile?

Be Consistent

"When writing your essay, be sure to make your story consistent with what your recommenders are saying about you."

— M.B.A., Stanford Graduate School of Business

WHAT MAKES AN ESSAY EFFECTIVE?

Writing effective essays requires serious self-examination and sound strategic planning. You will need to pay close attention to the content, style and mechanics, and distinctive qualities of your essay.

Content

Most B-school applications require that you write one to three essays. The essay questions asked probe for information the school thinks is important to know in evaluating future students. They often relate to characteristics of the program as a whole. You are, for example, more likely to find a question about your work in teams in the application of a program that emphasizes teamwork than in the application of one that does not. Reading the essay questions carefully is vital in constructing an effective essay. "Making do" by using an essay written in response to one question to answer a somewhat similar question posed by another school only indicates to the second school that you are not a serious applicant.

Think about what will set you apart, make you memorable and attractive as a student. If you are asked what your greatest strengths are, you don't want to say they are hard work and punctuality. Since no one will say he is lazy or late for work, hard work and punctuality do not distinguish you from the rest of the applicants. Instead of being just another financial analyst in a sea of financial analyst applicants, perhaps you are the financial analyst who raises dogs and volunteers at the local animal shelter, or the one who had to assume operational responsibilities during a strike, or the one who has applied her political science background to looking at emerging Eastern European markets. Whatever you say, be sure you have examples to back it up.

Much of this self-analysis should have occurred during your search for an M.B.A. program with an appropriate fit. If it didn't, you need to do it now. By cross-refer-

> ### Parts of a Package
>
> Most business schools require multiple essays. In order to put your candidacy in the strongest light, think of each response as part of a package rather than an individual statement on which your entire application hinges. Be bold; stick to the subject; use strong imagery; and let admissions officers get to know you.
>
> *— Adapted from "The Write Stuff,"* Newsweek/*Kaplan's* Careers 2000

encing your employment record, your personal characteristics, and desired M.B.A. program attributes, you should be able to find good examples and strong material for your essays.

Don't hesitate to go beyond your current job experience for essay topics. Although ignoring your job completely will raise a red flag, feel free to discuss other events that help define who you are. For example, if a question asks you to discuss three significant accomplishments, you might consider choosing one professional, one community, and one personal experience. Although this approach may not be exactly right for you, strategically, it does enable you to provide a range of personal insights as you answer a single question.

Style and Mechanics

Start by outlining your answers to each essay question. Consider what you want to say and take the time to outline the major points that you wish to make. Then write your first draft. Beginning with a strong lead will get the reader interested in what you are trying to say. Once you have written the first draft, put it away for a while before you begin to edit in successive rounds. Editing your essays is a very important step; you need to have gotten away from the essay and allowed it to settle before you sit down and take it apart.

Schools are pretty specific about how long they want your essays to be. Adhere to their guidelines. Short and clear is good; long and wordy is bad. One of the first mistakes that some applicants make is in thinking that "thorough" and "comprehensive" are sufficient qualities for their essays. They try to include as much information as possible, without regard for length limitations or strategic intent. Application officers dread reading these bloated essays. You're aiming for a crisp, precise style with which you can convey your message in the limited space allowed. You want to tighten your language to a point at which you have not used any extraneous words. At the same time, you want the essay to flow and be interesting to read. Extra-small margins and tiny type are not the solution, either. Keep your essays

One Draft Is Not Enough

"Feedback and revision are useful to any writer. Spell-check is only a starting point."

— *Pamela Curry, Assistant Director of Graduate Programs, Dolan School of Business, Fairfield University* reader-friendly. Remember that your essays are just two or three of thousands the reviewer may read.

Candidates who write well have an advantage in the application process because they can state their case in a concise, compelling manner. Write in an active voice; less effective writers commonly write passively. Strong writing will not compensate for a lack of substance, but poor writing can bring down an otherwise impressive candidate.

To deliver your message effectively, you must also strive for clarity of content. You should be clear in what you are trying to convey without using slang or jargon. Endeavor to make your sentences shorter, eliminate any repetition, and make sure you have articulated your thoughts well. Give the reader more information than can be found in the other parts of your application. You don't need to restate information that you have already provided.

Finding the right tone is an important component of writing effective essays. On the one hand, you want to tout your achievements and present yourself as a poised, self-confident applicant. On the other hand, arrogance and self-importance will not go over well with admissions officers. You're trying to convey a personal message, but don't refer to yourself in the first person too much. Tell the reader what you have learned or contributed without sounding pompous. Before you submit your application, be sure that you're comfortable with its tone as well as its content.

Do Quality Work

"Take the time to construct a well-written essay. Do not attempt to write a one-draft essay because you received an "A" in English 101; focus on what the school of business is requesting. Many students go off on some tangent and never answer the question. Quality is the operative word in these cases, not quantity."

– *Greg Gomez, Admissions Director, Southern Illinois University–Edwardsville*

If you choose to submit a humorous or creative application, you are employing a high-risk, high-reward strategy. You may not be the best judge of your creative talents, but if you're confident you can pull it off, go for it. Be aware, though, that what may work for one admissions officer may fall flat, or worse, with another. Admissions officers may consider your approach gimmicky or simply find it distracting. Remember, your challenge is to stand out in the applicant pool in a positive way. Don't let your creativity obscure the substance of your application.

Be sure to read your essays in the context of your entire application. Does the total package make sense? Does it represent you favorably? Is everything consistent? Have you demonstrated your intellectual ability, management skills, and personal characteristics? Most important, do you feel good about the application? After all, you don't want to be rejected with an application that you don't believe represents the real you.

Finally, get someone you trust to read over the essays. Make sure that you have conveyed what you were trying to convey. This is the one area of your application that you have complete control over and (with hope) ample time to do your best. Although a good essay cannot always overcome a poor academic record or GMAT, it is your chance to impress the admissions committee with your thoughtful, well-written response to the essay topic.

Making Your Essay Distinctive

The discussion above describes the qualities of a good essay, one that won't be dismissed by even the most critical reader. But what if you want or need a great essay? Depending on the amount of time you have and the amount of effort you're willing to put in, you can write an essay that will stand out from the crowd.

Like other parts of your application, your essay is a marketing tool. The difference is that the essay gives you more freedom than any other component to present yourself in the best possible light. This is not the time to be blasé. Unless they ask for it, don't dwell on your weak points. You want to highlight your most marketable qualities. Draw attention to your achievements and explain their significance so that the reader's potential questions are answered.

One of the best ways to be distinctive is to sell your image briefly and accurately, including real-life examples to back up your points. A strong essay, for example, about how much you learned in your current position and how the experience and knowledge you've gained inspired you to apply to business school

> **Remember Compliments**
>
> "One of my employers called me a "diamond in the rough" in one of my first annual reviews. I used this as the topic of one of my essays, which asked me to describe my strengths and weaknesses. I gave the essay to my employer to read and asked her for a recommendation. She was able to back up my story and was touched that I remembered her comment."
>
> — *M.B.A., Fordham University*

> **Use the Right Terms**
>
> "I thought I was merely selling art [at my previous job in catalog production at Sotheby's]. But in B-school terms, I was 'developing important communication skills, refining my ability to prioritize and demonstrating my potential to be a self-starter.'"
>
> – *M.B.A., Kellogg Graduate School of Management; quoted in* Newsweek/Kaplan's How to Choose a Career and Graduate School, *1999*

will give readers what they want—a quick image of who you are, how you got that way, and why you want to go to their school.

"Distinctive" means that your essay should answer the questions that admissions officers think about while reading essays: What's different about this applicant? Why should we pick this applicant over others? Authentic enthusiasm can be a plus, and writing about parts of your life or career that are interesting and relevant will help grab a reader's attention.

COMMON ESSAY QUESTIONS

Every application is unique, but most will include essay questions that fall into one of several basic types. The good news is that once you've crafted responses to these questions, you won't have to start each application from scratch. You will, however, need to make sure that every application (especially the ones with fewer questions) provides the level of insight that you wish to present. Here are the kinds of questions you can expect to see:

1. **Describe (one, two, or three) significant accomplishments, and discuss why you view them as such.**

   Here, the admissions committee is looking to get a sense of what you consider important. Throughout the application review process, the committee will be gauging not only your management aptitude but also the kind of person you are. The events you choose to write about say a lot about you, as do the reasons you consider them significant.

2. **Why are you pursuing an M.B.A.? Where do you hope to be five years from now? Ten years?**

   Admissions officers want to see that you've thought through the reasons for going to business school, that you're committed to it, and that you have a clear understanding of what the experience is all about. Although they don't expect you to necessarily map out your entire career path, they will look for you to demonstrate forward thinking.

3. **What are your strengths and weaknesses?**

   Answer truthfully. Don't settle for "pat" responses. When discussing your strengths, you may want to include a brief example of an experience that highlights your strengths, if length permits.

   Writing about weaknesses can be tricky. The committee is looking for evidence of self-awareness and maturity, but be careful about raising red flags. For example, if you apply to a case method school that requires classroom participation and you write that you are uncomfortable speaking in front of a group, the committee will question whether you can thrive in that environment. Of course, you should be asking yourself the same question, anyway. Describing a weakness that's really a strength ("I'm so honest that . . ." or "I'm so committed to my employees that . . .") is a common, safe approach, but doesn't provide much insight—and it may turn off some admissions officers.

   > **Don't Be Defensive**
   >
   > When dealing with weak aspects of your application, do so in a straightforward, nondefensive manner. Discussing the weak grades, unpleasant professional experiences, or difficult personal circumstances you've faced in the right way can help you turn a potential pitfall into a strength.

4. **Describe an ethical dilemma you've faced, and discuss how you handled it.**

   With this question, admissions officers will evaluate not just your ethical "compass," but also your thoughtfulness, maturity, and integrity. They want to see how you think through situations in which there are no easy solutions. Remember, not all dilemmas involve ethics, and not all ethical situations are dilemmas.

   Admissions officers know that applicants won't all have faced the same situations. What's most important is that you demonstrate your ability to exercise responsible judgment and learn from difficult personal circumstances.

5. **Is there anything else you would like the admissions committee to know about you?**

   If you believe that you've presented everything you need to make a strong case for admission, don't feel compelled to add anything here. With thousands of essays to read, admissions officers will not hold it against you. However, this question is also your opportunity to discuss anything you haven't yet had the chance to present. For example, if your undergraduate performance is the weak link of your application, you can use this space to explain it. Alternatively, if there's a gap in your employment record that is likely to attract attention, now is the time to discuss it.

Don't ignore something in your application that the admissions officers will question, thinking that they will not notice it. They read thousands of applications and are trained to notice the unexplained inconsistency. Write about it here—you may not get an interview to explain yourself.

6. **Describe a setback or failure and discuss what you learned from it.**

   This question acknowledges that people learn as much from their failures as they do from their successes. You may be asked to select a professional situation. Regardless of the event you choose to discuss, here is an opportunity to demonstrate your thoughtfulness and maturity, as well as your capacity for growth and change.

7. **If you could effect one change at your current job, what would it be?**

   Admissions officers recognize that some (especially younger) applicants have not yet reached levels at which they could make fundamental changes at work. This question lets you flex your brain power in talking about changes you'd like to see. It reveals how knowledgeable you are about business in general and your business in particular. It also provides clues about how you think. For example, do you think about big picture issues, or do you focus on the details?

8. **Describe a situation in which you demonstrated . . . (teamwork/leadership/ responsibility).**

   A question like this will give you insight into the personal qualities that a school considers especially important in its students. Be sure to discuss the specifics of the situation. Answer such questions as: How did you demonstrate it? Did you have group meetings? Individual meetings? How did you motivate people? What was the end result? By discussing the details, you'll provide the admissions committee with valuable insight into your management style and aptitude.

No Hurry

Don't rush to get your application out. Take time to carefully review your essay. Set it down, don't think about it for a week, and then reread it as though you were reading about someone you don't know. Be critical!

---

9. What do you do in your spare time?

This type of question provides admissions officers with information about your social skills and activities. Good managers should be good communicators, able to make friends and socialize easily. Show that you are committed to your leisure pursuits. Describe how you first became interested in your hobby or activity and identify any ways in which you have combined interests in unusual ways. Try to differentiate yourself. (Take, for example, the candidate who enjoys skydiving and poetry who published his work in a literary magazine and recited the poem at an "open mike" night in a local bar.)

COMMON MISTAKES

We've asked two admissions officials from different schools and with different backgrounds to list what they consider to be the most common mistakes that business school applicants make in their essays. The results of our mini-survey are reported below. Make sure you don't make these mistakes in your B-school applications!

Admissions Official #1:

1. Not Getting to the Point Right Away

Don't force your readers to plow through a lot of irrelevant material before they reach the meat of your essay—they will lose patience with you.

2. Not Getting to the Point at All

This is even more fatal than Mistake #1. Make sure that your essays are clear and concise.

3. Using Buzzwords and Business Clichés

Using the most ubiquitous phraseology possible won't set you apart from the other candidates.

4. Not Providing an Appropriate Level of Detail

Applicants often provide either too much or too little detail in their essays.

5. Failing to Proofread

Spelling and grammatical errors are unacceptable.

Admissions Official #2:

1. Writing What You Think Someone Wants to Read

This short-sighted strategy might gain you admission into an M.B.A. program, but beware. If you provide an inaccurate reflection of who you are, but are admitted and choose to enroll in a program, you may be very uncomfortable. This can impact your ability to do well and to develop academically and personally, and can also inhibit the establishment of valuable connections for the future.

2. Failing to Explain Crises in an Appropriate Level of Detail

There is a fine line between too much and insufficient in such cases. Explanations of crises and misfortune, for example, are essential if they impacted the student's personal and academic development and perspective. A superficial mention without providing the reader with insight is useless and often detrimental, but too much "gore" and destruction also impacts the reader negatively. I once read an essay that described how the death of a roommate affected the student's ability to concentrate. The circumstances were horrific, and they were described in "bloody" detail. There are better ways to accomplish the same purpose.

3. Failing to Relate Goals and Plans to a Realistic Time Table

You don't have to know it all, and it is naive to believe that you do. Naiveté, especially at the graduate level, is not a valued commodity.

4. Failing to Check Spelling and Grammar Carefully

This should go without saying, but many people omit this vital proofreading step.

5. Failing to Respond to the Questions Asked

Admissions officials pose certain essay questions in order to obtain answers to questions they have about you as a candidate. If you don't answer the questions asked, you will not be providing them with the answers they need, and it will appear that you can't follow instructions.

SAMPLE ESSAYS

In order to give you a better idea of the different kinds of things that a B-school admissions officer might be looking for in as essay, we asked the two admissions officers quoted above to read and critique three actual B-school application essays. Each sample essay is followed by two critiques.

Essay A

Question: What are your career goals? How will an M.B.A. help you achieve these goals? Why are you applying to ****? (Limit: 1,000 words)

During my senior year in college, while other students were making definitive decisions about their career paths, I decided to implement a five-year plan of development for myself. The plan was designed to allow me to examine any career path during that period that I thought might interest me. I chose to focus primarily on three different fields: marketing, education, and the law. Although I am currently only in year four of my plan, I have made my decision regarding which career path to follow. After sampling each of the three areas, I have discovered that the field of marketing provides the most enjoyment for me and best complements my skills and personality.

I am now embarking on another five-year plan, during which I hope to achieve a few specific career goals. First, I would like to be a part of the team that establishes an accurate metric for measuring Internet advertising effectiveness. As computers play a more important role in people's everyday lives, corporations have begun to look for a method to analyze the effectiveness of their interactive advertising dollars. To date, no one has been able to accurately measure the impact that interactive marketing has on consumers. Although there are a few systems of measurement currently in use, they are rarely comparable and therefore provide little information in terms of the effectiveness of an online advertisement. The development of a standardized metric, similar to the Nielson Rating for television viewers, is likely to revolutionize the way corporations advertize on the Internet. I hope to help develop this new metric and to consult with corporations about the metric's results. The advice that I will be able to offer clients through the use of this system will be as important as the system itself. After all, the system will only be as effective as the results that it drives.

Beyond the five-year scope, I plan to establish my own market research firm that will focus on the burgeoning technology sector. I believe that we have only seen the beginning of the growth that the technology industry will experience in the future. Personal computers have penetrated approximately 40 percent of American households, and only approximately half of those personal computers have the capacity to connect to the Internet. We have only scratched the surface of the advancements possible through the usage of technology, and I believe that this field will continue to grow with greater acceleration as we enter the twenty-first century. My market research firm will provide support and information to companies who are affected by the increased use of technology. This market has tremendous potential and I hope to provide a necessary resource that will enhance my clients' success as well as my own.

I believe that an M.B.A. is the cornerstone to achieving my goals. First, an M.B.A. will give me the academic background necessary to successfully return to the field of marketing. Through classroom instruction and interaction with marketing professionals, I will be better suited to participate in the ever-changing global marketing environment. Additionally, I believe that an M.B.A. will provide me with the management skills necessary to effectively run a business on all levels. Whether my position is as a member of a large corporation or as an entrepreneur, I believe that the skills garnered from an M.B.A. are essential to becoming a successful manager. In addition, I believe that an M.B.A. will provide me with an enhanced thought process or a better business sense. I feel that as a student, I will be continually challenged to "think outside the box" and to analyze all available options before making an informed business decision. I believe that this process of thinking, learning, and challenging preconceived notions is an important aspect of earning an M.B.A.

I am applying to **** for a number of reasons. I believe that **** is the best environment for me to achieve my goals while gaining exposure to, and experience with, a diverse student body and faculty. It is my belief that everyone continues to learn throughout their lives, and one of the most effective methods of learning is through interaction with others. ****'s diversity offers an environment for learning both inside and outside the classroom. I hope to share my diverse knowledge with classmates and to take from them a new understanding of topics that are currently foreign to me. I believe that no other business school provides students with the opportunity to share and learn in an environment similar to that which is fostered by ****.

Academically, **** offers a comprehensive curriculum that will allow me to focus on my Marketing concentration through classes like Marketing Research, Marketing Planning and Product Management, and Strategic Marketing Planning. In addition, through core courses such as Managerial Studies and Managing Human Behavior in Organizations, I will be able to learn about business from a broader perspective. I believe that the outstanding academic reputation of **** combined with its diverse environment and thriving **** location create an opportunity that is second to none.

I have many ambitions for myself as I embark on the next stage in my life. I believe that an education from **** will provide invaluable experiences and skills that will allow me to grow into a successful business leader for the next century.

Critiques of Essay A

Admissions Official #1:

Essay A asks the candidate to address career goals, the importance of an M.B.A. towards those goals, and the specific relevance of the particular program in attaining those goals. A successful response should address these points in order, and culminate in an explanation of why the program in question is an eminently suitable choice. The essay should also provide evidence of a focused career objective and examples of ways in which the candidate might stand out from other candidates. The accompanying example succeeds in setting forth clearly organized and well-ordered points. However, the candidate is less successful in setting herself apart from other applicants. Let's look at organization first, and then examine the content of this essay.

This candidate presents her points in a very well-organized manner. The first paragraph identifies marketing as a general career interest. The following paragraphs define short- and long-term goals respectively, in this case describing ambitions in Internet-related marketing research with the ultimate goal of setting up a new marketing research company. The candidate then indicates that an M.B.A. is useful in the pursuit of these objectives because coursework will provide a deeper understanding of marketing. The applicant then concludes by enumerating the reasons why the program in question is the right choice. It is easy for the reader to follow these points, and the supporting information clearly addresses the major points.

Unfortunately, the points themselves vary in terms of their effectiveness. In the topic paragraph, for example, the candidate asserts that she embarked on a five-year plan of unbridled exploration. This rings hollow—and suggests that some abortive forays into careers were in fact part of an intentional strategy. That's not much of a plan. It would be more credible simply to state that after some career exploration, the candidate discovered that marketing was a good fit, and that the Internet provided an interesting opportunity to explore.

In addition, the reasons the candidate provides for choosing the school are very generic, and could apply equally to most reputable M.B.A. programs. To assert that no other program offers a similar experience is not only patronizing, but probably untrue. Admissions officers expect that smart candidates will apply to multiple schools. In this particular case, the candidate missed an opportunity to incorporate the Internet-related or entrepreneurial goals in the reason for selecting the school in question. This might have helped set her apart from other applicants.

On a similar note, candidates are well advised to avoid clichés and buzzwords and to not parrot brochure copy. No admissions committee member will miss talk of "five-year plans" (fine for Stalin or *Star Trek*), being a "manager for the next century," or the "ever-changing global environment." Using the most ubiquitous phraseology possible won't set a candidate apart from anyone.

Admissions Official #2:

There is no one answer to the issue of addressing career goals. A variety of participants with a range of personalities and skill sets are required to ensure a functioning world. M.B.A. classes are no different. And beyond the crafting of a class, an institution is choosing a set of alumni to enhance and/or maintain its reputation. Thus regardless of what the applicant writes about her career goals, it must be real and logical.

This essay intelligently divides a complicated issue into short- and long-range goals. However, the respondent conveys a naive and superficial understanding of her chosen field. The goals of being involved in an initiative that breaks new ground, of meeting a need, and of being part of a team are admirable. But it is essential, in all cases, to identify the skills, expertise, and/or abilities that would enable you to accomplish those goals. Unfortunately, in this case, I see plans without strategies.

This point is also applicable as we move to the question, "Why an M.B.A.?" What is it about an M.B.A. that will enable the author to accomplish her goals? The sections should be linked in a logical manner. Just because questions are asked sequentially, the responses do not have to be given sequentially.

There are subtexts to these questions. It is important to provide a sense of who you are, what you will bring, and why we should feel confident that you will contribute to your fellow students and class interaction. The author does understand that the class is composed of people with different strengths and that learning does come from diversity. However, I have gained no sense of who the author is as a person from this essay. Thus an opportunity has been lost.

And finally, as to the question of why the author has selected the specific institution in question, I don't see that she has taken the argument to the next level. A citing of courses doesn't do anything for me. Are the cited courses distinctive? In this case, they aren't. What is "diverse" about this program's "environment"? Why is being in a thriving city important? The components of this section aren't bad; they just don't provide insight into why they are important to this person. Why this program?

In summary, this essay needs more integration, logic, and focus. Make it easy to understand; don't force complicated leaps and assumptions. The author didn't capitalize on the opportunity to make a case for admission and to differentiate herself from other applicants.

Essay B

Question: In reviewing the last five years, describe one or two accomplishments of which you are most proud. (Limit: 500 words)

> I have always had a sense of organization and order. As a child, every toy had its place and every book had its nook. I have consistently worked towards certain goals and implemented the appropriate plan to achieve them. Therefore, it was no surprise when I decided to develop a plan for my postcollegiate success in which I would sample a variety of different fields before deciding on which to focus. The manner in which I would execute this plan, however, was a challenge.
>
> In order for it to be a success, my plan necessitated that I switch companies and fields several times. Being a creature of habit, this was at first a very difficult notion for me to accept. At the time, I would have preferred to have taken a job with one company and worked there for my entire career. However, that plan of action would never result in the full realization of my goal. In order for me to be successful, it was necessary for me to break out of my comfort zone and to explore a variety of fields.
>
> As my plan progressed, I began to realize that I had created an opportunity for myself to gain a wealth of experience while also gaining new insights into my capabilities. As I faced each new experience, I was no longer daunted by its unfamiliar nature but rather enthused by its challenge. I began to relish the unknown as a chance to learn more about myself and my goals. As a result, I now understand that my plan was more than a quest for a career but also a journey of discovery and growth.
>
> I consider the completion of my plan to be a major accomplishment. The pursuit of new positions and opportunities required a great deal of hard work and dedication. I am proud of myself for accepting my self-initiated challenge and for seeing my plan to its fruition. More

importantly, I am proud that I encouraged myself to leave my comfort zone in order to achieve my goal.

In a different light, but also important to me, is my chili. I know that this sounds bizarre, but I am a dreadful cook. When I got engaged two years ago I decided that it was time to improve. I bought a cookbook and started at the beginning with the "Appetizers." I decided, however, to refocus my efforts when I unsuccessfully assembled a crudité platter. Instead, I planned to master one recipe. I chose chili because it is not overly complicated and I enjoy it. Throughout the entire winter, I toiled over my chili, perfecting the spices and the exact quantity of vegetables. Finally, when spring had arrived, I had done it: I had created the perfect chili. Although my chili has yet to win any accolades, I am proud nonetheless because I worked hard, achieved my goal, and I married a man who can cook!

Critiques of Essay B

Admissions Official #1:

Essay B asks the candidate to provide succinct accounts of one or two personal accomplishments. The candidate should begin by briefly describing the accomplishments in the topic paragraph. The body of the essay should then describe each of the accomplishments in more detail, providing insight into their significance. A concluding paragraph is probably not necessary, unless there is some common thread in the examples that the candidate wishes to underscore. The response should ideally provide the admissions committee with some insight into the candidate's values.

In this example, the candidate did not lay out the format of the essay in the topic paragraph. She instead commenced with a description of her first accomplishment. It was difficult to discern what she was describing because she didn't indicate that her "plan for postcollegiate success" was indeed one of her accomplishments until she wrapped up the description in the fourth paragraph. She spent the balance of the description saying little more than that she held jobs in a few different fields. This was not an effective tactic for differentiating herself from other applicants, since many candidates have held jobs that challenged them to grow professionally. Another problem with this accomplishment is that she provided no specific information or examples drawn from her experience.

The second "accomplishment" was also flawed. If the point of discussing her foray into cooking was to show her ability to rise above adversity, she did so by trivializing the process.

Beyond the issues of content, this essay used pronouns with unclear antecedents and preferred the passive over the active voice (i.e., "in order for it to be a success, my plan . . . ," instead of "In order for my plan to succeed . . . ").

The admissions committee was asked to consider a candidate whose greatest accomplishments were exploring several career paths and perfecting a chili recipe. If this essay does set the candidate apart, it does so at the expense of her candidacy relative to other candidates, who will have undoubtedly accomplished much more.

Admissions Official #2:

An essay can't address everything. The author made a choice as to topics and, in the process, she provided me with an insight into who she is. Willingness to break out of a comfort zone is a trait that I value because the business world is constantly changing and change necessitates the learning of new skills. The author recognizes that this is an uncomfortable process. I could see how she developed. I recognized that she can handle change, and even respond in positive, growth-producing ways.

Both this respondent and the previous one had a plan and experimented with different paths. But in this case, the author shared her internal conflicts, those created by personal preference and reality, and what she learned from the experience. The choice of this topic provided an answer to an unasked question. If I have a limited number of places in the class, and the world is constantly in flux, my best students and most successful alumni will typically be able to manage change and grow from it. The author provided evidence that she can do both. I also know that she can handle uncertainty, and that attention to detail and order are important to her. Since teams have become the predominant organizational structures in business school and business, the aforementioned abilities and values are ones that at least some team members must possess to bring a project to successful fruition.

The author's second accomplishment provided humor and addressed other dimensions. I now know that she is married and that, in her choice of a partner, she found someone who has skills that she doesn't have. That is the benefit of a team. I also know that she is organized and methodical as she assumes new tasks and responsibilities.

This was, to me, a relatively solid essay. It was informative and insightful. As a bonus, it was amusing which, while not essential, can be different. I do have one caution. This essay does not explain what experiences she had, how/why she chose them, how long she stayed, and what she learned from them. And it doesn't reassure me that the author doesn't assume that jobs and people are expendable—that once they serve their purpose you move on. The purpose of this essay was not to probe such issues. However, these questions arise as one reads the essay, and thus the answers to them should be integrated into the essay or created as an addendum if they don't appear elsewhere in the credentials.

Essay C

Question: Describe an ethical dilemma you have faced in the workplace. How did you resolve it? (Limit: 500 words)

One of the students I counseled while working for the Jewish Public School Youth Movement (JPSY) was a 16-year-old student named ****. **** had joined our club as a freshman and participated in almost all our events. When I first met him, **** seemed to be a well-adjusted teenager in good academic standing and with many friends. During his sophomore year, I noticed that **** seemed increasingly disturbed, and I was informed that his grades were suffering. Repeated attempts to question **** about his problems were rejected. I debated approaching some of his friends but decided that his desire for privacy was more important.

At 11 o'clock one night I received a call for help from ****. He was calling from a pay phone after wandering around town for hours. His parents had been fighting with each other consistently and had become directly hostile towards him. When he brought home a failing grade, his mother locked him out of the house. My first reaction was disbelief. Aren't a mother's instincts always correct—especially a mother who is trained as a child psychologist? Don't parents always do what they believe is best for their child? Was it right for me in my role as a friend to interfere with the way the parents were raising their son? But their son had confided in me and was asking for help. I could not bear to let him wander the streets all night. I picked up **** and took him to another advisor's apartment for the night. Meanwhile, I decided that I would speak to his mother the next day. I would approach her as an adviser of ****'s school club and offer to help him with his schoolwork. I was hoping to somehow learn the reasons for her behavior without seeming too inquisitive or intrusive.

When I contacted her the next day, she politely thanked me for the offer and informed me that it was no longer necessary since **** was being sent to reform school. Inquiries made at the public high school and of various JPSY officials confirmed that my involvement had to end. During the subsequent year I heard reports of ****'s deteriorating behavior. In the end, he ran away from the school, and has yet to be found. Unfortunately, I could not control the outcome of the situation, but it taught me two lessons: how naive certain childhood assumptions may be, and to be more confident in following my instincts.

Critiques of Essay C

Admissions Official #1:

This question poses two unusual problems. The first is that it's badly worded: A dilemma isn't just any difficult problem. By definition, a dilemma is a problem that requires a person to choose between equally undesirable alternatives. A dilemma cannot, therefore, be resolved. One school that uses an "ethical dilemma" question asks how the candidate managed and resolved the attending situation, and not the dilemma itself. That was probably the intent of this question as well.

The second problem is that the question assumes that all applicants have faced ethical dilemmas in the workplace. That may not be true unless the dilemma is sought out intentionally. Author Robert Reid, who recounted his first year in a top M.B.A. program in a recent book, noted that "have you had your ethical dilemma yet?" is something of a standard workplace joke among the M.B.A.-bound. Unfortunately, candidates don't have control of the questions, just their answers.

With these problems noted, a concise (approximately 500-word) response should describe the dilemma in an introductory paragraph or two, explain each of the alternatives and their consequences, and conclude with a paragraph describing the choice the author has made and why that choice, while imperfect, was nevertheless preferable to other choices.

Here's an example. Imagine that you are an M.B.A. applicant who has never encountered an ethical dilemma in your workplace. What are your choices in answering this question? You can deliberately stretch or misrepresent events to conform to the question (i.e., lie—unethical), or indicate that you haven't had such an experience, potentially hurting your chances for admission. Both alternatives are bad—hence, a dilemma.

To his credit, the candidate in the example chose a third alternative, to do the best he could with an actual situation, even though it wasn't truly a dilemma. In this essay, the candidate is counseling a high school student who is having problems at home. The candidate adheres to his advisee's right to confidentiality until the situation turns more serious, and then attempts to intervene with the parents when the advisee's welfare might be at stake. While the situation the candidate describes is certainly unfortunate and obviously difficult, it isn't a dilemma, since there isn't a forced choice between flawed alternatives. Instead, the candidate has followed the highly ethical practice in counseling of honoring confidentiality until the advisee's welfare may be compromised by continuing to do so.

While this response isn't perfect, it is certainly preferable to lying or dismissing the question. With any luck, the admissions committee will understand the limitations of its question.

Admissions Official #2:

Unfortunately, there is little that I liked about this essay. I would caution the reader, however, that an admissions committee is composed of a group of people with various values and orientations, and each member reacts, more or less strongly, to different issues.

The author never really, or at least not clearly at the beginning of the essay, outlined what the ethical dilemma was. What ethics were involved in this case? The recounting of the circumstances appeared to have no overarching point. This was unfortunate, because there were real tensions inherent in this story that could have been addressed. Among them are:

- Can we ever truly understand a situation to which we are outsiders, and what role do we play when we see problems?
- What happens when the world as you experience it is inconsistent with the world as you come to see it?
- What options exist to respond to the situation, and why was this particular option chosen?

It is appropriate to set the stage or lay out the situation (one-quarter of the essay) and then proceed to analysis (three-quarters of the essay). Since the author neglected to do this, I am unsure as to why certain items were included and why they were included in the ways that they were. There has to be logic. Why, for example, did the author say that he "picked **** up and took him to another adviser's house"? What really mattered is that the student was in need and the author found him a place to stay. It is a bad idea to provide opportunities for the reader to get side-tracked with other issues. In this case, the question arises as to why the author didn't just take the student home with him.

The essay's conclusion could have been interesting. Even when not in control, you can learn things. In the author's case, he learned that childhood assumptions could be naive and that sometimes you need to be more confident in following your instincts. Unfortunately, I don't know what his assumptions or instincts were.

This was a missed opportunity. I see someone who didn't know how to use resources that were there, i.e., a school-connected agency, and insisted on "going it alone" instead of being a member of a team. While independence is important, at times, it is essential to know when to use the resources of a system. I don't see clarity of thought; I don't see someone who knows what is important. I have no real sense of who this person is and what he values, and that is, in my opinion, part of the purpose for which this question was designed.

I am not saying that this student wasn't admitted to the schools to which he applied. But for me the admission would have occurred in spite of the essay, not because of it, and in a competitive environment where test scores, grades, and work experience were equal and spaces limited, this student would have suffered in comparison.

PART FOUR

Financing Your M.B.A.

CHAPTER 12

Planning Your Investment

The first step in financing your degree is to identify all the costs. Whether or not your company offers to reimburse your tuition, you should have a clear idea of the expenses that will be incurred over the next few years. Before accepting admission to one school over another, carefully consider whether the costs are the same, and whether you can really afford to attend the school of your choice.

The following page contains a sample chart of what you can expect to pay for your M.B.A., and, if you're participating in an employer-sponsored program, whether the expense is usually considered reimbursable. The charges certainly rack up!

What about the Books?

As you may recall from your undergraduate career, books are an essential—and expensive—part of a student's diet. Unfortunately, most companies do not pick up the bookstore tab as part of a reimbursement policy.

Item	Estimated cost	Reimbursable?
Prep Course for GMAT	Can range from $300 & up	No
GMAT	$165 ($210 for international students)	No
TOEFL	$100 (only for students with English as a foreign language)	No
Transcript Fee (from undergraduate school)	Varies per school; some do not charge	No
Application Fee	$50 per application (Estimate that you will apply to three schools.) Note: Some schools waive the application fee if you apply online; by doing so, you also save on postage.	No
Transportation to/from school	$80 per term	No
Books	$100–$200 per term	No
Misc. Fees (such as health insurance, student services fee, technology fee, library fee, etcetera)	$100 per term	No
Tuition	$500 per credit (each school is different)	Depends

As noted above, many of the "smaller" charges are not generally covered in a company's reimbursable policy. These fees can add up significantly, though, so be sure to consider them when estimating whether you can afford the degree.

Setting Boundaries

In many cases, the limit for tuition reimbursement reflects the former federal tax law in which the first $5,250 in company tuition reimbursement was exempt from taxes. This law has expired, although colleges and universities are still trying to have it reinstated.

Read the Fine Print

If you are fortunate enough to be employed at an organization that implements a tuition reimbursement policy, make sure you carefully investigate the terms.

- **Is the tuition reimbursement limited to areas of study approved by your company?** When restrictions on area of study exist, the primary criterion for approval is usually the direct applicability of the program to the requirements of your job.

- **Have you been employed at your firm long enough?** Tuition reimbursement benefits for a degree program may only be available to you after several years' service with your company. These requirements are usually spelled out in your employee handbook.

- **Are 100 percent of tuition expenses covered?** Some firms will reimburse you based on your grade (for example, 100 percent reimbursement for an A, 80 percent for a B, 70 percent for a C, etcetera). Remember that companies often only reimburse you after you've completed your courses and your grades are official. You may have completed your first term and started your second—and had to pay for it—before you receive any reimbursement.

That's Irrelevant!

"When I was looking into M.B.A. programs, I requested permission from my employers to pursue the M.B.A./J.D. program at Fordham University. Part of my job responsibilities in the bank where I was employed included the review of legal contracts for financial products. Although I saw the relevance of the M.B.A./J.D. program to my course of work, my employers didn't, and they refused to finance the degree."

– *M.B.A., Fordham University*

- **Is there a limit as to the amount you will be reimbursed?** Some employers may allocate a capped amount of tuition reimbursement offered or set a maximum reimbursement per year. Make sure that by taking two courses per term you do not exceed your annual maximum.

If, however, your company does not have a tuition reimbursement policy in place, and you still wish to get your M.B.A., there are a few financial aid options you can consider, such as financial aid, loans, scholarships, and your own savings. We will cover these alternatives in greater detail in the next chapter.

CHAPTER 13

Financial Aid, Scholarships, and Loans

Financial aid can be broken down into two general categories: funds that are lent to the student and require repayment, and "free funds" such as grants and scholarships. This chapter will give you an overview of the general application requirements, including the documentation, that's usually necessary. Even if you are not sure that you qualify for financial aid, it can't hurt to apply.

Forms

Financial aid application procedures can vary from school to school. The first step is to get the admissions materials from the school(s) and read them thoroughly. Usually, general financial aid information appears in the admissions application, including the financial aid deadline(s). These deadlines drive the rest of the process for you.

Key Materials

The Free Application for Federal Student Aid (FAFSA) form is always required to request any federal financial aid. This form is used for need analysis, the calculation that determines your financial need. The detailed financial information you provide on the FAFSA form is run through a federal formula to arrive at an expected family contribution (EFC) figure.

As its name indicates, the FAFSA form is free of charge and allows you to send your financial information to a maximum of six institutions. If you're applying to more than six schools, you need to list your top six choices. If you subsequently want to add a school to this list, you'll have to drop one from your list. Make your life easier—try to limit your financial aid application to just your six top choices.

Other required forms may include (but are not limited to):

- A separate school financial aid application
- Private need analysis form, such as the PROFILE from the College Scholarship Service or the NeedAccess disk
- Your prior year's IRS 1040 form
- Financial aid transcripts from every postsecondary school that you attended (this requirement has been replaced at many schools by the National Student Loan Database System (NSLDS); check with your school to see if it participates)

Once you've submitted all the required forms, you'll have to wait about a month before anything else happens regarding your financial aid. You might hear from admissions offices during this time.

Meanwhile, the federal processor, a number-crunching center for the government currently based in Iowa, is working on the information you provided on your FAFSA. They rub your numbers through a formula called Federal Methodology that is revamped every six years (although the numbers are changed yearly). Their calculations result in a Student Aid Report (SAR). You'll get a copy of it in the mail. Your SAR contains both the financial information that you provided on your FAFSA plus the results of the federal need analysis calculation. The schools that you listed on the FAFSA will receive the data electronically, but they may need you to sign an additional form to activate the financial aid process (especially if the school does not have its own financial aid application).

Remember to keep track of your financial aid applications in the same way that you're keeping track of your admissions application material. If you need money to attend school, this process is just as important as the process of getting admitted.

Your Financial Aid Package

Once the financial aid office has all the forms and data that they need, they'll wait for the admissions decision before they review your application. During this waiting period, it's a good idea to check with the schools to make sure that everything is complete and ready for processing once the admissions decision has been made.

When the financial aid office finds out that you've been admitted, they'll review your application and offer you an award package. This financial aid package can include funds you are required to pay back, such as: Federal Perkins Loans, Federal Stafford or Federal Direct Loans, and suggested private loans, as well as "free funds" such as scholarships and grants.

> **Before You Decide . . .**
>
> Get the answers to these questions about your financial aid package:
>
> - What is your contribution expected to be?
> - How much money will you be expected to borrow?
> - What kinds of loans are offered, and do they have attractive rates?

FUNDS YOU ARE REQUIRED TO PAY BACK

As a student, you may be eligible for federal or state student loans or private loans. Some student loans are need-based and some are not. So, as mentioned previously, you should apply even if you do not think you qualify.

It can take up to eight to 12 weeks from the date you apply to receive any loan proceeds, so planning is essential. Also, since the rules and regulations for borrowing through each of these programs differ, you should read each section carefully.

The good news is that educational loans typically have more favorable terms than consumer loans, particularly unsecured loans, and they're usually easier to obtain. However, you can't assume that you'll be able to get a student loan whatever your financial circumstances. Remember, federal student loan programs have eligibility requirements. Many private loan programs have some type of credit criteria that you must meet before you can borrow, and virtually all programs establish some borrowing limits.

The trick is to make sure that you don't borrow so much that you reduce the return on your investment once you graduate. With planning, you can avoid that problem.

Kaplan–American Express Educational Loan Program

A valuable resource for prospective borrowers is the Kaplan–American Express Educational Loan Program. This program provides students with information and step-by-step assistance in how to meet the high cost of business school. Through an affiliation with one of the nation's largest student loan lenders, the Kaplan–American Express Educational Loan Program connects you with a resource for the financing you need to reach your educational goals. Information and guidance is provided through seminars and written materials. Additional benefits include:

- Student loan experts who are available to answer questions seven days a week, 12 hours a day, at (888) 527-5626.
- Application editing by Kaplan–American Express experts who will review all entries, signatures, and figures on your application thoroughly to ensure accuracy and eliminate delays due to missing information.
- The Second Review[SM], Kaplan–American Express's credit re-evaluation program, which guides previously denied borrowers through the process of clearing incorrect and/or outdated credit report listings and, if possible, reverses a credit-denied status.

Credit and Credit Reporting

A poor credit history could be a large stumbling block to financing your M.B.A. degree. While the U.S. federal loan programs for graduate students don't really check your credit history, many of the private loan programs do. If your credit record is weak, your previous actions may come back to haunt you and make attending B-school a financial impossibility.

Federal Loans

In order to qualify for federal student loans (Federal Stafford or Federal Direct loans), you cannot be in default of any previous federal loans. If you are, you can't take out another federal student loan until you make six consecutive payments on the loan you're in default on, or completely pay it off. If you're only delinquent rather than in default on your loan payments, you must pay off any past-due balance before you can borrow again.

Private Loans and Credit Reports

Private loan programs are much stricter about their lending guidelines than the federal government. When a private loan program checks your credit history, it requests a credit report from one of the three major credit bureaus in the United States.

Your credit history shows a record of all your prior debts and your history of repayments. This list will

> **Check Your Credit Report**
>
> Credit reports can be incorrect! Obtain a copy of your credit report well before you apply for any loans and ensure that there are no errors. We've all heard horror stories about someone's bad credit history getting mixed up with someone else's good one. A word of caution: If you (or someone else on your behalf, such as a mortgage broker or bank) request a credit check too frequently, this can jeopardize your credit rating. How? It may raise a red flag to institutions considering lending you money—they may want to know why your credit has been checked so frequently.

include your credit cards, mortgage, and any other consumer loans you might have. Your repayment history on any previous student loans will be listed, too. Private loan programs look for a record of on-time, consistent repayment of any financial obligations. If your track record as a borrower is not up to its standards, a lender will deny your loan application.

Key Credit Terms

Most private loan programs require that you have no adverse credit and that you be at least credit-ready, if not credit-worthy. Credit-ready simply means that your credit record is clean, that there are no indications of credit problems. You can be credit-ready even if you have no credit history at all, because you have nothing adverse in your credit record. Some private loan programs may require that you get a co-signer if you have no previous credit history. Credit-worthy means that you have both a clean credit history and that you currently have the means to make payments on the loan. A mortgage is an example of a loan that requires you to be credit-worthy.

Federal Loan Programs

The two U.S. federal loan programs available to graduate business school students are generally considered the core loan programs, since they carry certain attractive features defined by law. These features include a low interest rate, low fees, and defined deferment provisions. The two programs are:

- Federal Stafford Student Loan Program (part of the Federal Family Education Loan Program)
- William D. Ford Federal Direct Student Loan Program

The terms of these loan programs are similar. The eligibility criteria, interest rates, fees, grace period, deferment and cancelation provisions, and other terms are all basically the same. There are, however, minor differences in the application process and certain repayment options.

The key differences lies in who provides the loan funds. The Federal Stafford Student Loan is part of the Federal Family Education Loan Program (FFELP), through which loans are made by a private lender (such as a bank, a savings and loan association, a credit union, or an insurance company) and are insured by a state or private guarantee agency sponsored by the U.S. federal government. Under the William D. Ford Federal Direct Student Loan Program, the U.S. federal government is the lender.

Many schools participate in the Stafford program, but some participate in the Ford Direct program. The school you attend will determine which of these two loans you can apply for.

In order to be eligible for these programs, you must:

- Be a citizen, a permanent resident, or eligible noncitizen of the United States
- Be enrolled at least half time (usually six credits)
- Be in good academic standing, and be making satisfactory progress towards the degree (as defined by the school)
- Not be in default of any previous loans without being in an approved repayment program
- Have progressed a class year since receiving your last Federal Stafford Loan (for example, fourth-year undergrad to first-year grad student)

- Never have been convicted under federal or state law of sale or possession of drugs (This new law was implemented on July 1, 2000; however, a conviction prior to 7/1/00 could still affect your eligibility.)
- Show financial need based on the information provided on your FAFSA in order to qualify for the interest subsidy

Federal Stafford Student Loans

The Federal Stafford Student Loan Program provides two types of loans: subsidized and unsubsidized. The subsidized loans are a better deal, but you have to meet the government's financial need criteria. For either type of loan, you may defer payments of principal and interest until you graduate or drop below half-time enrollment. Depending on when you first borrowed, there's a grace period of six or nine months before you'll have to start repayment.

The Federal Stafford Loan Program evolved from the Guaranteed Student Loan Program (GSL) that you may have borrowed under in college. The concept of a federal loan program originated in 1965 as the Federally Insured Student Loan Program (FISL). The Federal Stafford Loan Program has the same purpose as these previous programs—to make loan funds available for students to attend post-secondary school—but the amounts available, interest rates, and deferment provisions have been modified.

Federal Subsidized Stafford Loans are available to all students who meet the financial need criteria. A federally mandated needs analysis, based on information provided on the FAFSA, determines a student's Federal Subsidized Stafford Loan eligibility. Students who don't qualify for the subsidized loan or need to borrow beyond the limit can take out an Unsubsidized Federal Stafford Loan.

Borrowing Limits

Graduate students may borrow up to their demonstrated need with a maximum $8,500 per year in the Federal Subsidized Stafford Loan Program, with a total borrowing limit (including undergraduate Federal Stafford Loans) of $65,500. The Federal Unsubsidized Stafford Loan Program allows an eligible student to borrow up to $18,500 per year, minus any Federal Subsidized Stafford Loan approved. The total cumulative maximum is $138,500 (including the Federal Subsidized Stafford Loans).

Interest Rate

As the program's name indicates, the federal government subsidizes the interest on the Federal Subsidized Stafford Loan. You're not required to pay interest on these loans until after you leave school. If you have a Federal Unsubsidized Stafford Loan, you're responsible for the interest while you're in school, but most lenders will allow you to capitalize the interest, and not pay it until you leave school. Capitalization means that the interest accrues while you're still in school and is added to the principal at a predetermined time (often at the point of repayment). Applications and information about current interest rates and repayment schedules are available at participating lending institutions.

Fees

There's a loan origination fee that is equal to 3 percent of the loan. If you borrow $5,000, for example, the loan origination fee will be $150. The fee, required by law, is sent to the U.S. federal government to offset a portion of the federal interest subsidy. In addition, the guarantee agency may charge you an insurance fee of up to 1 percent of the loan. Both of these fees would be deducted from the loan proceeds when the check is issued. All lenders are required to deduct the federal government's 3 percent loan origination fee, but they're allowed to reduce or eliminate their own 1 percent guarantee fee. Some lenders reduce this fee as an incentive for borrowers. Shop around for the best deal.

Sources of Federal Stafford Student Loans

Federal Stafford Student Loans are made through participating banks, savings and loan associations, credit unions, pension funds, and insurance companies.

Application Procedures

To apply for a Federal Stafford Student Loan, you should complete the FAFSA and mail it to the federal processor, and fill out a Common Loan Application and submit it to the school you plan to attend. The B-school will certify your application and either mail it to the bank or electronically send them the certification information. The bank will electronically forward that information on to the guarantee agency who will approve or deny the loan and send that info back to the bank. The bank will either cut a check made payable to you and the school, or will transmit the funds to the school via Electronic Funds Transfer (EFT). Once the funds are available at the B-school, the funds are credited against any unpaid balance you have and the difference is refunded to you. This whole process can take up to three months, so plan for the time lag.

Repayment

The amount of your monthly payment will depend on the total amount you borrowed, the number of months in the repayment schedule, and whether or not you elected to pay interest on the unsubsidized portion of the loan while in school. The maximum repayment period is usually ten years, with repayment generally in equal monthly installments. You'll have a shorter repayment term if you borrow a small amount, since there's a minimum monthly installment of $50.

If you don't meet the repayment terms of the loan, you go into default and the entire balance of the loan becomes due. If your loan goes into default, your lender may refuse to allow you to borrow again until the entire debt is satisfied.

Deferments/Forbearance/Cancelations

Under certain circumstances you may be able to defer, or postpone, the payments of your Federal Stafford Loan. Deferments are not automatic; you must apply for them. You can also request forbearance in situations that aren't covered by normal deferments. Forbearance means the lender agrees to grant you a temporary suspension of payments, reduced payments, or an extension of the time for your payments. As a final option, you can get a portion of your loans canceled under special circumstances. Read your promissory note for details of all of these provisions. They should also have been covered in your entrance and exit interviews.

William D. Ford Federal Direct Loan Program

The Ford Federal Direct Loan Program was authorized by the U.S. Congress in 1993. In this program, the federal government is the lender. Individual schools, rather than banks or other financial institutions, originate the loans. This program includes two types of loans: the Federal Direct Stafford Loan and the Federal Direct Unsubsidized Stafford Loan.

The eligibility criteria, borrowing limits, interest rate, fees, grace period, and deferment and cancellation provisions for this program are the same as for the Federal Stafford Loan Program, covered above. The Federal Direct Loan Program has different application procedures and repayment options for students.

Application Procedures

The FAFSA and the other required documents that were discussed earlier must be completed. Usually, the Federal Direct Loan will be offered as part of your financial aid package. Once you accept the loan as part of the package, the financial aid officer creates a Loan Origination Record and electronically transmits it to the federal servicer for approval. The approval is transmitted back to the school, and the school produces a promissory note for you to sign. Once the promissory note is signed, the school can disburse the first semester portion of the loan (minus fees) to your student account. Any funds remaining after any unpaid balance you have with the university will be refunded to you. The entire process, from the point of loan certification to disbursement of the check, can take as little as a week to complete.

Repayment

Most of the conditions of repayment are the same as for the Federal Stafford Loan Program. Although the same standard repayment plan (fixed payment for up to ten years) is offered in both programs, students who participate in the Federal Direct Loan Program have three additional repayment options: the extended repayment plan, the income contingent repayment plan, and the graduated repayment plan.

Option 1: Extended Repayment

Similar to the standard repayment plan, it allows the student to repay a fixed amount over a period longer than ten years.

Option 2: Income Contingent Repayment

Students pay a percentage of their salary no matter how much they've borrowed. If they have large debts, this option requires many more years of repayment than the standard ten years. As their salaries increase, so do their loan repayments. The drawback to this option is that the longer they stay in repayment, the more interest they pay on the loan. Indeed, if their payment does not cover the current interest due, unpaid interest is capitalized, increasing the amount of principal they owe.

Option 3: Graduated Repayment

This allows students to opt for lower payments at the beginning of the repayment cycle when their salaries are lower. The payments automatically increase as the years progress. The repayment term remains ten years, but the payments are more manageable in the beginning.

No matter which repayment option you select, the plan will be explained in the promissory note you sign. Repayments will be made to a federal loan servicer contracted by the U.S. Department of Education.

Federal Perkins Student Loan

In addition to the Federal Stafford Student Loan Program and the William D. Ford Federal Direct Student Loan Program, there is another federal student loan program that merits your consideration. The Federal Perkins Student Loan Program is administered by colleges and universities. It is made possible through a combination of resources: an annual allocation from the U.S. Department of Education, a contribution from the participating institution, and repayments by previous borrowers. You may have taken advantage of this program under its previous name, the National Direct Student Loan (NDSL) Program. This program, one of the first federal financial aid programs, was instituted more than 30 years ago.

Eligibility

As with FWS, the college or university determines eligibility for Federal Perkins Loans based on your financial need (calculated through the FAFSA/SAR) and the availability of funds. Besides demonstrating financial need, you have to be enrolled at least half time, and maintain satisfactory progress towards a degree. Keep in mind that Federal Perkins Loans are reserved for the neediest students.

Borrowing Limits

Federal policy allows the maximum annual loan of $5,000 per graduate student. Actually, though, many schools lack the funds to allocate this much to any one student. A graduate student may borrow up to a cumulative total of $30,000, including all outstanding undergraduate and graduate Federal Perkins Loans.

Interest Rate

The terms are very good. The annual interest rate is currently 5 percent. Interest does not accrue while the borrower remains enrolled at least half time.

Fees

Another perk of the Federal Perkins Loan: no fees.

Application Procedures

Usually, you're automatically considered for this loan when you apply for financial aid. If you've been offered and have accepted a Federal Perkins Loan, you'll sign a promissory note for each semester of the loan. The promissory note lists the amount of the loan and states your rights and responsibilities as a borrower. When the signed note is received, either you will be credited for one semester's portion of the loan, or a check will be cut for you directly.

Deferments

You can defer payments of your Federal Perkins Loan while you are enrolled until you graduate or drop below half time. This deferment is not automatic; you must request the deferment forms from either your school or the billing agency to which you're repaying the loan.

Grace Period

A Federal Perkins Loan has a six-month grace period after a student graduates or drops below half-time attendance. During this period, no repayment is required and no interest accrues. If you borrowed under the NDSL Program, you may have a different grace period. You need to check with the school that granted you the loan to find out what the specific grace period for your loan is.

Repayment

Borrowers under the Federal Perkins Loan program repay the school, although there may be an intermediary. Many schools contract with outside agencies for billing and collection. Repayment may extend up to ten years, beginning six months (your grace period) after you cease to be enrolled at least half time. The amount of the monthly payment and the maximum number of months allowed for repayment is based on the total amount borrowed. The federal government has set the minimum monthly payment at $40. Under some special circumstances, borrowers may make arrangements to repay a lower amount or to extend the repayment period. There is no prepayment penalty.

Cancellations

The entirety of your Federal Perkins Loans and/or NDSLs will be canceled if you become permanently disabled or die. Check your promissory note. Your loan may have additional cancellation provisions. Also, if you have "old" Federal Perkins Loans or NDSLs, there may be some different conditions depending on when the original loan was made. Check with your previous school for any special circumstances.

Federal Loan Consolidation

Federal Loan Consolidation allows students with substantial debt to combine several federal loans into one larger loan with a longer repayment schedule. The new loan has an interest rate based on the weighted average of the rates of the consolidated loans. Students who borrowed under the Federal Stafford Loan (or the earlier Guaranteed Student Loan), the Federal Perkins Loan (or the earlier National Direct Student Loan), the Federal Supplemental Loan for Students, the Auxiliary Loan to Assist Students (ALAS), and the Health Professions Student Loan Program can consolidate all these loans into one new loan.

To qualify for federal loan consolidation, you must be in your grace period or in repayment of your loans, and not be delinquent by more than 90 days. Apply to one of the lenders of your current loans. They'll negotiate to purchase your other loans from the lenders who hold them so your loans will be consolidated. If none of your lenders offers federal loan consolidation, you can go to another lender who does. Arrange to have that lender purchase your loans.

You have the option of consolidating all or only part of your loans. Often, students consolidate their higher interest loans, but keep their Federal Perkins Loans separate since the interest rate is so low. No fees are charged to participate in this program.

Private Loan Programs

Many M.B.A. students find that scholarship funds and the federal loan programs are not adequate to meet their expenses in an M.B.A. program. Over the last few years, several private loan programs have emerged to fill the gap.

As the economic environment changes, new loan private programs are added and some older programs are discontinued. Check with the individual programs for their current provisions.

The TERI Supplemental Loan Program

This is a private educational loan program designed to help students make up the difference between their cost of education and their grants or loans. Approval is based on the credit-worthiness of the applicant.

Business Access

This is a private loan program sponsored by The Access Group. Business Access offers private and federal loan funds up to the cost of attendance to students attending graduate business schools accredited by the American Assembly of Collegiate Schools of Business. Although the rates and terms are subject to change, the current annual interest rate on these loans is the 91-day Treasury Bill rate plus 3 percent, and there is no origination fee. There is a loan minimum of $500.00, and students can take up to 20 years to repay. Visit their Website at http://www.accessgroup.org.

The GradEXCEL Program

This is an education loan program through Nellie Mae, a private loan agency, designed to meet the needs of students enrolled in graduate and professional degree programs. GradEXCEL offers graduate students an educational loan based on projected future earnings rather than on current credit-worthiness.

Tuition Loan Program (TLP)

This private educational loan plan was designed specifically as part of a service called M.B.A. LOANS for graduate business students who need additional funds to support their educational expenses. Students may borrow on their own or use a co-signer. The program was designed by the Graduate Admissions Management Council (GMAC), the people who bring you the GMAT, in association with Norwest Bank and HEMAR Insurance Corporation of America.

FUNDS YOU DON'T NEED TO PAY BACK

Unlike loans, scholarships and graduate fellowships do not have to be repaid. This type of funding is usually reserved for students with special qualifications including: merit (academic achievement), financial need, ethnic background or gender, or for students who will pursue a specific industry. Be advised that many scholarships and grants do not apply to part-time students, so research carefully.

Individuals, Businesses, and Philanthropic Organizations

These sources recognize the value of investing in the future of business professionals, and they provide fellowships and scholarships for outstanding students who otherwise would be unable to pursue graduate studies. You might receive this type of award through the school of your choice. Organizations often give money to schools to set up "named" scholarships. These scholarships usually go to students selected by the admissions/financial aid officers or faculty members. Often, you'll be considered for these scholarships on the strength of your admissions application or your interview. Sometimes a separate application is required. If so, the extra steps will be outlined in the admissions or financial aid application materials.

Students who receive named scholarships might also be offered internships or be honored at receptions where they meet the officers of the sponsoring organization. Some organizations and companies award scholarships directly to students. There are various free scholarship search databases on the Web which you can use to identify scholarship sources that you can pursue. This kind of research could turn up one or two small grants to help offset the cost of your M.B.A.

The most comprehensive scholarship search is FastWeb, the Internet's first, largest and fastest free scholarship search service. You can even submit a preliminary application to some of the scholarships listed here directly via the Web through FastWeb's E-Scholarships Program (http://www.fastweb.com).

Some other free scholarship databases that you may want to investigate are:

> ### Beware of Scholarship Scams
>
> Scholarships are free funds, so stay away from anyone or any organization offering to provide information on scholarships (or scholarship funds) for a fee. According to the Federal Trade Commission (FTC), you should be wary of any agency that guarantees or promises you scholarships or grants, as they are most likely not legitimate. Visit the FTC Website for further information at http://www.ftc.gov.

- Sallie Mae's Online Scholarship Service offers free access to the College Aid Sources for Higher Education (CASHE) database, which lists private sector awards from 3,600 sponsors.
- The College Board's Fund Finder scholarship database, also known as ExPAN Scholarship Search, lists scholarships and other types of financial aid programs from 3,300 national, state, public and private sources.

- CollegeNET MACH25 is a free Web version of the Wintergreen/Orchard House Scholarship Finder database. The database lists awards from 1,570 sponsors.

- SRN Express is a free Web version of the Scholarship Resource Network (SRN) database. The SRN database focuses on private-sector, non-need-based aid, and includes information about awards from more than 1,500 organizations.

All these scholarship databases can be accessed on the Internet through http://www.finaid.org, under "Scholarships." Another great source of information is your public library.

Financial Aid for Minority Applicants

There are a number of fellowships and scholarships available for specific ethnic groups. If you are an African American or Hispanic American applicant, for example, it might be worth your while to take the time to investigate fellowships offerings at your local chapter of the National Black M.B.A. Association and the National Society of Hispanic M.B.A.'s. You might also want to check into fellowships from the organizations listed below. The Consortium for Graduate Study Management provides fellowships at selected M.B.A. programs, while the Robert A. Toigo Foundation offers fellowships, internships, and mentorship for M.B.A.'s interested in the financial services industry.

Consortium for Graduate Study in Management
200 S. Hanley Rd., Suite 1102
St. Louis, MO 63105-3415
Phone: (314) 290-4565 or (888) 658-6814
Fax: (314) 290-4566
Website: www.cgsm.org

Robert A. Toigo Foundation
1211 Preservation Park Way
Oakland, CA 94612
Phone: (510) 763-5771
Fac: (510) 763-5778
E-mail: nsimsrtf@aol.com
Website: www.rtf.org

Reference Service Press publishes a number of guides on scholarships and other funding that are written with specific minority groups in mind, including:

- *Financial Aid for African Americans*
- *Financial Aid for Asian Americans*
- *Financial Aid for Hispanic Americans*
- *Financial Aid for Native Americans*

Veteran's Benefits

If you've served in the U.S. military, you may be eligible for educational benefits. Check with the Office of Veteran's Affairs at your school, if your school had one. If budget cuts have closed the Veteran's Affairs office at your school, you can obtain information through the following sources:

- Department of Veteran's Affairs
- On the Internet, you can access the Federal Benefits for Veterans and Dependents Website at http://www.va.gov/publ/benman95/.

SAVINGS

With interest rates on the rise, it may be a difficult decision to take money from your hard-earned savings. If this is your only source, carefully weigh the pros and cons of your choice.

OTHER SOURCES

Even if your company does not reimburse educational expenses, check whether they offer employee loans. Often, you can obtain funds from your firm (especially if they are a financial institution and/or have a good credit rating) at more favorable rates than you would obtain as an individual borrower.

Before cashing in your 401(k), mortgaging your home, or borrowing from credit cards, try asking a spouse or parent to lend you the money. If you are not able to finance your M.B.A., perhaps you should consider a cheaper means of obtaining the degree, such as an online degree or a shorter and less expensive route.

A last thought: If your company refuses to assist you in your endeavor to obtain an M.B.A., consider changing jobs. When you interview, be clear that you are looking for a firm that supports its employees in their academic pursuits and improvements.

For additional information regarding the financial aid process and products available, refer to Appendix A where we have listed some useful Website resources.

PART FIVE

The Part-Time Experience

CHAPTER 14

Opening-Night Jitters

You've progressed a long way down the road to B-school. You've learned how to gain admission to a program that fits your needs. You've explored how to find the money to pay for your education. But you may still have many questions. What's business school really like? Will my investment be worth it? Of course, your own answers to these questions lie in the future. In the meantime, however, we can show you how people who have been down the road to a part-time M.B.A.

For many of you, the first day of your M.B.A. program will be the first day in quite a while since you've set foot in a classroom. To help alleviate any anxiety you may be feeling about this big step, this section contains valuable advice for your school days, from the first to the last day and beyond.

THE FIRST DAY OF CLASS

The strongest memory from my first day of classes at Fordham University was the sense of urgency and anticipation prior to walking into the classroom. I'm not sure exactly what I was expecting—all eyes to turn on me? What I received upon the entrance to the classroom was the busy faces of about 30 students, most of whom were reading their *Wall Street Journals* or updating their Franklin Planners with the notes from the day's meetings. Did I expect to find a long-lost friend? Or maybe just hoping to find another eager first-day student?

It's a little like dating. You find things when you least expect them; don't push too hard. Yes, I was disappointed at first that other students were not a bit more friendly and interested in learning about the people who were going through the same process. But if you stop to think about it, everyone is there with a similar purpose: to learn, not to make best friends. Try to remember that for many students, the five-minute break before the start of class may be the only time during the day when your neighbor, sitting in the seat next to you, can have a few minutes alone, without the phones ringing, the baby crying, and that all-important client complaining. So relax, enjoy your first day, and know that before long you will be well entrenched in the day-to-day business of part-time student life.

Suggestions for Your First Day

Below are some ideas for your first day:

- Try to buy your books in advance and skim through them. Check with the registrar's office when you register that there are no reading assignments for the first day. If there are, don't think you can slack off because it's the first day. Getting behind on your homework from day one is a bad idea.

- Arrive very early. Since you are probably on unfamiliar terrain, allow yourself some extra time to get lost.

- Dress comfortably and wear comfortable shoes. Your first day will feel very long, especially after a full day's work.

- If your company does not provide you with a business card, have personal cards made up. To avoid the cost and time of having them printed up, you can design them yourself using presentation software, and purchase business-card paper at an office-supply store. This is an inexpensive and creative way of providing your fellow students with your phone numbers and addresses. Although the whole idea may sound a bit silly, sometimes it may be embarrassing if you *don't* have a business card.

- Explain to your classmates that you have personal cards made up because you are usually in meetings and cannot be interrupted during business hours. Try to find out where other students live and sit near those who live in your neighborhood. Many classes will require you to do group projects. Groups are usually assigned at the beginning of the term (sometimes the first day), and since you will be required to get together for projects after work and on weekends, it is really in your best interest not to have to commute too far.

- Don't try too hard, but do make the effort to talk to your classmates. Above all, be yourself.

- Lastly, take it easy. In general, when things start appearing unmanageable it is a good tactic to break down projects into smaller pieces. You have embarked upon a long and challenging journey—take it one day at a time!

Card Making

"Many word-processing software programs offer a template (a predesigned format) for making business cards. Usually these are found under the "Tools" and "Labels" indicators. You can also refer to the software user's manual for specific directions. There are several companies that produce finely perforated, 10-per-sheet business cards for laser and inkjet printers. The most preferable card stock is usually white or ivory–gray is also available, but I would not recommend it. Avery™ is probably the best-known brand name of business cards for computer generation and software, and you can purchased these items in almost any office supply store.

"A professional's business card should be clean and very readable. Look at others' cards that you have kept. Choose a standard format that you like from one of the business cards in your collection and re-create it for yourself. "Designed" card sheets are definitely a no-no as they are too commonly used, and you want to stand out in crowd! One last tip: The best colors of font (type) to use are black, dark navy, or dark gray."

*— Debbie Petersen, Graphic Designer
and Illustrator*

CHAPTER 15

What the Experts Say

In an effort to provide you with some insight on part-time M.B.A. programs from the people that stand at the gateway: admissions directors at select B-schools. Our survey included various schools from around the country, as well as one for-profit online university. Some of the issues touched upon by these contributors include: What is the marketability of the M.B.A.? What sort of criteria should prospective students look for in choosing a school? Which factors are weighed most heavily in the admissions process? How has the Internet revolution affected the M.B.A. degree? As experts, they were given the opportunity to provide their own interpretation of useful information and "do's and don'ts" for the part-time M.B.A. candidate. You will notice some consensus in their responses, specifically that the student should research carefully the options available to him or her and to prepare by speaking with others that have gone through the process as well. Some responses may sound more like a sales pitch to recruit you for their program, but they all offer invaluable and comprehensive advice to a future M.B.A. student. But we'll let our survey group speak for themselves.

Kim Corfman, Academic Director, The Langone Program: A Part-Time M.B.A. for Working Professionals (New York University's Stern School of Business)

Is a part-time M.B.A. right for you? If you want to stay in the business world yet at the same time are interested in moving ahead in your firm or industry, considering a career change, or preparing to launch an entrepreneurial venture, a part-time M.B.A. can be a valuable asset. Students in the part-time M.B.A. program at the Stern School earn the same degree as students in the full-time program, and a degree earned part-time has proven to be just as marketable as one earned in a full-time program. The requirements, the renowned faculty, and the academic curricula are identical for both programs.

Good part-time business programs combine the high-caliber, rigorous business education that working professionals desire with the flexibility they need to be successful while going to school and working full-time. Look for a school like Stern that offers a wide range of class times (evening and weekends) and formats, making the program very adaptable. Alternatively, Internet-based learning allows students in some classes to lessen the number of hours they spend on campus. In these courses a reduced number of traditional class meetings are supplemented by live online chats, moderated discussions, group meetings, lectures, assignment submission, and other Internet-based methods. Another popular format, intensive minicourses, allows students to accelerate the program, utilizing the down time in the standard academic calendar. These offerings make it possible for students who wish to attend only on Saturdays, as well as those who attend during the week, to graduate from the Langone Program in three years, if they choose.

The school's environment can play a big role in the learning process, as well. For instance, New York City itself serves as a "classroom" where the business, communications, and cultural worlds commingle to provide a truly dynamic learning environment. Because Stern is located close to Wall Street, Silicon Alley, and the entertainment and media industries, our students have numerous opportunities to enhance their education with exposure to executives from these industries, who are frequent guest speakers in classes and at conferences.

Students are attracted to part-time programs for several reasons. Many want to pursue an M.B.A. part-time so they can study business formally and advance their careers. Other students desire the degree to gain the skills, knowledge, and networking opportunities that will help them change careers at some time in the future. In both cases, students are not willing to give up their jobs to attend school full time. Because Stern's Langone Program is designed specifically for the working professional, it appeals to students who need to balance their studies with a full-time job.

For interested applicants, two years of work experience is the minimum prerequisite for admission to Stern, yet the average number of years among current students is between four and five. The admissions committee considers an applicant's essay, academic performance, letters of recommendation, and extracurricular activities. An applicant's GMAT, GPA, and work experience are used to take the application process to next level, to determine whether there is potential for admission.

In a time when many professionals want to stay on the fast track while getting a degree, a part-time M.B.A. may be the right choice.

Diane Dimeff, Director, Evening M.B.A. Program, Haas School of Business (University of California–Berkeley)

I've noticed that the market is more interested in part-time M.B.A. programs for two reasons. First, many years ago, business schools started revamping their part-time programs so that students would have a richer experience than traditional part-time programs have provided in the past. These programs are now concentrating on providing academic, professional, and social experiences that complement the classroom environment and approximate a full-time M.B.A. experience. This also includes a ramping up of student services so that part-time students can concentrate on the academic program and not the administrivia that is normally associated with attending school. Second, with the economy as strong as it is and the abundance of career opportunities, Part-time M.B.A. programs provide many fully employed individuals the opportunity to earn an M.B.A. while maintaining their career paths.

Because the classroom experience is enriched by the discussion of experienced people, it is best for students interested in part-time M.B.A. programs to have at least a few years of work experience. Students will get more out of the program and make a stronger contribution to their classmates' experience if they have that experience to draw upon.

The most important factors that individuals should consider when thinking about attending part-time M.B.A. program are (1) whether they have a work schedule that will allow them the appropriate amount of time, and (2) whether they have support from their family, supervisors, and colleagues. Obviously, it's critical, also, that the student have a sense of what they expect to get from the M.B.A.

For most schools, the application is divided into two major components: the quantitative component (GMAT, undergraduate and previous graduate records, and TOEFL, if applicable) and the qualitative component (work experience, outside activities, essays, letters of recommendation, and, if used, the interview). The quantitative component of the application gives the admissions committee a sense of how well the applicant will do academically in the program. The qualitative component will give the admissions committee a sense of the applicant's promise as a manager or leader.

Haas requires applicants to respond to two essays in our application. The purpose of the essays is to give applicants an opportunity to let us get to know them beyond their statistics. There are no right or wrong answers to the essay questions; rather, admissions committees are interested in how applicants think about the essay questions and how effectively they communicate their thoughts. The Haas Evening M.B.A. Program strongly encourages interviews, though they are conducted by invitation only.

My best advice is to be sure to get to know the schools to which you are applying. Talk to alumni and current students, observe a class, ask the placement center for placement statistics, and so forth. It's important for the applicant to know what kind of culture exists in the program and whether it offers what the applicant is looking for.

Joseph P. Fox, Associate Dean for M.B.A. Programs, Olin School of Business (Washington University)

Olin's Professional M.B.A. Program (P.M.B.A.) offers students the benefits of a top-quality M.B.A. program in a flexible format designed to fit their needs and schedules. Professionals develop knowledge and skills immediately applicable to the work environment and vital to overall career advancement.

The P.M.B.A. is designed to take a cohort of students through a 54-credit evening program in three years. This cohort system, in which students move through the core required courses with the same class of students, fosters a sense of community. The addition of teamwork within the new group system has greatly enhanced student satisfaction, cycle time, and graduation rate. (Note: Olin's cohort system was introduced in spring 1996. Program cycle time has improved from 4.5 years to 3 years, and the graduation rate has increased from approximately 50 percent to over 90 percent under the new design.) In contrast to the more traditional transient system, where students begin the program and move through at an individual pace, the cohort system dramatically enhances group interaction and meaningful class discussions.

A student-centered approach that emphasizes individual attention reflects the Olin culture, a close and caring community that empowers students to make strategic decisions early in their professional careers. With the increased flattening of organizations, this skill has grown increasingly important. The diversity of backgrounds and experiences represented in each class enriches the learning experience for professionals while preparing them to meet both immediate and long-term challenges.

Individuals considering enrollment in a part-time M.B.A. program should evaluate the reputation of the program, paying particular attention to the portability of the credential to new employers and/or to national or international locations. Look for accredited programs that will offer highly qualified colleagues, distinguished and accessible faculty, active alumni networks, world-class facilities, and additional programs within the university that have achieved distinction, and will thus improve name-recognition and the longer term value of your M.B.A.

Additionally, you should consider cycle time and graduation rate, as well as type of program (cohort versus transient), flexibility of the curriculum so that it can be tailored to personal goals, access to courses in technology and international business, student services and support, and employer sponsorship.

Olin requires three years of professional, postgraduate experience of their P.M.B.A. applicants. This work world experience ensures that each individual possesses the appropriate breadth and depth of experience to allow for substantial contributions to class discussions and projects, and that each student will have appropriate context for the information and perspectives shared by others. The most important criteria of the admissions application regards the quality of professional experience, the applicant's motivation and goals for pursuing the M.B.A., and academic preparation. Although no specific undergraduate path is required, previous academic success and readiness to embrace the quantitative challenges of an M.B.A. program are essential.

At Olin, two essays are required, and a third is optional. No writing formula exists for these essays, which instead are designed to offer applicants the opportunity to present themselves to the admissions committee in a personal, unique way. The essays also can serve as a means to addressing what might be perceived as a weakness in the applicant's background or credentials. For example, applicants can supply explanations for frequent job moves, weak GMAT scores, or gaps in employment.

Olin does not require P.M.B.A. applicants to interview with the Admissions Committee, although they are welcome to do so. Applicants wishing to provide additional information or discuss specific qualifications not well covered in their application will want to schedule an interview.

In selecting a part-time M.B.A. program, applicants should heed the following advice:

- Visit the programs that interest you.
- Talk with current students and alumni to learn more about the program.
- Network with professionals in the field that you intend to pursue postgraduation to see what additional considerations they believe are important in selecting an M.B.A. program.
- Adhere to deadlines.
- Retake the GMAT, if needed (the highest score is used in the admissions process).
- Maintain communication with the Admissions Office; don't hesitate to ask questions.

There is no one best program, nor is there one best type of student for a part-time M.B.A. The responsibility of a prospective student in the admissions process is similar to that of the school—to share information that allows both parties to assess the program's offerings in the context of the goals, professional priorities, and expectations of the would-be M.B.A. student. Ensuring the right fit is critical and will help lead to your happiness as a customer and a future alumni ambassador.

Katherine Gerstle Ferguson, Assistant Dean and Director of M.B.A. Programs, University at Buffalo School of Business

Part-time M.B.A. programs are most suitable for people who are currently working in their field of interest but need graduate-level education in order to make their next career step. This may mean, for example, an increase in decision-making responsibility, the addition of supervisory activity, or a move from a technical position to a manager of technical staff. Part-time programs are ideal for candidates who are in the relatively early stages of their careers but have high potential and are interested in improving their marketability and career options. If an individual is interested in dramatically changing his or her career path, a full-time M.B.A. program is more appropriate. Students immersed in full-time study have time to take advantage of internships and networking opportunities to a greater extent than part-time students, which is critical to a successful transition with significant career-path changes.

Over the past few years, many M.B.A. programs have moved from offering very flexible part-time programs to those that are cohort based. This shift has increased the opportunity for part-time students to develop competency in critical managerial areas such as team skills, leadership, oral communication, and conflict management. Because team activities are so essential in cohort programs, students are forced to learn how to work over a period of time (semester, year, or entire program) with assigned team members with different personalities, learning styles, and approaches to problem solving. These are invaluable skills.

In evaluating applications for admission to the part-time M.B.A. program, the Admissions Committee at the University at Buffalo reads each application in its entirety. Three factors most heavily influence the admission decision. The first is the applicant's academic record—overall GPA, performance in upper-level undergraduate courses and previous graduate work, and success with quantitative coursework—considered within the context of the institution(s) attended and the difficulty of the applicant's major. The second factor is the score on the GMAT. Our admissions decisions are based on a review the quantitative, qualitative, and the Analytical Writing Assessment (AWA) results, using the highest overall score as the point of reference. We rely heavily on the GMAT because validity studies that we conduct biannually with the assistance of ETS consistently demonstrate that the GMAT is an excellent predictor of success in our M.B.A. program (as measured by M.B.A. grade point average and placement results). Finally, the third of the most critical decision factors is the applicant's employment history. The Admissions Committee considers current employment as well as career progression. In cases where an application provides evidence of potential, but the dossier is not completely compelling, we request that an applicant meet with one or more faculty members for a personal interview.

The Internet in general has revolutionized the M.B.A. experience by making both course material and business information more immediately available for student consumption and by allowing faculty a wealth of excellent examples for practical application of theory. It has also dramatically altered the courses that students want to take (more MIS and marketing, less finance), the pace at which students desire to complete M.B.A. programs (faster), and the nature of employment opportunities students are pursuing. These changes have emerged more visibly in full-time programs but are quickly catching on among part-time programs and students.

The University at Buffalo is currently immersed in the developmental phase of an online M.B.A. that will utilize a variety of pedagogical methods including audio, video, voice, and text. The program will be very similar to our traditional M.B.A. programs in content and rigor; however, students will work in virtual groups and will communicate with faculty electronically. They will also take courses and complete assignments at a time and in a place that is convenient for them, not for us. We believe that the Internet provides a chance for excellent students who are bound to place or who have somewhat limited financial resources to pursue quality graduate management education. In addition, a forum for truly global student interaction can be much more easily achieved via electronic communication than if all the students must be in the same place at the same time.

Kathy Pattison, Assistant Dean of Admissions, Fordham University Graduate School of Business

Part-time students have different requirements and demands than full-timers. Fordham provides a flexible schedule that allows part-time students to attend classes in Manhattan or Tarrytown while maintaining their professional and personal responsibilities. Classes meet once a week for two hours, Monday through Thursday evenings. Limited Saturday classes are also available. In practice this means that most part-timers take two classes per trimester. On average, part-time Fordham students take between three and four years to complete their M.B.A. As of fall 2000, approximately two-thirds of the Fordham student body are pursuing their M.B.A. studies on a part-time basis.

General Advice for Part-Time Students

Do:

- Seek out colleagues at work who are currently attending an M.B.A. program. Ask what they have found to be positive and negative about their experiences in the program.

- Talk to your employer about your plans and schedules. Be prepared to describe how getting the M.B.A. will benefit all parties involved. Make sure to investigate whether your company has a tuition reimbursement program.

- Visit an evening class. Sit down to discuss the reality of the part-time program with a current M.B.A. student in each of the programs that you are considering.

- Attend an information session and/or part-time breakout session to learn about the benefits that part-time students have in each M.B.A. program.

- Obtain a Program of Study to decide what courses you are required to take and approximately how long you will need to commit to the program.

Don't:

- Delay completing your application. The sooner you have a decision, the more time you have to plan your M.B.A. program.

- Take your application lightly—plan it strategically like you would for a job interview. Know what credentials are valued by each admissions committee and make sure that you address these issues as they relate to your background.

- Forget about the GMAT. Allow enough time to study for the GMAT. Balancing GMAT preparation and a full-time work schedule is not only a good warm-up for a part-time program, but can indicate to an admissions committee that you are prepared for the rigors that lie ahead.

Jeanne Wilt, Assistant Dean of Admissions and Career Development, University of Michigan School of Business

Education is always valuable and always adds to your marketability. Investing in your education is certainly a good decision; that's been a truism for a long time and will probably remain true forever! The value of both the full-time and the part-time M.B.A. degrees have greatly increased in the last 20 years. There have been so many changes in the economy—globalization, technology, entrepreneurship, and greater management of diverse teams of people to achieve results—that the knowledge that comes with an M.B.A. degree is highly valued. The M.B.A. is, in many ways, seen as a gateway to leadership in business, a credential that puts you in an elite group of business people who deal with all aspects of business.

Individuals bring very different goals into their decisions about education. To some extent, individuals determine the value, as different M.B.A. programs fulfill somewhat different goals. So the objective is to ensure that your goals are aligned with the M.B.A. program you choose to apply to and then attend.

In general, companies are looking for talent, and your resume and interview will adequately highlight your ability to contribute to a firm. A part-time M.B.A. from a school with an overall excellent reputation for management education is definitely marketable. Occasionally, a part-time M.B.A. student may run into a firm or an individual that prefers graduates of a full-time program, but most people recognize the value of current work experience and the dedication it took to achieve the degree while working.

The right time to apply is when you feel the education and developmental experiences that come from an M.B.A. program will benefit you the most. Most M.B.A. programs recommend several years of work experience—with a usual minimum of two years—before applying, but today's average age of about 28 is just that, an average. Those several years provide a background of experiences and observations such that you will more fully appreciate what you learn in the M.B.A. program. You'll also be able to contribute to the learning of your classmates when you share your experiences in class discussions; likewise, you'll learn from their experiences. Your professional accomplishments during those years also provide admissions committees with a demonstrated record of achievement. As business is very much about producing results, admissions committees screen candidates rigorously for their proven ability to have an impact on the organizations they work for. Expectations for the length of work experience for part-time applicants are somewhat less demanding than those for full-time programs, as candidates will continue to gain experience while they are going to school.

As mentioned earlier, individuals have very different goals when it comes to furthering their decisions about education. The objective is to ensure that your goals are aligned with the M.B.A. program you choose to apply to and attend. Will the M.B.A. program you're considering help you reach your career objectives? Several years after graduation, your performance on the job is the most important factor in career success. These are some of the questions to ask yourself as you're determining whether you should apply to full-time or part-time programs:

- What is the profile of the students who are in the program? Will I feel comfortable there? Will I feel challenged there? How important is the diversity of classmates' background to my learning goals?

- What is the regional reputation of the school? The national reputation? The international reputation? If your life goals are to live in the same region as the school, you may not value the international reputation as much. If, however, you want to have maximum career flexibility and mobility, national and international reputation is important.

- What is the reputation of the faculty in the program? Are they available to students in office hours?

- What career services does the school provide? What are the placement statistics of the school, both in salaries garnered by their students and in the companies their students join?

- Am I ready for an M.B.A. program? What do I want to do after I get an M.B.A.?

- What are the strengths of the school's curriculum? How flexible is the curriculum in terms of course choices?

- What is my employer's policies regarding tuition reimbursement for the M.B.A. program?

Most admissions committees use the entire application to get a sense of a candidate, so you can't really say if any one element is more important than another. At Michigan, we believe we are about identifying leadership talent, and leadership comes in many forms. So we look at all aspects of an applicant's experiences and accomplishments as we review an application.

The most important thing to remember is this: What you are trying to do in the application is convey—coherently and concisely—a sense of who you are, where you've come from, where you hope to go, how you think an M.B.A. will get you there, and why you think there is a particularly good match between for you and the M.B.A. program to which you are applying.

We require four essays in our M.B.A. application; applicants have the option to answer more than four if they think the information presented will enhance their package. The best advice regarding the essays is to spend some time to do some introspection on possible ways to answer the essay question. When you've written your first draft, ask yourself a few questions. Does this essay answer the question? Is it written in a clear and concise manner? Does it convey important information about my goals, accomplishments, ability to lead others, and personality that will help the admissions committee know me better? Where appropriate, do I back up my statements with good examples?

Some "do's":

- Apply to schools that you're really interested in and that you feel are a fit for you.
- Apply to a range of schools that fit your needs so that you have several options to consider; some students only apply to one or two schools and that can be a limiting strategy, given the competitiveness of the application process.
- Apply in the earlier decision rounds.
- Visit the school and talk to as many current students and alumni as you can.
- Think deeply about where you are in your career right now, where you want to take your career and how the M.B.A. can help you achieve that transition.

The value of the M.B.A., as demonstrated through placement statistics, has risen. The use of technology has also increased in M.B.A. programs. The Executive M.B.A. has grown in popularity recently and generally attracts an older M.B.A. student with more experience and corporate sponsorship.

University of Michigan Business School does offer a Global M.B.A. to executives in selected companies in selected countries. The Global M.B.A. is an online M.B.A. program that uses technology extensively. In our regular M.B.A. programs, technology is used in a variety of ways to enhance the educational experience, such as:

- Web-enabled classes, which allow more flexibility in the scheduling of classes
- Web sites for individual courses, in which professors can post class notes and students can review problem sets

- M-Track, the Business School's Intranet site, in which students can view job postings, network with alumni, and bid on interviews
- E-lab, which serves as a research and teaching center on e-commerce and provides an incubator for developing e-business products and services

Broadly speaking, the Internet has revolutionized the M.B.A. degree because it has revolutionized business. Therefore, every M.B.A. course must consider how the use of technology has changed the fields of accounting, marketing, strategy, operations, business law, and so on.

Glenn Berman, Director of Admissions, Rutgers University Graduate School of Management

From my perspective, the value of the part-time M.B.A. has not changed dramatically. While changes in format, schedule, and mode of delivery may be required in order to meet the mobility and increasing time constraints of members of this segment, the demand for this degree remains strong. For many candidates, the full-time option is not viable, as family, personal, and professional responsibilities do not permit full-time attendance. As most part-time candidates are already employed, an M.B.A. adds value to their professional résumé and increases their value to their current or future employers.

For part-time candidates, the "right time" to go for an M.B.A. has many interpretations. At Rutgers, our typical part-time applicant is in his or her early to mid-20s and has had at least two years of full-time work experience. However, many part-time M.B.A. students begin their programs right out of college at schools that do not require prior work. In this instance, the "right time" is best defined as when the candidate finds a school and program which offers a curriculum and schedule that works and when he or she believes an M.B.A. program can be pursued successfully along with employment and other responsibilities.

In addition to wanting a program of quality with an excellent, experienced, and professional faculty (characteristics sought by most M.B.A. candidates), part-time candidates are generally most concerned with availability of programs they want to study, along with convenience and flexibility in class schedules. If the current employer offers tuition assistance of some kind, recognition and approval by the firm (usually the Human Resources Department) of the quality of the program in question is also important.

At the Rutgers University Graduate School of Management, we review and consider the entire application submitted by the candidate. This includes academic success (completion of a four-year bachelor's or equivalent, GPA, GMAT), work experience (résumé), essay, and letters of recommendation. Each element has an effect upon the outcome, and a strength in one area can often serve to provide balance for one in which the applicant was not as strong. We currently require one essay, but we may soon give applicants a choice among two topics.

Here's some general advice to those considering a part-time M.B.A.:

- Apply as early as possible. Don't wait until the deadline to send in the application.
- Be realistic in your choice of institutions. Apply to schools within your academic reach. Research each institution in which you have interest. Review the profile of the previous years' entering classes (average GPA, GMAT, years of work, etcetera).
- Compare programs and choose those which will best prepare you for your intended career or help you grow within your current company or industry.

Currently, we do not normally require interviews for applicants to our M.B.A. program. Occasionally, a particular program or scholarship opportunity may mandate an interview, or we may ask a candidate in to provide additional information about his or her application. The key to successful interviewing is preparation. Know everything you can about the institution, the graduate school, and the program. Be prepared to answer questions about why you want to attend and, if offered admission, what strengths and qualities you would bring to the program. Finally—although this should be obvious—dress professionally and be prompt. Treat the admissions interview as you would a job interview.

Although Rutgers does not currently offer any distance-learning M.B.A. classes, it may do so in the future. I believe that offering some courses online can be very beneficial, especially in the case of a part-time working student. However, I am not in favor of M.B.A. prgrams offered entirely on the Internet. Having students working together as a team, face-to-face, in the completion of a project that is vital to a business program experience. This is critical preparation for real-world business and cannot be achieved in chat rooms.

Brian Mueller, Chief Operating Officer, University of Phoenix Online

Should you earn your M.B.A. via the Internet?

The Internet is revolutionizing higher education. According to the International Data Corporation, over one million students are already taking courses via the Internet, and that number is projected to more than double by 2002.

The primary advantages of the Web-based educational format are convenience, flexibility, efficiency, and time savings. Many students also prefer the online learning environment because lectures and discussions are all in text form. This allows students to fully evaluate the information that is presented and more carefully consider their own responses. Numerous studies have indicated that the online students equal or outperform their on-campus counterparts in postgraduation test scores. In addition, the online degree is highly regarded by many employers today because it demonstrates a willingness to embrace new technology and an ability to apply innovative techniques to achieve success.

At University of Phoenix, our proven online format lets you earn your M.B.A. in the most efficient and convenient way possible—from your office during lunch time, at home in the evenings, or while traveling on business. You'll learn from instructors who currently hold leadership positions within the fields they teach. You'll study with other successful professionals from around the country. And you'll earn one of the most up-to-date and relevant M.B.A.'s offered anywhere. Best of all, most of our students complete their M.B.A. degree in just two years. In addition to the traditional Master of Business Administration, we offer M.B.A.'s in Accounting, Global Management, Technology Management, and E-Business.

What should you look for when choosing an online university?

I see seven major factors:

(1) Are they accredited? First and foremost, you want a degree that will be valuable and respected. The most important accreditation in the United States comes from one of six regional accrediting associations (Middle States, New England, North

Central, Northwest, Southern, and Western). These associations grant membership to all regionally accredited educational institutions (including Harvard, Princeton, and Yale), and acknowledge one another's accreditation. (University of Phoenix is accredited by the Commission on Institutions of Higher Education, which is part of the North Central Association of Colleges and Schools.)

(2) Do they have a proven online program? Most online degree programs haven't been around that long. Consequently they're still working out the bugs from their technology and their format. This can prove to very frustrating to students who are looking for convenience and efficiency. University of Phoenix was one of the first universities to offer an online degree program back in 1989. Today we are among the largest accredited online universities, with over 16,000 degree-seeking students. Our Web-based educational format has been proven and perfected for over a decade.

(3) Is the program 100 percent online? Many so-called "online" degree programs aren't entirely online. Instead they include instruction via other mediums, such as mail, telephone or videotape, or they require some on-campus attendance. These mediums are not as convenient or as effective as the purely online format. With University of Phoenix Online, you can complete 100 percent of your education at the times and places most convenient to you. All you need is a computer and an Internet Service Provider.

(4) Is the format asynchronous? Even among the online programs that are completely online, there are different formats. Some require the whole class to participate simultaneously in chat rooms, which means you must log on at prescribed times, and in this sense, there is no flexibility in scheduling. The more flexible formats are asynchronous, allowing students to participate whenever they want. Generally this is done through a system of bulletin board entries and e-mails. At University of Phoenix, all our classes are asynchronous.

(5) Do they have online faculty? Many online universities fail to fully utilize the Internet's global reach. Instead of recruiting the most qualified instructors from around the world, they simply give their local classroom teachers a computer with Internet access. The University of Phoenix Online faculty includes over 1,300 highly qualified instructors drawn from around the world. In addition to holding master's or doctoral degrees, our instructors hold high-level positions within the

fields they teach. When they are not teaching class, our instructors are successful CEOs, CFOs, CIOs, supervisors, managers, business owners, executives and professionals. What's more, all our instructors complete an extensive testing, training and mentoring program that prepares them to facilitate a productive and stimulating online learning environment.

(6) Do they offer financing and financial aid? Are they eligible for your company's reimbursement program? Earning your M.B.A. can require a substantial investment of money. Fortunately, many low-interest financing options are made available to students, even those with high incomes. Many of these financing options are only available, however, if the university is an eligible institution that participates in the funding process. University of Phoenix offers numerous options for financing your education, including low-interest student loans. We're also eligible for most company reimbursement programs. In fact, 59 percent of our students receive all or part of their tuition from their employer.

(7) What level of customer service do they offer? As a government-supported, non-profit organization, many state universities do not emphasize customer service—mostly because they don't have to. They leave it up to the student to figure out what he or she needs to do, and how to do it. Unfortunately, this lack of student assistance can often result in delays, confusion and wasted effort, lack of financing, enrollment in unnecessary classes, longer time to graduation, and other administrative complications. At University of Phoenix, you are assigned your own personal adviser who streamlines the process of returning to school, and answers all your questions regarding programs, start dates, financing and the application process. Once your application and fees have been received, your adviser will provide a detailed outline of your entire program, help you order your textbooks and course materials, and get you into class. From enrollment through graduation and afterwards, we're here to help you succeed.

What is the value of an online M.B.A.?

Without speaking for other universities, University of Phoenix can boast a great degree of satisfaction among our online graduates. In fact, in a recent post-graduation survey, an impressive 96 percent of our graduates expressed a high level of satisfaction with their online education and its positive impact on their career.

CHAPTER 16

What the Students Say

It's all well and good to be informed from the professionals at business schools, but the picture would not be complete without hearing from the students as well. What is the climate *really* like? What have they appreciated most about their experiences at school? Will they miss it? Has is proven useful yet? When reading the essays submitted below, consider that the author may one day be sitting next to you in a classroom, or sitting in your living room reviewing a class project.

With that said, here's what current students and recent alumni have to say:

Carmen Saleh, M.B.A., The University of Michigan Business School

As I recently sat through the commencement exercises at the University of Michigan, I reflected on my M.B.A. experience as a part-time student. Two years earlier, I had enrolled in the program while working as an internal change management consultant for a large marketing services company. I negotiated a flexible schedule with my employer that allowed me to scale back my hours to roughly 30 a week so that I could increase my academic load and finish faster. Although this flexibility had financial repercussions (i.e., no tuition reimbursement, a smaller salary), it did afford me the opportunity to finish in two years, take elective courses during the day, and increase my involvement in club and leadership activities. Although my strategy may not work for all students, it was perfect for me. I was able to progress in my career and apply the skills I learned to my job all while finishing in two years and enjoying the program every step of the way.

Many part-time students view obtaining a graduate degree as a means to an end: They plan on remaining with their current employer, so they grudgingly go to class with only one goal in mind—to get the degree. I did not want my M.B.A. experience to be like this. One of the reasons I chose the University of Michigan's program is because of the opportunities it offers from both a social and networking perspective. I quickly became involved in the Consulting Club and the student government, for which I held leadership positions in both. As the president of the student government for part-time students, I implemented numerous programs that improved communication among students and facilitated a new student's transition into the program. For instance, I created an Ambassador Program in which current and recent graduates of the part-time program offer advice and guidance to new or prospective students. They, therefore, serve as ambassadors of the school and the program. As a vice president in the Consulting Club, I worked to improve the relationship that consulting firms have with part-time students. Now, more consulting firms are marketing recruiting and educational events specifically to part-time students. Outside of club activities, I also attended many guest speaker events and conferences. These events at the University of Michigan, which draw influential business people from around the world, were truly top-notch and definitely impacted the quality of my education. These are the types of out-of-classroom events that all M.B.A. recruiting brochures preach about but that Michigan truly delivers on.

A big reason why many students return to school is for the opportunity to make a career or job transition. Having recently gone through recruiting season, I was thoroughly impressed with the quantity and quality of the companies recruiting on campus. Before entering the program, I knew that obtaining an M.B.A. degree would open doors for me, but I never imagined the full extent of that opportunity until I was bombarded with invitations from firms from around the country. Many part-time students worry that companies will not be interested in them since they pursued their degree while working, but this is not the case! Those I spoke to were impressed that I worked and went to school concurrently. Part-time students have sacrificed a lot to obtain their degree, and companies recognize and reward that.

Obtaining a graduate degree on a part-time basis has its challenges. At times, you will feel like you are being pulled in a million directions. It is up to you though to balance the demands of work, school, family, and community. Although this may be difficult at times (i.e., recruiting season), it can be done with good prioritization and time management skills. Don't get me wrong: There will be occasions when you need to take a day off of work to study for an exam or give up those Red Wing tickets to meet for a group assignment, but in the end, it will be well worth it. If you do decide to pursue an M.B.A. degree, my advice to you is to make the most of your school's program. Get involved, network with everyone you meet, and last but not least, have some fun!

Ivy Epstein, M.B.A. Candidate, The Langone Program: A Part-Time M.B.A. for Working Professionals (New York University's Stern School of Business)

When I decided to apply to Stern, I was ready to take on the commitment of an M.B.A. program, but I didn't want to be a full-time student again. I wanted to continue to pursue my career so I would have the ability to apply the new knowledge and skills I gained in the classroom to my job on an everyday basis.

Not only did I know that I only wanted to go to business school part-time, but the only school I applied to was NYU's Stern School of Business. The part-time program is formally called The Langone Program: A Part-Time M.B.A. for Working Professionals. I'm very proud to be a student at Stern, the part-time business school consistently ranked number one in the nation. At Stern, I'm not only getting an excellent education, but I've also become part of a community and am developing long-term relationships with the people in my classes and study groups. There is a tremendous sense of support; everyone here is dedicated to learning more and helping each other succeed in learning together, which enhances the experience.

Since starting the program, I have gained a greater sense of confidence, and I feel that my employer views me in a new way because I am pursuing this degree. But to use a metaphor, to me, the overall M.B.A. experience is like cake: The academic challenges, the community and network of people and the opportunity for leadership are the core of the experience; what comes after my time at Stern, my future career potential, is just the icing. I'm here for the M.B.A. experience.

I think back to my first day, sitting in Schimmel Auditorium with all of my soon-to-be classmates, thinking, "Who am I going to be here? How will this experience change my life?" That day, the possibilities seemed endless, which was so exciting.

In addition to the high academic quality of the program, I think one of the aspects I value most is its flexibility. The program is really geared towards working professionals. Classes are not only held in the evenings and on weekends, but mini-intensive courses can be taken during school breaks. Also, services for students are available when we're on campus during the later hours, and online communication makes everything possible. Although I haven't taken a course that formally incorporates distance learning, alternative course delivery systems are being used to enhance the experience and make the program even more accessible to students who work. For me, e-mail and the Web are critical for the teamwork and projects required by the program.

After completing three semesters, I can say that I wish someone had given me some guidance to help me better prepare for business school. Having learned some of the things the hard way, I'd like to offer some advice.

- First, start eating well as soon as possible. You'll need the energy.
- Practice working in groups and learn to enjoy it. It becomes a way of life, and it truly brings value to the learning and working experience.
- Prioritize, prioritize, prioritize . . . down to the minute.
- Take advantage of your M.B.A. experience. Get involved in your community because it can truly be rewarding.
- And remember, you're a student now—again. Flash that ID and take advantage of the discounts!

If you're looking for a tremendous experience to grow both intellectually and personally and are ready for the commitment that this type of experience will require, an M.B.A. may be right for you. I'm happy to say that I know it's right for me.

Maureen Oates, M.B.A. Candidate, Boston University

Since I started my M.B.A., I've taken on a new role as manager of training and development. I'm working on a leadership development program using a lot of the content from my courses. Last summer I had the opportunity to guide our executive team through Michael Porter's "What is Strategy?" article that was drilled into my head in my first class. (Michael E. Porter is the C. Roland Christensen Professor of Business Administration at the Harvard Business School and the premier authority on strategy and competition. His article "What is Strategy?" appeared in the 1996 *Harvard Business Review* and is essentially required reading for all M.B.A. students.) This year I'm helping to facilitate the long-term strategy-planning process. I've had a lot of opportunities to do new things at work and expose people to new ideas.

I am also incredibly organized now. I try to be ruthlessly efficient. Today, everything—exams, papers, team meetings, dates with my husband—goes into my Palm Pilot™ so I know exactly what my responsibilities are at work, school, and home.

The most significant change in my life, however, is that I think differently now. There isn't a day that goes by that I don't wonder how we can alleviate the bottleneck in the process (and sometimes find out it's me!), service our internal and external customers more effectively, position ourselves more successfully in the marketplace, or create a richer culture and environment for employees. I dream of Porter's 5 forces models, find myself referring to customer intimacy and the 7S model on a regular basis, and can even bear financials . . . very scary.

As far as the marketability of the M.B.A., I don't think a degree by itself gets you anything, whether it's full-time or part-time. It's what you do with it—how you carry yourself, present yourself, think and analyze things—that makes a difference. Knowledge in a vacuum or in your head is not much, but knowledge applied to a situation to create an impact is what matters.

My first day of school was pretty amusing. I had my book, parking pass, course packet, and so on, but I didn't bring anything to write in—no paper, no pen, nothing. The thought didn't even cross my mind. I had to quickly run to the bookstore to scrounge up a notebook and was sweating by the time I made it to class.

The M.B.A. program has definitely met my expectations. I wanted to gain a broad understanding of business principles, and I have. The funny thing I found out is that I already knew many of them—maybe not in depth, but I knew what they were. My company is great about exposing its employees to marketing and financials, making sure we all understand topics like our revenue recognition model. It gave me a leg-up walking into the program.

I also have an incredible network today. I can pick up the phone and call any one of my professors and get connected to leaders in particular industries. I feel very fortunate to have those links.

My advice to prospective students is get your support group on board. My boss was all for it, my friends and coworkers were thrilled, and my husband was, and still is, incredibly supportive. (In fact, he now edits most of my papers.) It's tough, though. It's not a piece of cake, and it takes a lot of initiative and drive to get the most out of the program and try to balance your life. It took me until my second semester to really get in the groove and learn what I needed to know to be successful, and now I'm cruising. In fact, this spring, I ran the Boston Marathon on top of everything else.

I'm plowing straight through my courses so I'll be finished in less than three years, but I'm doing that for a reason. As I like to say, "I don't want to get a glimpse of the 'good life,' or I may never go back to school." I've had to miss a bunch of nights out with my friends, and I've studied right through date night with my husband. But when you finish a case, a paper, an exam, or a presentation, and you really know the content inside and out, you feel great. You feel even better when you use your learning at work the next day, week, or month. This is what you need to remember.

Although I don't have any kids, I'm told that getting an M.B.A. can be compared to childbirth. There's a buildup, although you're never quite prepared. The pain is temporary, but very real, and once it's done you have this lasting imprint. Some day I guess I'll find out if that's the truth, but not before I get finished with school!

Michael R. Slade, M.B.A., Dolan School of Business (Fairfield University)

The first issue the part-time M.B.A. candidate needs to address is at the office. Obviously, one's supervisor must be made aware of the time demands placed on a graduate student, but he or she also needs to understand the level of course work support required, in the form of survey requests, student visitations, and company financial and product data. (Many of these support issues will not only improve the student's performance, but it will promote the company corporate image as well.) If a lack of support is found, I think it is time to leave the company. My advice, in that situation, would be to get out as soon as you can and find a M.B.A.-friendly employer.

I would also advise the part-time candidate to determine if the business school offers a tuition payment plan that will accept your company's reimbursement structure without requiring the student to provide the tuition upfront. This is an excellent opportunity to minimize finance charges on frequently used credit cards. Add up what is saved in finance charges over a couple years, and it can easily equal a well-deserved graduation vacation.

During my graduate school career, I do not remember hearing a fellow student state that he could not keep up with the part-time program and needed to switch to a full-time status. In fact, if a student would like to expedite the completion of the program, many schools offer accelerated semesters that include trimesters, intersession courses, and summer courses. Completing your master's program in two years is not unheard of—I personally completed each of my M.S. and M.B.A. degrees in approximately two years by always taking two courses per semester and luckily always having courses available during the summer sessions and intersession. One of my fellow classmates followed a very similar M.B.A. program of study and also completed his M.B.A. part-time in roughly two years. It's a rigorous but clearly obtainable goal. On average, I am sure most students take between three to four years to complete the program part-time. Regardless of the length of time, I have found that most M.B.A. graduates feel, in retrospect, that their time was extremely well utilized, and they typically feel like it went by so quickly.

Most graduate schools of business are clearly geared towards the part-time student. That is, most business schools structure their graduate course offerings based on evening and weekend classes. In addition, many of the course registration and student information bulletins are posted online to keep the student informed about course availability, university events, and support resources. If the school has a staff that advocates the use of the Internet for communicating university activities, this is a tremendous benefit to the part-time student.

Fairfield University does a great job of keeping their students well informed. Almost on a weekly basis, Colleen from the School of Business would electronically mail course offerings, inquiries regarding student interest in special interest courses, conference offerings, and updates about the graduate student association. This frequent communication tends to keep the part-timer tuned in to campus activities and thus maintains a bond or relationship with the university.

A benefit of a part-time M.B.A. program is the opportunity to integrate courses with work projects. Certainly, many of the M.B.A. concepts taught in graduate school are quite current. You can take courses with subject matter which is coincident with new or ongoing projects. When the graduate student has the opportunity to apply those concepts immediately on the job, it literally make both tasks easier while possibly justifying the high cost of tuition.

I believe the use of team-based projects opens up the learning process. Team projects obviously broaden the analysis process to account for multiple opinions, talents, personalities, and solutions. They also promote time management, presentation skills, team dynamics, and genuine cross training. Some of my most memorable activities include the different phases of team projects.

Using case studies offers the graduate student the opportunity to investigate real-world cases and experiment with newly found technical and management skills. While working with other students, you genuinely get the opportunity to understand the different opinions and problem-solving techniques, as you stretch the limits of your own ideas and talents.

One of the initial hurdles of the part-time M.B.A. program is the first day. The first day is typically spent in a financial management or accounting class. In these courses there is a clear pecking order: Those who have a strong background in these disciplines are the most vocal with regard to answering all of the questions, since many of their classmates have never taken the class nor read the book. Obviously, these are the most sought after study partners. And a part-time M.B.A. candidate must establish effective study partners, usually within the first couple class sessions. You need to learn how to acclimate or transfer your free time to graduate studies (thus eliminating leisure pursuits) and understand the culture, rhythm, and character of the student body. A classmate of mine refers to this activity as "face time." How well one handles this period can greatly simplify the next couple years of your graduate school life.

One characteristic I found quite favorable when forming my study team was experience: Classmates who have completed prior graduate work clearly understand the effort and time demands of a successful student. Also, team up with those who have a clear purpose and time frame for completing their degree program, since the M.B.A. program consists of a rather broad subject matter, and the level of work is academically very challenging and typically requires a three- or four-year commitment.

I also recommend seeking out students with a broad skill set. That is, include in your core group members with, say, finance, marketing, technical, and operations backgrounds. Gathering knowledge in different areas clearly is a great help as you work through the M.B.A. program.

Would I recommend pursuing a degree part-time? I, for one, repeatedly received acknowledgement for the effort necessary to complete my degree work while handling my family and career responsibilities. Typically this recognition was understood to represent maturity, goal setting, responsibility, and strong time-management skills. When a prospective candidate is considering the tremendous effort necessary to complete a part-time M.B.A., he or she should remember that the extra effort might represent greater value to an employer.

Regarding the marketability of the M.B.A. program, now that I am in a corporate environment versus plant operations, I have found that essentially all of the middle- and upper-management promotions have been awarded to those with M.B.A. degrees. It is reasonable to believe that career opportunities for M.B.A. graduates are quite strong at one's present company as well as in the open market.

In the real world, those who expect to lead a business into the future will have completed their graduate degree. The bottom line is to perform well at work and obtain additional graduate training that can be applied to your career.

John MacKay, M.B.A. Candidate, Fordham University

Over the past three years, I have had the opportunity to pursue an employer-sponsored, part-time M.B.A. in Finance at the Fordham University Graduate School of Business. This experience has been both challenging and rewarding, and has changed my entire outlook on the business world, while at the same time opening many doors which would have been closed to me had I not undertaken this effort. I highly recommend part-time M.B.A. study to any business professional interested in expanding his horizons and enhancing future career prospects.

I decided to enroll on a part-time basis for financial reasons. As far as I was concerned, borrowing to finance high tuition and living costs in New York City would have had a negative impact on my future financial security. My employer was willing to sponsor me for M.B.A. study through a program wherein I pay the tuition up front, and then am reimbursed based on my performance. While this plan was an additional challenge to my part-time study, it proved to be a motivating force throughout.

In addition, I felt strongly that a part-time M.B.A. would allow me to apply what I was learning to a professional context, and to glean more out of the experience than if I were to simply stop working and study full-time. In my current position, I have been able to apply both managerial and financial techniques learned in class to my work environment. I feel that a part-time degree is more marketable than a full-time degree to prospective employers for the simple reason that learning is enhanced when it is immediately applied.

When I initially began my program of study at Fordham University, I was concerned with several issues. I wondered if I would be able to handle the additional workload imposed by the program and still perform well at work. I saw the M.B.A. as a major, long-term, life-changing commitment that would limit my social life as well as my mobility. Also, I worried about the backgrounds of other students and how competitive the environment would be. I found that the solution to these concerns was discussing them with other part-timers. This helped me to allay my fears of failure as well as to realize that other students were in fact allies, not competitors. By developing relationships with fellow students, I was able to learn who the best professors were, and how to gauge the number of hours I would need to devote to the M.B.A. outside of the classroom. I would suggest to any new part-time student that seeking out other students with similar backgrounds and interests is as important as devoting a substantial amount of time to studying.

There are several pieces of advice I would like to share with both prospective and new part-time students. First, it is important to attend a school's orientation session before beginning the application process. Some schools are more committed to part-time students than others, and it is important to establish this on day one.

New students should take advantage of automatic course waivers and placement exams. I was exempted from three courses in which I had excelled at the undergraduate level. Many M.B.A. programs offer waivers from courses if the student did well in the course and took it within a recent time period. For students who have been out of the undergraduate arena for a long time, the placement exam option is often available.

Also, I would suggest that students start out by taking two courses in the first semester. This will allow time to adapt to the challenges posed by nighttime study. However, if able, I recommend moving up to three classes per semester. This is a serious decision that depends on the student's ability, as well as his or her work schedule and social obligations.

It is also important to make sure that your employer and coworkers understand the extent of the challenge you are undertaking—but don't expect too much sympathy for challenges you have willingly imposed upon yourself. When I began the program of study at Fordham, I was fortunate enough to have an immediate supervisor who knew what I was experiencing, as she had pursued a part-time M.B.A. at the same school. You will have to leave work on time on school nights, as lectures tend to be jam-packed with information, and missed classes definitely have an impact on both learning and final grades. Your employer needs to understand this.

Finally, if your employer is reimbursing you after you pay the tuition to your school, I recommend that you get a credit card sponsored by an airline mileage program. I paid tuition on my credit card, and accumulated airline miles that I was able to apply towards much-needed vacations during the program.

I highly recommend part-time M.B.A. study to any businessperson interested in expanding his or her horizons. However, I cannot stress enough that pursuing an M.B.A. while working is very challenging, and only you can determine if your perceived future benefits of M.B.A. study outweigh the sacrifices you will make. Best of luck!

Dawn Taketa, M.B.A. Candidate, Haas School of Business (University of California–Berkeley)

I weighed the pros and cons of attending business school at night very carefully before applying. My career was just taking off; I was asked to lead the project team to develop online stores for Gap Inc. During my first semester at Haas, I launched online stores for GapKids and babyGap; in the following year, I took on additional responsibilities for the launch of the Banana Republic online store and Old Navy online marketing Website. Just over a year into the M.B.A. program, I helped lobby for the creation of a new department that would focus on the customer experience, which was inspired by my Competitive Strategy class. Knowing that I would be taking on so much added responsibility, I understood that returning to school would be difficult. I was also convinced that I could apply much of the theory directly to my line of work.

Since all of my work experience had been at one company, I decided on an evening program to broaden my horizons and expose myself to new business situations. The Evening M.B.A. Program at Haas was a perfect match for me. I wanted a top-notch education, and I wished to continue working. There were so many exciting things happening in our online business, and I wanted to be a part of it. But I also had heard about the energy and excitement that Haas had been generating around entrepreneurship and high-tech fields.

The Evening M.B.A. Program has truly exceeded my expectations. I had always heard that one of the most valuable aspects of business school is the people you meet. My classmates brought a wealth of knowledge to the program, and, through conferences and events sponsored by the school, I have been able to tap into an amazing network.

What's more, I was able to take advantage of once-in-a-lifetime opportunity: to study business in the Netherlands, Belgium, and Ghana. The International Business Seminar (an elective) consisted of about four weeks of presentations by expatriates from each of the countries that were living in the San Francisco Bay Area, and by the student themselves—the goal being to understand the history, culture, and economic conditions of each country prior to our trip. Then, 30 students and two professors were off to spend two weeks to meet with Haas alumni working in these countries. Many of these alumni had returned to their native countries and therefore brought an interesting perspective to our conversations . . . one that you could never get from reading a book or newspaper.

We were exposed to flowers and broadband in Holland, speech recognition software and the European Commission in Belgium, and personal-care manufacturing and gold mining in Ghana. Many of our hosts were eager to pick our brains, as we brought a wealth of experience in areas ranging from high technology and e-commerce to finance and marketing. The trip exemplified all that is wonderful about being in a part-time M.B.A. program: the excitement of taking part in a learning environment while being able to apply new skills and knowledge in real time.

Juggling a family, career, and school is a small price to pay for the opportunities that the program has helped me discover. The Haas program provides assistance—ranging from transportation to assistance purchasing textbooks—to help students keep up with their hectic schedules. I also found that my company has been very supportive; they saw the benefits immediately from my contributions. For example, I worked on projects directly related to online marketing in both my Business and Public Policy course and the International Business Seminar. By integrating my experiences at work, home, and school, I was able to make new business connections and friendships.

It has been quite an experience so far and I expect that I will really miss the program when it is over, believe it or not!

CHAPTER 17

The M.B.A. at Work

By now, you've heard opinions and advice from current and former B-school students, school officials, and, most likely, various people in your own life about your pursuit of a part-time M.B.A. Perhaps you've enrolled in a program that's perfectly tailored to your needs, you've secured means for tuition, and you've purchased and skimmed through all your textbooks. You're on top of things—but are you? Are you prepared to weather the changes that will inevitably enter into the picture?

It cannot be stressed enough that attending school while maintaining a full work schedule is a daunting task. It may be tempting, especially in the beginning, to let your responsibilities at work slip a little. You must remember that, even though your company may fully support your decision financially and emotionally, they are in a business and you are their employee. Your first and foremost responsibility during work hours is to them.

So, imagine yourself rushing out the door at 5:00 for a Futures and Options midterm as your boss stops you in the hall to request additional documentation for a presentation scheduled for 8:00 the following morning.

Imagine a professor refusing your Business Law final booklets because they were written out in pencil. (This actually happened to me. In the accounting department where I worked, we wrote everything in pencil. Apparently, at the beginning of a class I was late to, the professor had mentioned that all finals should be written in ink.)

Imagine not having any vacation time left but needing days to finish two research papers that are due next Monday.

Imagine colleagues giving you the evil eye for constantly being on the phone with your classmates or for always leaving early on Mondays and Wednesdays.

I think by now you are getting the general idea: The bottom line is that there is no way to please everyone. Accept the fact that you will need to juggle many priorities and handle difficult situations. Just remember to be true to yourself.

Perhaps, however, after an honest introspection, you have decided that the life of a part-time student and full-time employee is not beneficial or feasible for you. Or it may be your company that has put the future of your M.B.A. degree in jeopardy—perhaps they need you to be available more consistently, or they have restructured their tuition reimbursement policy. In situations such as these, you may find yourself in a situation where you have to choose between work and school.

HAVE FORESIGHT

When I first started my M.B.A. program, most of my fellow students were enrolled part time as well. Interestingly enough, as my studies progressed, I noticed this ratio change. Why? There were several reasons. First, some found the program too rigorous and decided to complete their degree on a full-time basis. The second reason was the surge of mergers and acquisitions in the financial arena in the late 1980s that left many of my colleagues and classmates out of work. Lastly, some students decided to run off and make their fortune by hooking up with a dot-com or starting up their own business—a fate that continues today.

When you start your M.B.A. program, don't necessarily assume that you will complete your degree on a part-time basis. As we mentioned earlier, a very important question to address when applying to graduate school is whether you are able switch your status without needing to apply to the full-time program.

There are other precautions you can take as well. Career counselors recommend that M.B.A. students meet with a counselor early in their educational career. Do not make the same mistake that many students do by using the counseling center only when it's absolutely necessary. Too many part-time students wait until either they have lost their job or they are concerned about their job security—and by then it may be too late to effectively make a campaign for their employment prospects. Even if you are happily employed at present, make an appointment to introduce yourself to a member of your school's career services staff. You never know when their resources will prove useful!

> ### Long-Term Effects
>
> No one can predict what the future will hold, but you can research schools and programs carefully so that you are adequately prepared for a successful professional life and not just the next step in your career.

OUT OF WORK, NOT OUT OF OPTIONS

What can you do if you find yourself suddenly out of work once you have begun the part-time M.B.A. program? First, don't panic. Identify your options and realistically determine which one is right for you. There is no correct answer; everyone's situation is different. Before evaluating your options, you should consider the following:

- **The number of credits remaining until you complete your degree.** Does your school allow you to take time off or transfer to a full-time program?

- **The length of time it will take you to find a job at your level.** Unless you are in a very specific market with highly marketable skills, the more experience you have (or the higher level you are at), the longer it will take to find a new position.

- **Your financial circumstances.** When assessing your monetary situation, don't forget to include your cost of living. In addition to school, you will still have to pay your monthly overhead (rent, electricity, and job-searching expenses, for example). How much money do you need to complete your degree, including the incidentals, such as books and activity fees? How much disposable income is available to you, like savings or severance funds, if applicable? How credit-worthy are you? Are you eligible for loans (bank or personal), financial aid, and credit cards? How long can your savings support you? What is your threshold for finding a new job?

Once you have determined the above, you can consider your options. You can (1) continue your part-time program while searching for a new job; (2) take time off from your schooling to search for a job on a full-time basis; or (3) complete your degree full time.

Continuing the Part-Time Program

You have weighed the alternatives and determined that maintaining your part-time status at school is the best way to approach your new situation. You will need to reassess your finances and your job prospects.

Financial Implications

If you find yourself out of work due to cutbacks or downsizing, you may be entitled to a severance package. Depending on the length of employment with your company, a severance can be a substantial amount of money that you will be able to apply towards your studies. If, on the other hand, you're in a position where you are unable to meet your current financial obligations in addition to footing the bill for school, student loans are available to assist you make ends meet. Visit the M.B.A. Loans Web site at www.salliemae.com, or make an appointment to meet with a dean at your school to discuss alternatives. Work-study programs or tutoring are a few options that may be at your disposal.

Before taking out any loans, consider whether your employers have legally obligated themselves to pay for your degree. Do you have a contract? Some firms require you to sign a contract when you start your program, stating that you will remain employed with them for a certain time period after completing your degree. Read your contract carefully: Has your company committed themselves to paying for your completed degree? Consider this point when you sign the agreement at the beginning of your program.

Employment Considerations

If you decide to continue your program on a part-time basis while you are out of work, you will find yourself with huge blocks of free time to job search. So where do you start?

First, if you've been laid off, check with your company to see whether they have arranged to assist you with placement services such as résumé workshops or recruiter connections. Tap in to your available connections and make sure to request references letters from them early (i.e., before your last day).

Make an appointment to visit your school's career counselor. As we mentioned earlier, this is a step that should be taken at the beginning of your program. Imagine how helpful it would be—especially if you're out of work—to have an open line of communication with a career counselor who knows you and your aspirations.

Finally, do your research. Although this book was not intended as a guide to searching for employment, there are many such resources available. Investigate at your library and on the Internet to find the company that is right for you.

Taking Time Off

Perhaps you can not or wish not to finance the remainder of your degree yourself. In this case, you will need to take some time off. The first step is to notify your school. Some institutions may limit the amount of time students can take off without having to reapply to the program. The most efficient manner of informing your school is to send a formal letter indicating that you are not "dropping out" but rather "stopping out"—that you do intend to resume courses in the near future. If this step is not taken and your school alters its curriculum, you may be required to take a class that you have already completed.

You should remain in contact with your school periodically and keep them advised of your situation. Each school has its own policy regarding career counseling, and although you may no longer be an active registered student, you may be eligible to participate in the career placement services offered at your school.

Weighing the Alternative

In comparing the full- and part-time programs at your school, make sure you know the following:

1. Do part-time students need to apply to the full-time program? If so, is there one admissions committee and one set of admissions standards for part-time and full-time programs?

2. Do the same faculty members teach both full and part time?

3. Is the curriculum the same? If not, is it still appropriate to your goals?

Switching to Full-Time Status

Depending on the number of credits required to complete your degree, the most efficient stance to take in this situation is to finish your M.B.A. on a full-time basis.

Can it be done?

The very first question you should consider is whether you can transfer to the full-time program at your school. Again, this is something that needs to be checked out with your school. Some programs distinguish between full-time and part-time programs while others do not. You may find yourself in a position where you will be required to reapply to your school.

Cost/reward evaluation

If you have the financial ability to finish off your degree in a short period of time (say, one term or semester) it may be in your best interest to concentrate your efforts on finishing your studies. Searching for a new job is stressful enough without the extra burden of school considerations. In addition, you don't want to jeopardize a potential new employment by requesting tuition reimbursement from day one. Keep in mind the added bonus: When you do start your job hunt, you will be able to add "M.B.A." to your résumé!

LESSONS LEARNED

To recapitulate, here are the most important lessons learned and the steps you can take to ensure that there are no snags along the path to your successful completion of the M.B.A. program:

1. Keep an open mind and take the time to network while in school. You never know when connections or insights into other firms may prove useful.

2. When selecting a school and program, ensure that there is the flexibility of transferring between programs without reapplying to the school.

3. Visit your career counselor at the beginning of your M.B.A. program—and keep in contact. Make this an introductory meeting; don't start your part-time M.B.A. program by applying for jobs. This is premature. Additionally, some schools may consider this a conflict of interest, since your employers are paying for your degree.

4. Before signing a contract for tuition reimbursement with your employer, make sure your interests are covered.

5. If your employment situation changes, be sure to notify your school in writing.

But let's be optimistic, and assume you obtained your part-time M.B.A. as planned, with no major snags. Congratulations! You have achieved a terrific goal. So how will those three letter after your name affect your chances of moving up or moving on? The fact that you pursued the degree on a part-time basis speaks very highly of your motivation, stamina, intelligence, organization, and much more—and employers recognize this.

HOW EMPLOYERS VIEW THE PART-TIME STUDENT

What employers admire in part-time students is their obvious loyalty and stick-to-it-ness. The full-time student usually uses the M.B.A. as a stepping-stone or a career changer; the part-timer uses the degree as a career booster. Many employers especially appreciate the "experienced hire" that has become synonymous with the more seasoned part-time M.B.A. candidate.

If or when you look for a job, remember to market the skills that are highly valued in the part-time M.B.A. profile. These skills include: experience, flexibility, dedication, ability to work in teams, practical and theoretical knowledge, exposure to other companies and company practices, motivation, ability to work under pressure, and a genuine interest in learning and applying new concepts. Here's a brief sampling of industry opinion:

"When interviewing a prospective candidate who has either completed or is currently attending an M.B.A. program part-time, I am impressed not so much by the knowledge acquired through the M.B.A. process, but by the personal sacrifice and commitment necessary to work full time and attend school at night. I believe this work ethic and career development transcends itself to the workplace, and more often than not result in an employee who is extremely driven, focused, and goal-oriented."

— *Director, Deutsche Bank*

High Market Value

"Managers cannot afford to be operating on outdated information or faulty models of the business environment. Information and strategic decision-making skills are of utmost value. A superior M.B.A. program provides both. I believe a part-time degree is more marketable than a full-time M.B.A., all other factors being equal. In today's market, if you are out of the loop for a year, you are far gone."

— Pamela Curry, Assistant Director of Graduate Programs, Dolan School of Business, Fairfield University

---

"As an employer, I appreciate candidates who have earned the part-time M.B.A. because they tend to be effective employees sooner. There is no need for them to get acclimated to the business world; they already have a keener sense of how the principles can be applied. The advantage of being in a business context is enormous.

"As an educator, I notice that students with current business experience perform very skillfully in our Simulation Program. In fact, they tend to perform better than those full-time students in the honors class."

— *President and Chief Executive Officer, Parnassus Associates, International; Adjunct Professor at Baruch College*

Remember to market these qualities when you are on your job search, either to get your foot in the door or at the interview itself!

Before jumping to the task of looking for a new job, take the time to assess the attributes that you have enjoyed in your prior work experiences. Your list may include specific tasks as well as the kinds of environments you enjoy. Once you are confident about the type of employment you want to target, you will be on your way!

USEFUL RESOURCES IN THE JOB SEARCH PROCESS

You have many useful tools that are readily available, such as your colleagues at school and your work, the Internet, and recruiters.

Schools

We cannot stress the point enough: You must develop a relationship with a career counselor at your school. You'll be that much better off when the time comes to ask for their assistance in the job hunt. The valuable services a school's career placement center usually provides include:

- On-campus recruiting
- Group workshops or one-on-one assistance with résumé writing, interview skills, and general job search skills
- Internet sites with job boards (listing candidate résumés and linking to other career resources)
- Résumé books
- Résumé referral services
- Employer and alumni database services
- Job search workshops
- Career fairs

> **Take Advantage of Advisers**
>
> "I fully utilized my school's career center from the start of my M.B.A. experience. Advisers helped me build my résumé, research companies, even improve my interviewing skills."
>
> – *M.B.A graduate*

Other Students/Alumni

Because the M.B.A. experience can be so significant, many current students and alumni will feel an immediate bond with you and will be very open to talking with you, mentoring you, and assisting you with contacts. Conduct an informal poll

> **Off Campus**
>
> Research your school's affiliates! Students at Loyola University in Chicago who are seeking employment outside Chicago are eligible for reciprocal career planning and placement assistance at any of the 27 other Jesuit Universities located across the United States.

among your classmates: Ask them about their companies, what the corporate culture is like, and if they in a hiring mode. Many organizations post job openings in the office itself; see if you can get a copy. As you know, no matter how much research on a company you complete, getting an insider's scoop is always more insightful, especially if it is from someone you know and trust. Lastly, remember that school ties are very strong—don't forget to refer to your undergraduate and graduate school alumni directory.

Colleagues

Perhaps the best referral you can obtain is from a current colleague or boss. The people who work with you are the most competent to recommend you to a new employer. Ask around; perhaps they can recommend some useful connections.

The Internet

Job searching on the Internet has become commonplace. There are many useful sites, including job placement sites specifically designed for M.B.A.'s. Appendix A in the back of this book includes a listing of some of the most popular Web addresses.

Referrals

It's always key to maintain your relationships with friends, ex-colleagues, and acquaintances, as they represent a good source of information on potential job availability. Make lunch dates to sustain your contact. Once caveat: In today's tight job market many companies offer their employees a referral fee for bringing in new staff. Do not rely solely on someone else's opinion, since there may be ulterior motives, as the referral fees can be substantial. Always do your own research on a firm; what may be utopia for one person can be hell for another.

Recruiters

Recruiting firms can also be a very useful for the prospective employee. Although it is imperative to research a company thoroughly, many recruiters will have additional insights into the workings of a firm. A recruiter's allegiance is twofold: to the corporation, who needs the position filled, and to the candidate searching for a new position. Their expertise lies in their ability to make the perfect match and satisfy all concerned.

We asked a top recruiter, Evan Lee, President at Accent International (www.accentjob.com), a recruiting firm in New York that has serviced financial institutions and Fortune 500 companies over the last 12 years, a few questions about the idiosyncrasies of job search.

When is a good time to start looking for a new job?

If you are about to complete an M.B.A., it would be prudent to give yourself three months to start looking for a new position. Obviously, it depends on the level and nature of the position you are looking for; a very specialized type of job, for instance, may take longer to fill. We work with a great many universities via job fairs and on-campus recruiting. These are wonderful tools for candidates looking for a new position, so be sure to use them.

Do most of the firms you service offer the tuition reimbursement benefit?

Most of our financial services firms do offer tuition reimbursement benefits. I would add that while many of these firms are aggressive about financing an M.B.A., it does depend on which position you are applying for. Does the company need you to receive the degree? How it will complement the skills that you are already bringing to the table? It really depends on the fit.

What would you suggest to the candidate who wants the tuition reimbursement benefit from Day One (i.e., for those who are enrolled in a program and find themselves out of work or wanting an immediate change)?

It is important to be flexible. Research the company and see if the fit is right. For example, if the perfect match is there, you may be in a position in which the prospective employer woos you, perhaps even offering a signing bonus (usually only offered to candidates who are currently employed). The bonus can carry you financially until you are eligible for the tuition reimbursement benefits. Remember that it is the fit that is crucial. If the prospective employer really wants you, they may be able to find ways to accommodate your requirements and circumvent their current policy. Most importantly, remember not to walk into an interview demanding tuition reimbursement benefits. No one reacts well to ultimatums, and it is premature to discuss these issues until you are convinced the position is right for you and you are in the negotiations stage.

Have you noticed any trends vis-a-vis the M.B.A. candidate? Are they more or less in demand than they used to be?

I believe the M.B.A. is much more in demand in terms of the work that I do. In fact, I would say that for many positions, the M.B.A. is now a prerequisite. Most financial analysts either have the degree or are in the process of pursuing it, and the companies I work with have indicated a strong preference for all analysts to have the degree—and these are mostly entry-level positions. Let's say you are a vice president position in charge of credit. It's important for you to possess the M.B.A. for the additional incentive of competitiveness. In your next job, the candidates who you'll go up against will certainly have the degree, so you need to stay competitive. I have worked with many people who have tremendous amounts of responsibility in their current position, but if they were out in the job market today they would need an M.B.A. to complete their experience and have the type of résumé that employers want to see.

What skills do you and your clients appreciate in the part-time M.B.A. candidate?

Employers really appreciate the balance between the analytic skills and business development skills that the M.B.A. with work experience can bring to the table. Employers will always value the amount of work that went into obtaining the degree. They recognize the motivation and focus of the candidate. They may have many employees with managerial talent or top quantitative skills, but they really appreciate the candidate that possesses both. Overall, I would say that the dedication required of an M.B.A. student is the attribute my clients seem to rate the highest. This never goes overlooked and is always respected.

Can you provide any advice to M.B.A. candidates who are contemplating a job change?

The best advice I could give is to do your research. I believe that the company you choose to work for is oftentimes even more important than the actual position you are filling. Look what the company can offer you down the line. Most importantly, make sure that the chemistry is right.

A FINAL THOUGHT . . . OR IS IT?

Although you can only get one M.B.A., many schools are offering add-ons! For instance, Syracuse University offers an M.B.A. Upgrade, an executive education program designed for experienced managers and executives who have earned an M.B.A. five or more years ago. So if you have already earned your M.B.A. but fear you may be getting a little stale, check with your school about auditing classes or updating your degree.

For Your Information

Frequently Asked Questions

When it comes to an endeavor as significant as your education, there is no such thing as too much information, and no question too foolish to ask. Indeed, in my discussions with students, administrators, educators, and employers, I often heard the same questions about the M.B.A. The following is my attempt to answer some of the more frequently asked questions and lead you to some resources I found very helpful in researching this book.

Do I need to have an undergraduate degree in business to pursue an M.B.A.?

The initial answer to this question is no. In fact, many schools appreciate candidates with a diverse background; it makes the classroom more interesting. However, some schools or programs may require their students to have some previous coursework in fundamental business courses such as mathematics, statistics, economics, and financial accounting. If this is the case, and you have not yet fulfilled the requirements, do not give up. If the program is right for you, consider taking the prerequisites before applying. Just be sure that the credits can be transferred.

Why doesn't work experience count towards coursework?

According to admissions officers, work experience in itself does not necessarily represent a structured, thorough understanding of business principles and concepts. Business schools provide a product to their students as well as to the corporations that hire the M.B.A. degree. Keep in mind, though, that prior work experience is vital to classroom discussion and eases the transition of theory to practice.

Are the standardized tests (GMATs/TOEFL) really necessary to gain admission?

If I can give prospective students any advice, it would probably be to never, ever ask this question. If the school you are interested in identifies that GMATs (or TOEFL) are necessary, that means they are. If you are applying to graduate school on a part-time basis and have been out of school for many years, you may be quite unaccustomed to taking standardized tests. You should realize that many other people are in the same situation. Take a preparatory course and practice for the exam—Kaplan, for one, offers classes throughout the United States as well as retail books such as *GMAT CAT*. Apply yourself and you'll do fine.

Once in a part-time program, can I transfer to a full-time program?

This is an important question that needs to be addressed when you decide which programs and schools to apply to. Some schools consider the full- and part-time programs as separate and distinct programs, whereas others treat both as one and the same. In the first instance, if you wish to expedite the completion of your degree, you must realize there is a separate admissions process for the day program.

As a part-time student, am I eligible for financial aid?

The answer will vary from school to school, so you should broach this topic with the admissions department. Although you may not be eligible for financial aid, U.S. students are entitled to student loans. As soon as possible, consult with the financial aid professional at the school of your choice and they will indicate which aid, loans, or scholarships you may be qualified to receive.

When do I find out about waived coursework and credit requirements to graduate?

Usually this is a process that is determined after admission, although some schools may notify you with your admission letter if you can be "placed out of" a class as a result of previous credit in college. If you are required to take a placement exam, your school will notify you of its testing dates.

Do not be confused between "waived" courses and those courses which you can be "placed out of." For example, some schools will require a certain number of credits in order to graduate, and being "placed out of" a class will not reduce the total number of credits required to graduate.

Is there a maximum number of classes that can be waived?

This answer will vary from school to school. Most schools will allow you to waive only prerequisite courses such as calculus, marketing, business law, economics, statistics, or accounting. There is usually a maximum number of credits/courses that you can waive or be placed out of; it can range from two to five courses.

As a part-time student, am I authorized to use the school's facilities?

Although most schools will not prohibit the part-time student from utilizing the school facilities, such as the gym and the library, there may be fees associated with some amenities. Also, you may find that due to scheduling obstacles, certain facilities are inaccessible.

How much time apart from the classroom should I expect to spend on my M.B.A. activities?

This will depend on you (are you a speed reader?) and on the classes in which you are enrolled. You should probably budget on average an extra 4 or 5 hours per week for each class for study time. You also have to allow for commuting time and hiccups, like when you can't find the book you need at the library or the printer's down.

If I am required to travel for business, can I make up classes?

It's never a good idea to miss classes. You may find that for every class you miss, you will wind up spending more than double the normal amount of time trying to catch up for the missed lecture. Obviously, you will probably miss some classes, so here's some advice:

- If you know in advance that you may miss a significant number of classes, talk to the professor and review your schedule before registration. Knowing the syllabus may assist you in determining when to take a specific class.

- Pick a "buddy" or two and ask them to take meticulous notes and record the lecture in your absence, if your professor agrees. Be sure to agree to cover for them when they are away.

- If you will miss just one class, be sure to notify your professor in advance. This can serve two purposes: It's an introduction to your teacher, and it may unearth some additional insight on the missed class (will it be focused on the exam? is the lecture material covered in the readings?). Your professor may in fact offer his or her notes.

How important are grades once I am admitted to business school? Isn't the degree the only thing that counts?

This is a loaded question. Many companies offer tuition reimbursement based on results, and therefore you have additional financial incentives (and your pride!) to perform well. Also, your employers may consider your grades when evaluating your work performance. Realizing that most students enroll in B-school to learn and not necessarily to get the grades, there is a degree of satisfaction though from achieving good scores. Many schools will apply a course towards your degree only if you have received a C (or the school's equivalent) or better. Additionally, if you plan to leave your current job, many new employers will check your records and may only consider the top 10 percent from a graduating class for their job openings.

As a last note, if you are in school solely to get the degree, you may want to rethink your motivation for going to B-school. You should apply for the education and the experience—grades are part of the process.

What is the difference between full-time faculty and adjunct professors?

Full-time instructors are academics by profession. They may be tenured or under contract. Adjunct professors usually work in business as well as teach several courses. They are able to successfully blend theory and practice. Visiting professors may only be on the teaching staff for a short duration; perhaps they are from a specific industry or "borrowed" from another program. A good mix of these teaching staff will ensure that you have a well-rounded B-school experience.

Are my chances of gaining admission to a school better if I get my application in early?

The earlier you apply, the earlier you should find out if you are accepted. Additionally, the sooner you submit your application package, the sooner you will be notified if you are missing any required documentation such as recommendations and transcripts. Here's a good piece of advice: If you are happy with your application package, submit it once it is complete. Do not send in a sloppy package just to get it in on time—this will ruin your chances of acceptance.

Is there any advantage or disadvantage to submitting my B-school application over the Internet?

There should be no favoritism in terms of acceptance to a program. Applying via the Internet is a marketing tool used in order to facilitate the application process for the prospective candidate. Some schools may offer to waive the application fee if you apply online. Check it out!

I have three great references for my application package, but the school I am applying to requires only two. Will it help or hinder my chances of admission is I submit all three?

This will vary from school to school, so ask the admissions department. Some may say that the more information about yourself you can submit, the better. Others may require you to stick to the letter of the law.

I was not born in the United States but am fluent in English. Am I required to take the TOEFL test?

If English is not your native language, the TOEFL test will be required. The TOEFL test is now a computer-based test and is offered frequently. A TOEFL is valid for two years from the expected entrance date. Although you should check with each school, the test is usually not required if a candidate satisfies certain requirements, some of which are:

1. Citizenship of Australia, Canada, Great Britain, Ireland, New Zealand, Guyana, and Anglophone countries of Africa or English-speaking countries of the Caribbean.

2. A college or university degree earned in the United States or in one of the countries listed above.

3. A degree earned from American universities abroad.

These are general rules. You should confirm your status with your school before assuming you are exempt from the TOEFL requirement.

Useful Resources

We have just listed some of the most common concerns, but most likely, you still have some issues you'd like to research further. To get all your questions answered, check out these resources. Following some of these guidelines will help steer you though the often confusing task of selecting, applying, and successfully completing business school.

Below are some of the resources you can use to obtain information such as the location of schools in your area, available part-time programs, school and program rankings, and student discussion groups.

Visit the Schools/M.B.A. Forums

The series of M.B.A. school fairs known as M.B.A. forums, sponsored by the Graduate Management Admission Council (GMAC) each year, are a wonderful resource and an excellent way to browse the programs. Representatives of more that 75 graduate management schools from the United States and abroad are on hand at each Forum to answer questions about their programs.

These events can be helpful in numerous ways:

- They are a source of general information about M.B.A. programs that will help you to identify the attributes of a program and if it will meet your needs.

- Once you have decided which characteristics of a graduate management program are most important to you, they can help you find schools that meet your profile.

- If you have identified a group of programs to which you plan to apply, it may be possible for you to arrange an individual meeting with a school representative before or after an M.B.A. Forum to talk at greater length about the program and your qualifications.

Kaplan M.B.A. Forums

Kaplan M.B.A. Forums are held annually in several cities. Visit the Kaplan Website at kaptest.com, or call (800) KAP-TEST to get additional information about these forums and other related events.

The schedule of M.B.A. Forums typically includes eight cities in the United States, and sites in Asia, Europe, and Canada. Six U.S. Forum sites are permanent, with events each year; these are Boston, New York, Chicago, Los Angeles, and Washington, D.C. Two additional Forums rotate amount cities in various regions of the country. The exact calendar of sites and dates is determined annually.

Information about the M.B.A. Forums is available on the M.B.A. Explorer Web Site http://www.gmat.org, or by calling (800) 537-7982 (or (609) 683-2230 from outside the United States or Canada). You may also send an inquiry by fax to (609) 279-9149.

The M.B.A. Forums also include "Destination M.B.A.," a series of half-day workshops designed to acquaint underrepresented minorities with graduate management education and career possibilities. Scheduled in cities around the United States, the Destination M.B.A. programs are often held in conjunction with the M.B.A. Forums, allowing attendance at both the same day. In those cities in which no M.B.A. Forum is scheduled, a school fair or other activity often complements the Destination M.B.A. workshop.

Kaplan, Inc. holds several events and seminars throughout the year on the secrets of the GMAT, how to get into business school, women and M.B.A.'s, and several other topics. At these forums, attendees will meet representatives from individual business schools, learn about the application process, and listen to panelists discuss how an M.B.A. has enhanced their career.

Graduate Management Admission Search Service

The Graduate Management Admission Search Service (GMASS™) is a free service that makes your name available to schools whose specifications for applicants match the profile you furnish when you register for the Graduate Management Admission Test (GMAT). This automatic service will send you mailings from many schools about their M.B.A. programs, admissions procedures, and financial aid.

Schools: Program Brochures and Material

M.B.A. programs prepare a wide variety of materials to assist prospective students in learning about them. When you request information from a school, make sure to ask for a brochure as well as an application package. If you are requesting information via the Internet, be advised that some schools will reply automatically and will put your name on a list for their next mailing. Go directly to the school's Website, where you will be able to access more up-to-date information without being prejudiced by the beauty (or lack thereof) of a glossy brochure cover—remember never to judge the book by its cover. A school's Website also contains a lot of informative data such as class offerings and schedules. As a part-time student, the class schedule will be a major factor in determining which program is right for you.

Once you have narrowed your search of schools to a small handful, visit the campuses, and determine the atmosphere and facilities. Ask for a guided tour and visit the library. Oftentimes there are student evaluations of the professors and courses available in the reference area. If there is no student available to give you a guided tour, ask the admissions office if you can contact a current student to discuss the school from an insider's point of view.

Guidebooks

A wide variety of guidebooks have appeared on the shelves of bookstores in recent years. Although many are oriented primarily towards dispensing advice, they often include pieces of both objective and subjective information about M.B.A. programs. However, most books cover only a very small subset of the programs you can consider. It is important that you not limit your search to these few profiled programs, since there may be many more suited to your goals and aspirations.

Nonetheless, various guides may offer new perspectives to you, or they may contain a quote or piece of data that will shed some light on a specific area of interest. In using these sources, you need to remember that admissions officers providing advice to any guide are doing so in the hopes of expanding their marketing reach to qualified and eligible candidates.

Library Reference Section

Check your local library reference section (or your favorite bookstore) for a variety of books that detail the programs available nationwide. Here are some books of particular interest:

How to Get into the Top M.B.A. Programs, by Richard Montauk (Prentice Hall Press, 1996).
A detailed overview of the top M.B.A. programs nationally and internationally with admissions strategies.

Marketing Yourself to the Tops Business Schools, by Phil and Carol Carpenter (John Wiley & Sons, 1995).
How to develop a personal marketing program to get into business school.

Gravy Training: Inside the Business of Business School, by Stuart Crainer and Des Dearlove (Jossey-Bass, 1999).
A critical look at the past, present, and future of B-schools.

Here are some titles that focus on distance-learning programs specifically:

Bears' Guide to the Best M.B.A.'s by Distance Learning, by John Bear, Ph.D., and Mariah Bear, M.A. (Ten Speed Press, 2000).

Get Your Degree Online, by Matthew Helm and April Helm (McGraw-Hill, 2000).

College Degrees by Mail and Internet, by John Bear, Ph.D. and Mariah Bear, M.A. (Ten Speed Press, 2000).

M.B.A. Websites

These days there is very little that you can't find on the Internet. The following is just a sampling of some useful M.B.A. sites.

www.mbainfo.com

The M.B.A. Program Information Site. An international business school site containing a database with details on 2,250 M.B.A. programs from 1,160 business schools and universities in 127 countries as well as advice pages for the prospective candidate.

www.gmac.com

The M.B.A. Explorer. This site includes links to business schools on the Web, a school search engine, information about the M.B.A. Computer Adaptive Test, and order forms for GMAC publications. You can register online for the Graduate Management Admissions Test (GMAT).

www.kaptest.com

The nation's test-preparation leader, Kaplan offers extensive GNMA preparation. Also available is a business school admissions consulting service to help you wow admissions officers.

www.bschool.com

Marr/Kirkwood Official Guide to Business School Webs. This site links to business school sites, detailed reviews of these sites, and side-by-side comparisons of published rankings. Includes a variety of business education articles and financial aid information.

www.mbaus.com

The Official M.B.A. Guide. The electronic version of the *M.B.A. Guidebook*, published by Unicorn Research Corporation.

www.embark.com/mba/

Search for an M.B.A. program that meets your requirements and apply online.

www.accepted.com

Accepted.com's professional editors can advise you and edit your essays and résumés.

www.educationindex.com

A guide to education-related sites on the Web, sorted by subject and life stage. Click on life stage, then distance learning or grad school.

www.mbadepot.com

M.B.A. Depot provides an open line of communication between students and alum to share experiences and resources for B-school.

www.uwex.edu/disted/home/

Distance Education Clearing House. This site contains definitions of interactive delivery systems as well as links to distance-learning programs, articles and newsgroups.

www.gnacacademy.org

Global Network Academy. This site provides information on distance-learning programs.

www.multi-app.com

The leading M.B.A. application software. For a fee, users can complete their M.B.A. applications on their personal computer.

www.ft.com

The *Financial Times* site provides advice for those looking to complete an M.B.A. The site links you to their interactive M.B.A. rankings listing the global ranking of M.B.A. programs. There is also a guide to getting your M.B.A., including how to apply, prepare for, and finance your M.B.A. There are also M.B.A. discussion forums discussing the latest topics within the M.B.A. community.

Websites for School Books and Supplies

A frequently overlooked expense of attending business school is the high price tag associated with the textbooks and required material for each class. You school will make these books available to you in their bookstore, although the only discounts that are usually offered on premises are on used books. Beware of purchasing prior editions of textbooks. Ask your professor if there are substantial differences in editions that would prohibit you from gaining the most from an older edition. Here are some alternatives to the campus bookstore:

www.classbook.com

A site that offers discounted new and used books.

www.varsitybooks.com

Enter the school, author, title, or ISBN to order your textbooks online. Most titles are readily available, but if they don't have want you're looking for right away, book-pager™ will e-mail you when the book you need is in stock. If the book cannot be found altogether, Varsity Books will let you know.

www.collegebooks.com

Another site with discounted textbooks and reference materials.

www.amazon.com and www.bn.com also offer a very large selection of discounted books.

Websites for Career Advice/Searching/Planning

Many magazines and books have online versions that provide insight and advice on career advancement and new job opportunities.

www.careermag.com

Career Magazine's Website presents a comprehensive resource for the job seeker. You can also post your résumé free of charge.

www.nyt.com

The *New York Times* offers an online version of their Sunday employment section which lists hundred of jog openings.

There are too many job-posting sites to list here. Your browser can link you to some of the most visited sites. Here are a few:

www.monster.com

One of the largest and most visited, this site offers thousands of job listings, a career center, and résumé listings.

www.M.B.A.freeagents.com

A small, up-market site that offers links for M.B.A.'s with full-time and freelance positions.

www.vault.com

In addition to job postings, this site includes some interesting articles as well as inside industries and insider company research.

www.careerbuilder.com

A host for other career sites. These are articles on writing cover letters, juggling work and life, and special sections for the self-employed, women, and human-resource professionals.

www.dbm.com/jobguide/

The Riley Guide, one of the most comprehensive job sites available.

Financial Aid

www.estudentloan.com

If you are looking for a student loan, this free site lets you instantly compare loans that match your specific needs and provides online applications.

www.finaid.com

This site has everything you ever wanted to know about financial aid, including free scholarship and fellowship search services and descriptions of financial-aid sources. Sponsored by the National Association of Student Financial Aid Administrators.

Directory of U.S. Business Schools

The Business School Directory

This section includes several listings to be used as a guide to available part-time M.B.A. programs.

ALPHABETICAL INDEX OF BUSINESS SCHOOLS

Here you'll find a comprehensive list of all U.S. universities, arranged alphabetically, with their respective business school name and state. Deciphering and remembering each institution's B-school name can sometimes be a maze—this listing will help steer you in the right direction.

BUSINESS SCHOOLS WITH PART-TIME M.B.A. PROGRAMS

This section, arranged by state, provides the contact information for all AACSB accredited universities that offer part-time M.B.A. programs. An asterisk (*) following the school name in this directory indicates that the school offers both a part-time M.B.A. program and an Executive M.B.A. program. A dagger (†) indicates that the B-school's part-time offerings are limited to the E.M.B.A. only. Contact the admissions office of the school for further information.

DISTANCE LEARNING M.B.A. PROGRAMS

Currently, there are many universities that offer M.B.A. degrees via distance learning. The listing assembled in this directory represents a sampling of such schools. All of the programs included in the directory are accredited (either regionally or professionally, or both) and require little or no on-campus residency. The teaching mediums may vary, but they include the Internet, video, television, CD-ROM, e-mail, and text (traditional methods).

Alphabetical Index of Business Schools

University	Business School	State
American University	Kogod College of Business Administration	DC
Appalachian State University	John A. Walker College of Business	NC
Arizona State University	College of Business	AZ
Arkansas State University	College of Business	AR
Auburn University	College of Business	AL
Auburn University—Montgomery	School of Business	AL
Babson College	F.W. Olin Graduate School	MA
Ball State University	College of Business	IN
Baylor University	The Hankamer School of Business	TX
Bentley College	McCallum College Graduate School of Business	MA
Boise State University	College of Business & Economics	ID
Boston College	Wallace E. Carroll School of Management	MA
Boston University	School of Management	MA

University	Business School	State
Bowling Green State University	College of Business Administration	OH
Bradley University	Foster College of Business Administration	IL
Brigham Young University	Marriott School of Management	UT
California Polytechnic State University—San Luis Obispo	College of Business	CA
California State University—Bakersfield	School of Business & Public Administration	CA
California State University—Chico	College of Business	CA
California State University—Fresno	The Craig School of Business	CA
California State University—Fullerton	School of Business Administration & Economics	CA
California State University—Hayward	School of Business & Economics	CA
California State University—Long Beach	College of Business Administration	CA
California State University—Los Angeles	School of Business & Economics	CA
California State University—Northridge	College of Business Administration & Economics	CA
California State University—Sacramento	College of Business Administration	CA
Canisius College	Richard J. Wehle School of Business	NY
Carnegie Mellon University	Graduate School of Industrial Administration	PA
Case Western Reserve University	Weatherhead School of Management	OH
Central Michigan University	College of Business Administration	MI

University	Business School	State
City University of New York—Baruch College	Zicklin School of Business	NY
Claremont Graduate University	Peter F. Drucker Graduate School of Management	CA
Clark Atlanta University	School of Business Administration	GA
Clark University	Graduate School of Management	MA
Clarkson University	School of Business	NY
Clemson University	College of Business & Public Affairs	SC
Cleveland State University	College of Business Administration	OH
College of William and Mary	Graduate School of Business	VA
Colorado State University	College of Business	CO
Columbia University	Columbia Business School	NY
Cornell University	Johnson Graduate School of Management	NY
Creighton University	College of Business Administration	NE
Dartmouth College	Amos Tuck School of Business Administration	NH
DePaul University	Kellstadt Graduate School of Business	IL
Drake University	College of Business & Public Administration	IA
Drexel University	Bennett S. LeBow College of Business	PA
Duke University	The Fuqua School of Business	NC
Duquesne University	A.J. Palumbo School of Business Administration John F. Donahue Graduate School of Business	PA
East Carolina University	School of Business	NC
East Tennessee State University	College of Business	TN
Eastern Michigan University	College of Business	MI
Eastern Washington University	College of Business & Public Administration	WA
Emory University	Goizueta Business School	GA

University	Business School	State
Fairfield University	Charles F. Dolan School of Business	CT
Florida Atlantic University	College of Business	FL
Florida International University	College of Business Administration	FL
Florida State University	College of Business	FL
Fordham University	Graduate School of Business	NY
George Mason University	School of Management	VA
George Washington University	School of Business & Public Management	DC
Georgetown University	The Robert Emmett McDonough School of Business	DC
Georgia Institute of Technology	DuPree College of Management	GA
Georgia Southern University	College of Business Administration	GA
Georgia State University	J. Mack Robinson College of Business	GA
Gonzaga University	School of Business Administration	WA
Harvard University	Graduate School of Business Administration	MA
Hofstra University	Frank G. Zarb School of Business	NY
Howard University	School of Business	DC
Idaho State University	College of Business	ID
Illinois State University	College of Business	IL
Indiana State University	School of Business	IN
Indiana University— Bloomington	Kelley School of Business	IN
Indiana University—Northwest	Division of Business & Economics	IN
Indiana University– Purdue University at Fort Wayne	School of Business & Management Sciences	IN

University	Business School	State
Indiana University– Purdue University at Indianapolis	Kelley School of Business	IN
Indiana University—South Bend	School of Business & Economics	IN
Iowa State University	College of Business	IA
James Madison University	College of Business	VA
John Carroll University	Boler School of Business	OH
Kansas State University	College of Business Administration	KS
Kent State University	Graduate School of Management	OH
Lamar University	College of Business	TX
Lehigh University	College of Business & Economics	PA
Louisiana State University	E.J. Ourso College of Business	LA
Louisiana State University in Shreveport	College of Business Administration	LA
Louisiana Tech University	College of Administration & Business	LA
Loyola College in Maryland	Joseph A. Sellinger School of Business & Management	MD
Loyola Marymount University	College of Business Administration	CA
Loyola University Chicago	Graduate School of Business	IL
Loyola University New Orleans	Joseph A. Butt, S.J., College of Business Administration	LA
Marquette University	College Business Administration	WI
Marymount University	School of Business Administration	VA
Massachusetts Institute of Technology	Sloan School of Management	MA
McNeese State University	College of Business	LA
Miami University	Richard T. Farmer School of Business	OH

University	Business School	State
Michigan State University	The Eli Broad Graduate School of Management	MI
Middle Tennessee State University	College of Business	TN
Millsaps College	Else School of Management	MS
Mississippi State University	College of Business & Industry	MS
Mount Saint Mary College	Division of Business	NY
Murray State University	College of Business & Public Affairs	KY
New Mexico State University	College of Business Administration & Economics	NM
New York University	Leonard N. Stern School of Business	NY
Nicholls State University	College of Business Administration	LA
Northeastern University	College of Business Administration	MA
Northern Arizona University	College of Business Administration	AZ
Northern Illinois University	College of Business	IL
Northwestern University	Kellogg Graduate School of Management	IL
Oakland University	School of Business Administration	MI
Ohio State University	Max M. Fisher College of Business	OH
Ohio University	College of Business	OH
Oklahoma State University	College of Business Administration	OK
Old Dominion University	Graduate School of Business & Public Administration	VA
Oregon State University	College of Business	OR
Pace University	Lubin School of Business	NY
Pacific Lutheran University	School of Business	WA
Pennsylvania State University	The Smeal College of Business Administration	PA
Portland State University	School of Business Administration	OR

University	Business School	State
Purdue University	Krannert Graduate School of Management	IN
Rensselaer Polytechnic Institute	Lally School of Management & Technology	NY
Rice University	Jesse H. Jones Graduate School of Management	TX
Rochester Institute of Technology	College of Business	NY
Rollins College	Crummer Graduate School of Business	FL
Rutgers University	Graduate School of Management	NJ
Saint John's University	The Peter J. Tobin College of Business	NY
Saint Joseph's University	Ervian K. Haub School of Business	PA
San Diego State University	Graduate School of Business	CA
San Francisco State University	Graduate School of Business	CA
San Jose State University	College of Business	CA
Santa Clara University	Leavey School of Business & Administration	CA
Seattle University	Albers School of Business & Economics	WA
Seton Hall University	W. Paul Stillman School of Business	NJ
Southeastern Louisiana University	College of Business	LA
Southern Illinois University— Carbondale	College of Business & Administration	IL
Southern Illinois University— Edwardsville	School of Business	IL
Southern Methodist University	Edwin L. Cox School of Business	TX
St. Cloud State University	College of Business	MN
St. Louis University	School of Business & Administration	MO
Stanford University	Graduate School of Business	CA

University	Business School	State
State University of New York—University at Albany	School of Business	NY
State University of New York—Binghamton	School of Management	NY
State University of New York—Buffalo	School of Management	NY
State University of West Georgia	Richards College of Business	GA
Stephen F. Austin State University	College of Business	TX
Suffolk University	Frank Sawyer School of Management	MA
Syracuse University	School of Management	NY
Temple University	Fox School of Business & Management	PA
Tennessee Technological University	College of Business Administration	TN
Texas A&M University	Lowry Mays College & Graduate School of Business	TX
Texas A&M University—Commerce	College of Business & Technology	TX
Texas Christian University	M.J. Neeley School of Business	TX
Texas Tech University	College of Business Administration	TX
Thunderbird, The American Graduate School of International Management		AZ
Tulane University	A.B. Freeman School of Business	LA
University of Akron	College of Business Administration	OH
University of Alabama	Manderson Graduate School of Business	AL
University of Alabama—Birmingham	Graduate School of Management	AL
University of Alaska—Fairbanks	School of Management	AK
University of Arizona	Eller Graduate School of Management	AZ

KAPLAN

University	Business School	State
University of Arkansas—Fayetteville	Sam M. Walton College of Business Administration	AR
University of Arkansas—Little Rock	College of Business Administration	AR
University of Baltimore	Robert G. Merrick School of Business	MD
University of Bridgeport	School of Business	CT
University of California—Berkeley	Haas School of Business	CA
University of California—Davis	Graduate School of Management	CA
University of California—Irvine	Graduate School of Management	CA
University of California—Los Angeles	The Anderson School	CA
University of Central Arkansas	College of Business Administration	AR
University of Central Florida	College of Business Administration	FL
University of Chicago	Graduate School of Business	IL
University of Cincinnati	Graduate School of Business	OH
University of Colorado—Boulder	Graduate School of Business Administration	CO
University of Colorado—Colorado Springs	College of Business & Administration	CO
University of Colorado—Denver	Graduate School of Business & Administration	CO
University of Connecticut	School of Business Administration	CT
University of Dayton	School of Business Administration	OH
University of Delaware	College of Business & Economics	DE
University of Denver	Daniels College of Business	CO
University of Detroit Mercy	College of Business Administration	MI

University	Business School	State
University of Florida	Warrington College of Business Florida M.B.A. Programs	FL
University of Georgia	Terry College of Business	GA
University of Hawaii at Manoa	College of Business Administration	HI
University of Houston	Bauer College of Business	TX
University of Houston— Clear Lake	School of Business & Public Administration	TX
University of Illinois—Chicago	College of Business Administration	IL
University of Illinois— Urbana Champaign	College of Commerce & Business Administration	IL
University of Iowa	Tippie School of Management	IA
University of Kansas	School of Business	KS
University of Kentucky	Carol Martin Gatton College of Business & Economics	KY
University of Louisiana at Monroe (formerly Northeast Louisiana University)	College of Business Administration	LA
University of Louisville	College of Business & Public Administration	KY
University of Maine	Maine Business School	ME
University of Maryland— College Park	The Robert H. Smith School of Business	MD
University of Massachusetts— Amherst	Eugene M. Isenberg School of Management	MA
University of Massachusetts— Lowell	College of Management	MA
University of Memphis	Fogelman College of Business & Economics	TN
University of Miami	School of Business	FL
University of Michigan	University of Michigan Business School	MI

University	Business School	State
University of Michigan—Dearborn	School of Management	MI
University of Michigan—Flint	School of Management	MI
University of Minnesota	Carlson School of Management	MN
University of Mississippi	School of Business Administration	MS
University of Missouri—Columbia	College of Business	MO
University of Missouri—Kansas City	H.W. Bloch School of Business & Public Administration	MO
University of Missouri—St. Louis	School of Business Administration	MO
University of Montana	School of Business Administration	MT
University of Nebraska—Lincoln	College of Business Administration	NE
University of Nebraska—Omaha	College of Business Administration	NE
University of Nevada—Las Vegas	College of Business	NV
University of Nevada—Reno	College of Business Administration	NV
University of New Mexico	Robert O. Anderson Graduate School of Management	NM
University of New Orleans	College of Business Administration	LA
University of North Carolina—Chapel Hill	Kenan-Flagler Business School	NC
University of North Carolina—Charlotte	The Belk College of Business Administration	NC
University of North Carolina—Greensboro	Joseph M. Bryan School of Business & Economics	NC
University of North Dakota	College of Business & Public Administration	ND
University of North Florida	College of Business Administration	FL

University	Business School	State
University of North Texas	College of Business Administration	TX
University of Notre Dame	College of Business Administration	IN
University of Oklahoma	Michael F. Price College of Business	OK
University of Oregon	Charles H. Lundquist College of Business	OR
University of Pennsylvania	The Wharton School	PA
University of Pittsburgh	Joseph M. Katz Graduate School of Business	PA
University of Portland	Dr. Robert B. Pamplin Jr. School of Business Administration	OR
University of Rhode Island	College of Business Administration	RI
University of Richmond	Richard S. Reynolds Graduate School The E. Claiborne Robins School of Business	VA
University of Rochester	William E. Simon Graduate School of Business Administration	NY
University of San Diego	School of Business	CA
University of San Francisco	McLaren Graduate School of Management	CA
University of Scranton	Kania School of Management	PA
University of South Alabama	Mitchell College of Business	AL
University of South Carolina	Darla Moore School of Business	SC
University of South Dakota	School of Business	SD
University of South Florida	College of Business Administration	FL
University of Southern California	Marshall School of Business	CA
University of Southern Mississippi	College of Business Administration	MS
University of Tennessee—Chattanooga	School of Business Administration	TN

University	Business School	State
University of Tennessee—Knoxville	Graduate School of Business	TN
University of Texas—Arlington	College of Business Administration	TX
University of Texas—Austin	The Texas Graduate School of Business	TX
University of Texas—El Paso	College of Business Administration	TX
University of Texas—Pan American	College of Business Administration	TX
University of Texas—San Antonio	College of Business	TX
University of Toledo	College of Business Administration	OH
University of Tulsa	College of Business Administration	OK
University of Utah	David Eccles School of Business	UT
University of Vermont	School of Business Administration	VT
University of Virginia	Darden Graduate School of Business Administration	VA
University of Washington	University of Washington Business School	WA
University of Wisconsin—La Crosse	College of Business Administration	WI
University of Wisconsin—Madison	School of Business	WI
University of Wisconsin—Milwaukee	School of Business Administration	WI
University of Wisconsin—Oshkosh	College of Business Administration	WI
University of Wisconsin—Whitewater	College of Business & Economics	WI
University of Wyoming	College of Business	WY
Utah State University	College of Business	UT

University	Business School	State
Vanderbilt University	Owen Graduate School of Management	TN
Villanova University	College of Commerce & Finance	PA
Virginia Commonwealth University	School of Business	VA
Virginia Polytechnic Institute and State University	Pamplin College of Business	VA
Wake Forest University	Babcock Graduate School of Management	NC
Washington State University	College of Business & Economics	WA
Washington University	John M. Olin School of Business	MO
Wayne State University	School of Business Administration	MI
West Virginia University	College of Business & Economics	WV
Western Carolina University	College of Business	NC
Western Illinois University	College of Business & Technology	IL
Western Michigan University	Haworth College of Business	MI
Western Washington University	College of Business and Economics	WA
Wichita State University	W. Frank Barton School of Business	KS
Willamette University	Atkinson Graduate School of Management	OR
Winthrop University	College of Business Administration	SC
Wright State University	College of Business	OH
Xavier University	Williams College of Business	OH
Yale University	School of Management	CT

Business Schools with Part-Time M.B.A. Programs

ALABAMA

Auburn University*
College of Business
503 Lowder Business Building
Auburn University, AL 36849
Phone: (334) 844-4060
Fax: (334) 844-2964
E-mail: mbainfo@business.
auburn.edu
Web: www.mba.business.
auburn.edu

Auburn University—Montgomery
School of Business
7300 University Drive
Montgomery, AL 36117
Phone: (334) 244-3565
Web: www-biz.aum.edu/
graduate.htm

University of Alabama[†]
Manderson Graduate School of
Business
P.O. Box 870223
Tuscaloosa, AL 35487
Phone: (205) 348-6517,
(888) 863-3622
Fax: (205) 348-4504
E-mail: mba@cba.ua.edu
Web: www.cba.ua.edu/~mba/

University of Alabama—Birmingham
Graduate School of Management
1330 3rd Avenue South
Birmingham, AL 35294-4460
Phone: (205) 934-8817
Fax: (205) 934-9200
E-mail: gradschool@uab.edu
Web: main.uab.edu/sob/

University of South Alabama
Mitchell College of Business
182 AD
University of South Alabama
Mobile, AL 36688-0002
Phone: (334) 460-6418
Web: www.southalabama.edu/
graduateprograms/business.html

ALASKA

University of Alaska—Fairbanks
School of Management
P.O. Box 757480
Fairbanks, AK 99775-7480
Phone: (907) 474-7500
Fax: (907) 474-5379
E-mail: fyappply@uaf.edu,
famba@som.uaf.edu
Web: www.uafsom.alaska.edu

An asterisk (*) indicates that the school offers both a part-time M.B.A. program and an Executive M.B.A. program. A dagger (†) indicates that the school offers an Executive M.B.A. only.

ARIZONA

Arizona State University*
College of Business
P.O. Box 874906
Tempe, AZ 85287-4906
Phone: (480) 965-3332
Fax: (480) 965-8569
E-mail: asu.mba@asu.edu
Web: www.cob.asu.edu/mba/
mba.html

Northern Arizona University
College of Business Administration
Box 15066
Flagstaff, AZ 86011-5066
Phone: (520) 523-7342
Fax: (520) 523-7331
E-mail: cba-mba@mail.cba.nau.edu
Web: www.cba.nau.edu/
mbaprogram/

Thunderbird, The American Graduate School of International Management†
15249 North 59th Avenue
Glendale, AZ 85306-6000
Phone: (602) 978-7210
Fax: (602) 439-5432
E-mail: tbird@t-bird.edu
Web: www.t-bird.edu

University of Arizona
Eller Graduate School of
Management
P.O. Box 210108
Tucson, AZ 85721
Phone: (520) 621-4008
Fax: (520) 621-2606
E-mail: ellernet@bpa.arizona.edu
Web: www.bpa.arizona.edu/mba/

ARKANSAS

Arkansas State University
College of Business
P.O. Box 970
State University, AR 72467
Phone: (870) 972-3744
E-mail: colbus@cherokee.astate.edu
Web: www.astate.edu

University of Arkansas—Fayetteville
Sam M. Walton College of
Business Administration
BADM 475
Fayetteville, AR 72701
Phone: (501) 575-2851
Fax: (501) 575-8721
E-mail: gsb@comp.uark.edu
Web: waltoncollege.uark.edu/mba/

University of Arkansas—Little Rock*
College of Business Administration
Little Rock, AR 72204
Phone: (501) 569-3206
Fax: (501) 569-8898
Web: cba.ualr.edu/mba/

University of Central Arkansas
College of Business Administration
201 Donaghey Avenue,
Burdick #222
Conway, AR 72032
Phone: (501) 450-3124
Fax: (501) 450-5339
E-mail: dougc@mail.uca.edu
Web: www.business.uca.edu/mba/
mbaprogram.htm

CALIFORNIA

California Polytechnic State University—San Luis Obispo
College of Business
Graduate Management Programs
San Luis Obispo, CA 93407
Phone: (805) 756-2637
Fax: (805) 756-0110
E-mail: spahlow@calpoly.edu
Web: www.cob.calpoly.edu

California State University—Bakersfield
School of Business & Public
Administration
9001 Stockdale Highway
Bakersfield, CA 93311
Phone: (661) 664-3036
Fax: (661) 664-3389
Web: www.csub.edu/bpa/dept-info/
mba.html

California State University—Chico
College of Business
Graduate & International Programs
Chico, CA 95929-0680
Phone: (530) 898-6880
Fax: (530) 898-6889
E-mail: grin@csuchico.edu
Web: www.cob.csuchico.edu

California State University—Fresno
The Craig School of Business
5245 North Backer Avenue
Fresno, CA 93740-8001
Phone: (559) 278-2107
Fax: (559) 278-4911
E-mail: pennyt@csufresno.edu,
mkeppler@csufresno.edu
Web: www.craig.csufresno.edu/
mba/

California State University—Fullerton

College of Business Administration
& Economics
800 North State College Boulevard
P.O. Box 34080
Fullerton, CA 92834-9480
Phone: (714) 278-2300
E-mail: admissions@fullerton.edu
Web: sbaeweb.fullerton.edu

California State University—Hayward*

School of Business & Economics
Hayward, CA 94542
Phone: (510) 885-3964
Fax: (510) 885-2176
Web: sbegrad.csuhayward.edu

California State University—Long Beach

College of Business Administration
M.B.A. Program
1250 Bellflower Boulevard
Long Beach, CA 90840
Phone: (562) 985-1797
Fax: (562) 985-5590
Web: www.csulb.edu/colleges/cba/
NM.htm

California State University—Los Angeles

School of Business & Economics
5151 State University Drive
Los Angeles, CA 90032-8120
Phone: (323) 343-2980
Fax: (323) 343-2813
E-mail: deansbe@calstatela.edu
Web: sbela.calstatela.edu/mba/

California State University—Northridge

College of Business Administration
& Economics
18111 Nordhoff Street
Northridge, CA 91330-8380
Phone: (818) 677-2467
Fax: (818) 677-3188
E-mail: hfbus033@csun.edu
Web: www.csun.edu/cobaegrad/

California State University—Sacramento

College of Business Administration
Office of Graduate Programs
Sacramento, CA 95819-6088
Phone: (916) 278-6772
Fax: (916) 278-5767
E-mail: sbagrad@sbaserver.csus.edu
Web: www.csus.edu/sbagrad/

Claremont Graduate University*

Peter F. Drucker Graduate School
of Management
1021 North Dartmouth Avenue
Claremont, CA 91711
Phone: (909) 607-7810,
(800) 944-4312
Fax: (909) 607-9104
E-mail: drucker@cgu.edu
Web: drucker.cgu.edu/programs/
1_2_1_1m.html

Loyola Marymount University*

College of Business Administration
M.B.A. Program
7900 Loyola Boulevard
Los Angeles, CA 90045-8387
Phone: (310) 338-2848
Fax: (310) 338-2899
E-mail: mbapc@lmumail.lmu.edu
Web: www.lmu.edu/colleges/
cba/mba/

San Diego State University*

Graduate School of Business
5500 Campanile Drive
San Diego, CA 92182
Phone: (619) 594-5213
Fax: (619) 594-1863
E-mail: sdsumba@mail.sdsu.edu
Web: www.rohan.sdsu.edu/dept/
cbaweb/MBA/

San Francisco State University

Graduate School of Business
1600 Holloway Avenue
San Francisco, CA 94132
Phone: (415) 338-1935
Fax: (415) 338-6237
E-mail: mba@sfsu.edu
Web: www.sfsu.edu/~mba/

San Jose State University*

College of Business
One Washington Square
BT 250
San Jose, CA 95192-0162
Phone: (408) 924-3421
Fax: (408) 924-3426
Web: www.cob.sjsu.edu/graduate/

Santa Clara University*

Leavey School of Business &
Administration
200 Kenna Hall
Santa Clara, CA 95053
Phone: (408) 554-4523
Fax: (408) 554-2332
E-mail: mbaadmissions@scu.edu
Web: www.business.scu.edu

University of California— Berkeley
Haas School of Business
M.B.A. Admissions
Berkeley, CA 94720-1902
Phone: (510) 642-1405
Fax: (510) 643-6659
E-mail: mbaadms@haas.
berkeley.edu
Web: www.haas.berkeley.edu

University of California— Davis
Graduate School of Management
One Shields Avenue
Davis, CA 95616
Phone: (530) 752-7399
Fax: (530) 752-2924
E-mail: gsm@ucdavis.edu
Web: www.gsm.ucdavis.edu

University of California— Irvine*
Graduate School of Management
M.B.A. Admissions
202 GSM
Irvine, CA 92697-3125
Phone: (949) UCI-4MBA
Fax: (949) 824-2944
E-mail: gsm-mba@uci.edu
Web: www.gsm.uci.edu

University of California—Los Angeles*
The Anderson School
110 Westwood Plaza, Suite B201
Box 951481
Los Angeles, CA 90095-1481
Phone: (310) 825-6944
Fax: (310) 825-8582
E-mail: mba.admissions@
anderson.ucla.edu
Web: www.anderson.ucla.edu

University of San Diego
School of Business
5998 Alcala Park
San Diego, CA 92110
Phone: (619) 260-4524
Fax: (619) 260-4158
E-mail: grads@acusd.edu
Web: usdbusiness.acusd.edu

University of San Francisco*
McLaren Graduate School of
Management
Ignatian Heights
2130 Fulton Street
San Francisco, CA 94117-1080
Phone: (415) 422-6314
Fax: (415) 422-2502
E-mail: mbausf@usfca.edu
Web: www.usfca.edu/mclaren/
MBA/

University of Southern California*
Marshall School of Business
BRI 101B
Los Angeles, CA 90089-1421
Phone: (213) 740-7846
Fax: (213) 740-8520
E-mail: uscmba@marshall.usc.edu
Web: www.marshall.usc.edu

COLORADO

Colorado State University*
College of Business
160 Rockwell Hall
Fort Collins, CO 80523
Phone: (970) 491-3704
Fax: (970) 491-0596
Web: www.biz.colostate.edu

University of Colorado— Boulder*
Graduate School of Business
Administration
Campus Box 419
Boulder, CO 80309-0419
Phone: (303) 492-1831
Fax: (303) 492-1727
E-mail: busgrad@colorado.edu
Web: bus.colorado.edu/graduate/

University of Colorado— Colorado Springs*
College of Business &
Administration
P.O. Box 7150
1420 Austin Bluffs Parkway
Colorado Springs, CO 80933-7150
Phone: (719) 262-3408
Fax: (719) 262-3494
E-mail: busadvsr@uccs.edu
Web: web.uccs.edu/business/
mbamain.htm

University of Colorado— Denver*
Graduate School of Business &
Administration
Campus Box 165S
P.O. Box 173364
Denver, CO 80217-3364
Phone: (303) 556-5900
Fax: (303) 556-5904
E-mail: Valerie_Dobbs@maroon.
cudenver.edu
Web: www.cudenver.edu/public/
business/

University of Denver*

Daniels College of Business
2101 South University Boulevard
Denver, CO 80208
Phone: (303) 871-3416,
(800) 622-4723
Fax: (303) 871-4466
E-mail: dcb@du.edu
Web: www.dcb.du.edu

CONNECTICUT

Fairfield University*

Charles F. Dolan School of Business
Fairfield, CT 06430-5195
Phone: (203) 254-4180
Fax: (203) 254-4029
E-mail: mba@fair1.fairfield.edu
Web: www.fairfield.edu

University of Bridgeport*

School of Business
126 Park Avenue
Bridgeport, CT 06601
Phone: (203) 576-4368
Fax: (203) 576-4941
E-mail: admit@bridgeport.edu
Web: www.bridgeport.edu

University of Connecticut†

School of Business Administration
368 Fairfield Road, U-2041 MBA
Storrs, CT 06269-2041
Phone: (860) 486-2872
Fax: (860) 486-5222
E-mail: mbagen@sba.uconn.edu
Web: www.sba.uconn.edu

DELAWARE

University of Delaware*

College of Business & Economics
103 MBNA America Hall
Newark, DE 19716
Phone: (302) 831-2221
Fax: (302) 831-3329
E-mail: mbaprogram@udel.edu
Web: www.mba.udel.edu

DISTRICT OF COLUMBIA

American University*

Kogod School of Business
Administration
4400 Massachusetts Avenue, NW
Washington, DC 20016
Phone: (202) 885-1913
Fax: (202) 885-1078
E-mail: dswol@american.edu
Web: www.kogod.american.edu

**George Washington
University***

School of Business & Public
Management
710 21st Street, NW
Washington, DC 20052
Phone: (202) 994-6584
Fax: (202) 994-6382
E-mail: sbpmapp@gwu.edu
Web: www.sbpm.gwu.edu

Georgetown University†

The Robert Emmett McDonough
School of Business
105 Old North Building
Box 571148
Washington, DC 20057-1148
Phone: (202) 687-4200
Fax: (202) 687-7809
E-mail: MBA@msb.edu
Web: www.msb.edu

Howard University

School of Business
Office of Graduate Studies
2600 Sixth Street, NW
Washington, DC 20059
Phone: (202) 806-1576
Fax: (202) 806-1625
Web: www.bschool.howard.edu

FLORIDA

Florida Atlantic University*

College of Business
Graduate Studies
Admissions, ADM 297
777 Glades Road
Boca Raton, FL 33431-0091
Phone: (561) 297-2618
Fax: (561) 297-2117
E-mail: gradadm@fau.edu
Web: www.fau.edu

**Florida International
University***

College of Business Administration
University Park
Charles E. Perry Building
Miami, FL 33199
Phone: (305) 348-2751
Web: www.fiu.edu/~mba/

Florida State University

College of Business
Graduate Office
Room 318 RBA
Tallahassee, FL 32306-1110
Phone: (850) 644-6458
Fax: (850) 644-0915
E-mail: smartin@cob.fsu.edu
Web: www.cob.fsu.edu/grad/mba/

Rollins College*

Crummer Graduate School of
Business
1000 Holt Avenue 2722
Winter Park, FL 32789-4499
Phone: (407) 646-2405
Fax: (407) 646-2402
E-mail: sgauthier@rollins.edu
Web: www.crummer.rollins.edu

University of Central Florida*

College of Business Administration
Suite 240
Orlando, FL 32816-0991
Phone: (407) 823-2766
Fax: (407) 823-6442
E-mail: graduate@mail.ucf.edu
Web: www.bus.ucf.edu

University of Florida*

Warrington College of Business
Florida M.B.A. Programs
134 Bryan Hall
P.O. Box 117152
Gainesville, FL 32611-7152
Phone: (352) 392-7992
Fax: (352) 392-8791
E-mail: floridamba@notes.cba.
ufl.edu
Web: www.floridamba.ufl.edu

University of Miami*

School of Business
P.O. Box 248505
Coral Gables, FL 33124-6520
Phone: (305) 284-4607
Fax: (305) 284-1878
E-mail: mba@miami.edu
Web: www.bus.miami.edu/gdp/

University of North Florida

College of Business Administration
4567 St. John's Bluff Road South
Jacksonville, FL 32216
Phone: (904) 620-2624
Web: www.unf.edu/coba/

University of South Florida*

College of Business Administration
4202 East Fowler Avenue,
FAO 100N
Graduate Admissions
Tampa, FL 33620-7910
Phone: (813) 974-8800
Fax: (813) 974-7343
Web: www.coba.usf.edu

GEORGIA

Clark Atlanta University*

School of Business Administration
323 James P. Brawley Drive at Fair
Street, SW
Atlanta, GA 30314
Phone: (404) 880-8479
Fax: (404) 880-6159
E-mail: cechols@sbus.cau.edu
Web: www.cau.edu

Emory University*

Goizueta Business School
1300 Clifton Road, NE
Atlanta, GA 30322
Phone: (404) 727-6311
Fax: (404) 727-4612
E-mail: admissions@bus.emory.edu
Web: www.emory.edu/BUS/

Georgia Institute of Technology†

DuPree College of Management
755 Ferst Drive
212 DuPree College of
Management
Atlanta, GA 30332-0520
Phone: (404) 894-8722,
(800) 869-1014
Fax: (404) 894-4199
E-mail: msm@mgt.gatech.edu
Web: www.mgt.gatech.edu

Georgia Southern University*

College of Business Administration
P.O. Box 8050
Statesboro, GA 30460-8050
Phone: (912) 681-5767
Fax: (912) 486-7480
E-mail: mba@gasou.edu
Web: www2.gasou.edu/mba/

Georgia State University*

J. Mack Robinson College of
Business
Office of Master's Admissions
Atlanta, GA 30303
Phone: (404) 651-1913
Fax: (404) 651-0219
Web: www.cba.gsu.edu

State University of West Georgia

Richards College of Business
The Graduate School–Cobb Hall
1600 Maple Street
Carrollton, GA 30118-4160
Phone: (770) 836-6419
Fax: (770) 830-2301
E-mail: gradsch@westga.edu
Web: www.westga.edu/~gradsch/

University of Georgia
Terry College of Business
351 Brooks Hall
Athens, GA 30602-6264
Phone: (706) 542-5671
Fax: (706) 542-5351
E-mail: terrymba@terry.uga.edu
Web: www.cba.uga.edu/mba/

HAWAII

University of Hawaii at Manoa*
College of Business Administration
2404 Maile Way
BUSAD, A303
Honolulu, HI 96822
Phone: (808) 956-8266
Fax: (808) 956-9890
E-mail: osas@busadm.cba.hawaii.edu
Web: www.cba.hawaii.edu/grad/mba.asp

IDAHO

Boise State University
College of Business & Economics
1910 University Drive
Boise, ID 83725
Phone: (208) 426-1126
Fax: (208) 426-4989
E-mail: ranchust@boisestate.edu
Web: cobe.boisestate.edu/mba/

Idaho State University
College of Business
Box 8020
Pocatello, ID 83209
Phone: (208) 282-2150
Fax: (208) 236-4367
E-mail: mbaadmin@isu.edu
Web: cob.isu.edu

ILLINOIS

Bradley University
Foster College of Business
Administration
Baker Hall, Room 118
Peoria, IL 61625
Phone: (309) 677-2375
Web: www.bradley.edu/fcba/mba/

DePaul University
Kellstadt Graduate School of
Business
One East Jackson Boulevard
Suite 7900
Chicago, IL 60604-2287
Phone: (312) 362-8810
Fax: (312) 362-6677
E-mail: mbainfo@wppost.depaul.edu
Web: www.depaul.edu/~kgsb/

Illinois State University
College of Business
327 Williams Hall
Campus Box 5500
Normal, IL 61790-5500
Phone: (309) 438-8388
Fax: (309) 438-7255
E-mail: isumba@ilstu.edu
Web: gilbreth.cob.ilstu.edu/MBA/

Loyola University Chicago*
Graduate School of Business
820 North Michigan Avenue
Chicago, IL 60611
Phone: (312) 915-6120
Fax: (312) 915-7207
E-mail: mba-loyola@luc.edu
Web: www.gsb.luc.edu

Northern Illinois University*
College of Business
Graduate Studies in Business
Wirt Hall 140
De Kalb, IL 60115-2897
Phone: (815) 753-1245
Fax: (815) 753-3300
E-mail: cobgrads@niu.edu
Web: www.cob.niu.edu/grad/grad.html

Northwestern University*
Kellogg Graduate School of
Management
2001 Sheridan Road
Evanston, IL 60208-2001
Phone: (847) 491-3308
Fax: (847) 491-4960
E-mail: mgmtadmissions@kellogg.nwu.edu
Web: www.kellogg.nwu.edu

Southern Illinois University—Carbondale*
College of Business &
Administration
133 Rehn Hall
Mail Code 4625
Carbondale, IL 62901-4625
Phone: (618) 453-3030
Fax: (618) 453-7961
E-mail: mbagp@siu.edu
Web: www.siu.edu/~mba/

Southern Illinois University—Edwardsville
School of Business
Box 1086
Edwardsville, IL 62026-1086
Phone: (618) 650-3840
Fax: (618) 650-3979
E-mail: ggomez@siue.edu
Web: www.siue.edu

University of Chicago*

Graduate School of Business
6030 South Ellis Avenue
Chicago, IL 60637
Phone: (773) 702-7369
Fax: (773) 702-9085
E-mail: admissions@gsb.
uchicago.edu
Web: gsb.uchicago.edu

University of Illinois—
Chicago

College of Business Administration
UIC, MBA Programs (MIC 077)
817 West Van Buren Street, Ste. 220
Chicago, IL 60607-3525
Phone: (312) 996-4573
Fax: (312) 413-0338
E-mail: mba@uic.edu
Web: www.uic.edu/cba/mba/

University of Illinois—
Urbana-Champaign[†]

College of Commerce & Business
Administration
MBA Program
410 David Kinley Hall
1407 West Gregory Drive
Champaign, IL 61801
Phone: (217) 244-7602
(800) MBA-UIUC
Fax: (217) 333-1156
E-mail: mba@uiuc.edu
Web: www.mba.uiuc.edu

Western Illinois University

College of Business & Technology
School of Graduate Studies
One University Circle
Macomb, IL 61455
Phone: (309) 298-1806
Fax: (309) 298-2245
E-mail: Grad_Office@wiu.edu
Web: www.wiu.edu/grad/

INDIANA

Ball State University

College of Business
Graduate Business Programs
WB 146
Muncie, IN 47306
Phone: (765) 285-1931
Fax: (765) 285-8818
E-mail: mba@bsu.edu
Web: www.bsu.edu/business/

Indiana State University

School of Business
M.B.A. Office
Terre Haute, IN 47809
Phone: (812) 237-2002
Fax: (812) 237-8720
E-mail: bssmba@befac.indstate.edu
Web: web.indstate.edu/schbus/
mba.html

Indiana University—
Northwest

Division of Business & Economics
3400 Broadway
Gary, IN 46408
Phone: (219) 980-6821
Web: www.iun.edu/~busnw/

Indiana University–Purdue
University at Fort Wayne

School of Business &
Management Sciences
Neff Hall Suite 330
Fort Wayne, IN 46805-1499
Phone: (219) 481-6498
Web: www.ipfw.edu/bms/

Indiana University–Purdue
University at Indianapolis

Kelley School of Business
801 West Michigan Street, BS 3028
Indianapolis, IN 46202-5151
Phone: (317) 274-4895
Fax: (317) 274-2483
E-mail: mbaindy@iupui.edu
Web: www.kelley.iu.edu

Indiana University—
South Bend

School of Business & Economics
1700 Mishawaka Avenue
P.O. Box 7111
South Bend, IN 46634
Phone: (219) 237-4138
Fax: (219) 237-4866
Web: www.iusb.edu/~buse/

Purdue University[†]

Krannert Graduate School of
Management
1310 Krannert Building
West Lafayette, IN 47907-1310
Phone: (765) 494-4365
Fax: (765) 494-9481
E-mail: krannert_ms@mgmt.
purdue.edu
Web: www.mgmt.purdue.edu

University of Notre Dame[†]

College of Business Administration
276 College of Business
Adminstration
P.O. Box 399
Notre Dame, IN 46556-0399
Phone: (219) 631-8488,
(800) 631-8488
Fax: (219) 631-8800
E-mail: mba.1@nd.edu
Web: www.nd.edu/~mba/

IOWA

Drake University

College of Business & Public
Administration
2507 University Avenue
Des Moines, IA 50311
Phone: (515) 271-2188
Fax: (515) 271-4518
E-mail: cbpa.gradprograms@
drake.edu
Web: www.drake.edu/cbpa/

Iowa State University

College of Business
Graduate Programs Office
218 Carver Hall
Ames, IA 50011-2063
Phone: (515) 294-8118
Fax: (515) 294-2446
E-mail: busgrad@iastate.edu
Web: www.bus.iastate.edu/grad/

University of Iowa*

Tippie School of Management
108 Pappajohn Business
Administration Building
Suite C140
Iowa City, IA 52242-1000
Phone: (319) 335-1039
Fax: (319) 335-3604
E-mail: iowamba@uiowa.edu
Web: www.biz.uiowa.edu/mba/

KANSAS

Kansas State University

College of Business Administration
110 Calvin Hall
Manhattan, KS 66506-0501
Phone: (785) 532-7190
Fax: (785) 532-7216
E-mail: flynn@ksu.edu
Web: www.cba.ksu.edu/cba/
grad/MBA/

University of Kansas

School of Business
206 Summerfield Hall
Lawrence, KS 66045
Phone: (785) 864-4254
Fax: (785) 864-5328
E-mail: dcollins@bschool.wpo.
ukans.edu
Web: www.bschool.ukans.edu

Wichita State University*

W. Frank Barton School of
Business
Graduate Studies in Business
Box 48
Wichita, KS 67260-0048
Phone: (316) 978-3230
Fax: (316) 978-3767
E-mail: harpool@twsuvm.uc.
twsu.edu
Web: www.business.twsu.edu

KENTUCKY

Murray State University*

College of Business & Public Affairs
University Station
P.O. Box 9
Murray, KY 42071
Phone: (270) 762-6970
Fax: (270) 762-3482
E-mail: ladonna.mccuan@
murraystate.edu
Web: www.murraystate.edu

University of Kentucky

Carol Martin Gatton College of
Business & Economics
237 Business & Economics Bldng
Lexington, KY 40506-0034
Phone: (606) 257-3592
Fax: (606) 257-3293
E-mail: drball01@pop.uky.edu
Web: gatton.gws.uky.edu

University of Louisville*

College of Business & Public
Administration
Department AO
Louisville, KY 40292
Phone: (502) 852-7439
Fax: (502) 852-6256
Web: cpba.louisville.edu

LOUISIANA

Louisiana State University*

E.J. Ourso College of Business
Baton Rouge, LA 70803
Phone: (225) 388-1641
Fax: (225) 388-5256
E-mail: busmba@lsu.edu
Web: www.bus.lsu.edu

Louisiana State University in Shreveport

College of Business Administration
One University Place
Shreveport, LA 71115
Phone: (318) 797-5276
Fax: (318) 797-5127
E-mail: tvines@pilot.lsus.edu
Web: www.lsus.edu/mba/

Louisiana Tech University

College of Administration &
Business
The Graduate School
P.O. Box 7923 TS
Ruston, LA 71272
Phone: (318) 257-4528
Fax: (318) 257-4487
E-mail: cabgrad@latech.edu
Web: www.cab.latech.edu

Loyola University New Orleans
Joseph A. Butt, S.J., College of
Business Administration
6363 St. Charles Avenue, Box 15
New Orleans, LA 70118
Phone: (504) 864-7944
Fax: (504) 865-3496
E-mail: mba@loyno.edu
Web: www.cba.loyno.edu

McNeese State University
College of Business
M.B.A. Program Office
P.O. Box 91660
Lake Charles, LA 70609
Phone: (337) 475-5576
Fax: (337) 475-5986
E-mail: mbaprog@mail.
mcneese.edu
Web: www.mcneese.edu

Nicholls State University
College of Business Administration
P.O. Box 2015
Thibodaux, LA 70310
Phone: (504) 449-7014
Fax: (504) 448-4922
E-mail: ba-mba@mail.nich.edu
Web: www.nich.edu

**Southeastern Louisiana
University***
College of Business
SLU 735
Hammond, LA 70402
Phone: (504) 549-2146
Fax: (504) 549-5038
E-mail: bohara@selu.edu
Web: www.selu.edu/Academics/
  Business/MBA/

Tulane University*
A.B. Freeman School of Business
7 McAlister Drive, Suite 400
New Orleans, LA 70118-5669
Phone: (504) 865-5410,
(800) 223-5402
Fax: (504) 865-6770
E-mail: freeman.admissions@
Tulane.edu
Web: freeman.tulane.edu

**University of Louisiana at
Monroe (formerly Northeast
Louisiana University)**
College of Business Administration
700 University Avenue
Monroe, LA 71209-0100
Phone: (318) 342-5252
Web: ele.ulm.edu/mba/

University of New Orleans*
College of Business Administration
Lakefront
New Orleans, LA 70148
Phone: (504) 280-6393
Web: www.uno.edu/~coba/

MAINE

University of Maine
Maine Business School
5723 Donald P. Corbett Business
Building
Orono, ME 04469-5723
Phone: (207) 581-1973
Fax: (207) 581-1930
E-mail: mba@maine.edu
Web: www.umaine.edu/business/

MARYLAND

Loyola College in Maryland*
Joseph A. Sellinger School of
Business & Management
4501 North Charles Street
Baltimore, MD 21210
Phone: (410) 617-2407
Fax: (410) 617-2002
Web: sellinger.loyola.edu

University of Baltimore
Robert G. Merrick School of
Business
1420 North Charles Street
Baltimore, MD 21201
Phone: (410) 837-4200
Web: business.ubalt.edu

**University of Maryland—
College Park**
The Robert H. Smith School of
Business
M.B.A./M.S. Admissions
2308 Van Munching Hall
College Park, MD 20742
Phone: (301) 405-2278
Fax: (301) 314-9862
E-mail: mba_info@rhsmith.
umd.edu
Web: www.rhsmith.umd.edu

MASSACHUSETTS

Babson College
F.W. Olin Graduate School
M.B.A. Admission
Babson Park, MA 02457-0310
Phone: (781) 239-5591
Fax: (781) 239-4194
E-mail: mbaadmission@
babson.edu
Web: www.babson.edu/mba/

Bentley College
McCallum Graduate School of
Business
175 Forest Street
Waltham, MA 02154-4705
Phone: (781) 891-2108
Fax: (781) 891-2464
E-mail: gradadm@bentley.edu
Web: www.bentley.edu/graduate/

Boston College
The Wallace E. Carroll School of
Management
140 Commonwealth Avenue
Fulton Hall 315
Chestnut Hill, MA 02467
Phone: (617) 552-3920
Fax: (617) 552-8078
Web: www.bc.edu/mba/

Boston University*
School of Management
595 Commonwealth Avenue
Boston, MA 02215
Phone: (617) 353-2670
Fax: (617) 353-7368
E-mail: mba@bu.edu
Web: management.bu.edu

Clark University
Graduate School of Management
950 Main Street
Worcester, MA 01610
Phone: (508) 793-7406
Fax: (508) 793-8822
E-mail: clarkmba@clarku.edu
Web: www.mba.clarku.edu

**Massachusetts Institute of
Technology†**
Sloan School of Management
50 Memorial Drive, E52-126
Cambridge, MA 02142
Phone: (617) 253-3730
Fax: (617) 253-6405
E-mail: mbaadmissions@sloan.
mit.edu
Web: mitsloan.mit.edu

Northeastern University*
College of Business Administration
350 Dodge Hall
Boston, MA 02115
Phone: (617) 373-5992
Fax: (617) 373-8564
E-mail: grba@cba.neu.edu
Web: www.cba.neu.edu

Suffolk University*
Frank Sawyer School of
Management
8 Ashburton Place
Boston, MA 02108-2770
Phone: (617) 573-8302
Fax: (617) 523-0116
E-mail: grad.admission@admin.
suffolk.edu
Web: www.suffolk.edu

**University of Massachusetts—
Amherst**
Eugene M. Isenberg School of
Management
209 Isenberg School of
Management
Amherst, MA 01003
Phone: (413) 545-5608
Fax: (413) 545-3858
E-mail: gradprog@som.umass.edu
Web: www.som.umass.edu

**University of Massachusetts—
Lowell**
College of Management
One University Avenue
Pasteur Hall
Lowell, MA 01854-9985
Phone: (978) 934-2380
Fax: (978) 934-4058
E-mail: graduate_admissions@
uml.edu
Web: www.uml.edu/grad/

MICHIGAN

Central Michigan University
College of Business Administration
Graduate Business Studies
112 Grawn Hall
Mount Pleasant, MI 48859
Phone: (517) 774-3150
Fax: (517) 774-2372
E-mail: Pamela.Stambersky@
cmich.edu
Web: www.cmich.edu/MBA.HTML

Eastern Michigan University
College of Business
Admissions Office
401 Owen Building
Ypsilanti, MI 48197
Phone: (734) 487-4140
Fax: (734) 487-1484
Web: www.emich.edu

Michigan State University*
The Eli Broad Graduate School of
Management
215 Eppley Center
East Lansing, MI 48824-1121
Phone: (517) 355-7604
Fax: (517) 353-1649
E-mail: mba@pilot.msu.edu
Web: mba.bus.msu.edu/mba/

Oakland University
School of Business Administration
Office of Graduate Business
Programs
416 Varner Hall
Rochester, MI 48309-4401
Phone: (248) 370-3287
Fax: (248) 370-4275
E-mail: gbp@oak.oakland.edu
Web: www.sba.oakland.edu

University of Detroit Mercy
College of Business Administration
Bahaman Mirshab
P.O. Box 19900
Detroit, MI 48219-0900
Phone: (313) 993-1202
Fax: (313) 993-1052
E-mail: mirshabb@udmercy.edu
Web: business.udmercy.edu

University of Michigan
University of Michigan Business
School
701 Tappan Street
Ann Arbor, MI 48109-1234
Phone: (734) 763-5796
Fax: (734) 763-7804
E-mail: usmbusmba@umich.edu
Web: www.bus.umich.edu

University of Michigan—Dearborn
School of Management
4901 Evergreen Road
Dearborn, MI 48128-1491
Phone: (313) 593-5460
Fax: (313) 593-5636
E-mail: mba-umd@umd.umich.edu
Web: www.som.umd.umich.edu

University of Michigan—Flint
School of Management
M.B.A. Admissions
Room 346 CROB
Flint, MI 48502-2186
Phone: (810) 762-3160
Fax: (810) 762-0736
Web: www.flint.umich.edu

Wayne State University*
School of Business Administration
103 Prentis Building
Detroit, MI 48201
Phone: (313) 577-4505
Fax: (313) 577-5299
Web: www.busadm.wayne.edu

Western Michigan University
Haworth College of Business
1201 Oliver Street
Kalamazoo, MI 49008
Phone: (616) 387-5075
Web: spider.hcob.wmich.edu

MINNESOTA

St. Cloud State University
College of Business
720 Fourth Avenue South
St. Cloud, MN 56301-4498
Phone: (320) 255-3213
Fax: (320) 255-2243
E-mail: grads@condor.stcloudstate.edu
Web: www.stcloudstate.edu

University of Minnesota*
Carlson School of Management
2-210 Carlson School of
Management
321 19th Avenue South
Minneapolis, MN 55455
Phone: (612) 625-5555
Fax: (612) 626-7785
E-mail: mbaoffice@csom.umn.edu
Web: www.carlsonmba.csom.umn.edu

MISSISSIPPI

Millsaps College
Else School of Management
1701 North State Street
Jackson, MS 39210
Phone: (601) 974-1253
Fax: (601) 974-1260
E-mail: mbamacc@millsaps.edu
Web: elseschool.millsaps.edu

Mississippi State University
College of Business & Industry
Office of the Graduate School
P.O. Box 5288
MSU, MS 39762
Phone: (601) 325-7400
Fax: (601) 325-1967
E-mail: gsb@cobilan.msstate.edu
Web: www.cbi.msstate.edu

University of Mississippi
School of Business Administration
253 Holman Hall
University, MS 38677
Phone: (662) 232-5483
Fax: (662) 232-5821
E-mail: jholleman@bus.olemiss.edu
Web: www.bus.olemiss.edu

University of Southern Mississippi

College of Business Administration
Graduate Business Programs
Box 5096
Hattiesburg, MS 39406-5096
Phone: (601) 266-4653
Fax: (601) 266-4639
E-mail: Ernest.King@usm.edu
Web: www-dept.usm.edu/~cba/

MISSOURI

St. Louis University*

School of Business &
Administration
3674 Lindell Boulevard
St. Louis, MO 63108
Phone: (314) 977-2013
Fax: (314) 977-1416
E-mail: mba@slu.edu
Web: mba.slu.edu

University of Missouri— Columbia

College of Business
303D Middlebush Hall
Columbia, MO 65211
Phone: (573) 882-2750
Fax: (573) 882-0365
E-mail: grad@missouri.edu
Web: business.missouri.edu

University of Missouri— Kansas City*

H.W. Bloch School of Business &
Public Administration
120 Administrative Center
5100 Rockhill Road
Kansas City, MO 64110-2499
Phone: (816) 235-1111
Fax: (816) 235-2312
Web: www.bsbpa.umkc.edu

University of Missouri— St. Louis

School of Business Administration
Graduate Admissions
8001 Natural Bridge Road
St. Louis, MO 63121
Phone: (314) 516-5458
Fax: (314) 516-5310
E-mail: gradadm@umsl.edu
Web: mba.umsl.edu

Washington University*

John M. Olin School of Business
Campus Box 1133
One Brookings Drive
St. Louis, MO 63130
Phone: (314) 935-7301
Fax: (314) 935-6309
E-mail: mba@olin.wustl.edu
Web: www.olin.wustl.edu/mba/

MONTANA

University of Montana

School of Business Administration
Missoula, MT 59812
Phone: (406) 243-4983
Fax: (406) 243-2086
E-mail: spritzer@selway.umt.edu
Web: www.business.umt.edu

NEBRASKA

Creighton University

College of Business Administration
2500 California Plaza
Omaha, NE 68178-0130
Phone: (402) 280-2829
Fax: (402) 280-2172
E-mail: cobagrad@creighton.edu
Web: cobweb.creighton.edu/grad/

University of Nebraska— Lincoln

College of Business Administration
Administration 301
Lincoln, NE 68588-0434
Phone: (402) 472-2338,
(800) 742-8800
Fax: (402) 472-5180
E-mail: grad_admissions@unl.edu
Web: www.unl.edu/gradstud/

University of Nebraska— Omaha*

College of Business Administration
60th and Dodge Streets
Room 414
Omaha, NE 68182-0048
Phone: (402) 554-2303
Fax: (402) 554-3747
E-mail: mba@unomaha.edu
Web: cba.unomaha.edu/mba/

NEVADA

University of Nevada— Las Vegas

College of Business
4505 South Maryland Parkway
Las Vegas, NV 89154-6001
Phone: (702) 895-3970
Web: cob.nevada.edu/Cob_www/

University of Nevada—Reno

College of Business Administration
Reno, NV 89557
Phone: (775) 784-4912
E-mail: mgraham@unr.edu
Web: www.coba.unr.edu/
graduate/mba/

NEW JERSEY

Rutgers University*
Graduate School of Management
Engelhard Hall Room 115
109 University Drive
Newark, NJ 07102
Phone: (973) 353-1234
Fax: (973) 353-1592
E-mail: admit@business.
rutgers.edu
Web: business.rutgers.edu/
graduate/

Seton Hall University*
W. Paul Stillman School of
Business
400 South Orange Avenue
South Orange, NJ 07079
Phone: (973) 761-9222
Fax: (973) 275-2465
E-mail: busgrad@shu.edu
Web: www.business.shu.edu

NEW MEXICO

New Mexico State University
College of Business Administration
& Economics
MSC 3GSP
P.O. Box 30001
Las Cruces, NM 88003
Phone: (505) 646-8003
Fax: (505) 646-7977
E-mail: mbaprog@nmsu.edu
Web: cbae.nmsu.edu/~mba/

University of New Mexico*
Robert O. Anderson Graduate
School of Management
Albuquerque, NM 87131
Phone: (505) 277-3147
Fax: (505) 277-9356
E-mail: lchast@unm.edu
Web: asm.unm.edu

NEW YORK

Canisius College
Richard J. Wehle School of Business
2001 Main Street
Buffalo, NY 14208
Phone: (716) 888-2140
E-mail: gradbus@canisius.edu
Web: www.canisius.edu

**City University of New York—
Baruch College***
Zicklin School of Business
17 Lexington Avenue
Box H-0880
New York, NY 10010
Phone: (212) 802-2330
Fax: (212) 802-2335
E-mail: graduate_admissions@
baruch.cuny.edu
Web: www.bus.baruch.cuny.edu

Clarkson University
School of Business
P.O. Box 5770
Potsdam, NY 13699-5770
Phone: (315) 268-6613
Fax: (315) 268-3810
E-mail: gradprog@clarkson.edu
Web: phoenix.som.clarkson.edu

Columbia University†
Columbia Business School
Office of Admissions
105 Uris Hall, 3022 Broadway
New York, NY 10027
Phone: (212) 854-1961
Fax: (212) 662-6754
E-mail: gohermes@claven.gsb.
columbia.edu
Web: www.columbia.edu/cu/
business/

Cornell University†
Johnson Graduate School of
Management
111 Sage Hall
Ithaca, NY 14853-6201
Phone: (607) 255-4526,
(800) 847-2082
Fax: (607) 255-0065
E-mail: mba@cornell.edu
Web: www.johnson.cornell.edu

Fordham University*
Graduate School of Business
113 West 60th Street
New York, NY 10023
Phone: (212) 636-6200
Fax: (212) 636-7076
E-mail: gbaadmin@mary.
fordham.edu
Web: www.bnet.fordham.edu

Hofstra University*
Frank G. Zarb School of Business
134 Hofstra University
Hempstead, NY 11550
Phone: (516) 463-5683
Fax: (516) 463-5268
E-mail: humba@hofstra.edu
Web: www.hofstra.edu

Mount Saint Mary College
Division of Business
330 Powell Avenue
Newburgh, NY 12550
Phone: (914) 569-3582
Fax: (914) 562-6762
Web: www.msmc.edu

New York University*
Leonard N. Stern School of
Business
44 West Fourth Street,
Ste. 10-160
New York, NY 10012-1126
Phone: (212) 998-0600
Fax: (212) 995-4231
E-mail: sternmba@stern.nyu.edu
Web: www.stern.nyu.edu

**Rensselaer Polytechnic
Institute***
Lally School of Management &
Technology
Pittsburgh Building, Room 3218
Troy, NY 12180-3590
Phone: (518) 276-6586
Fax: (518) 276-2665
E-mail: management@rpi.edu
Web: lallyschool.rpi.edu

Pace University*
Lubin School of Business
One Pace Plaza
New York, NY 10038
Phone: (212) 346-1532
Web: www.pace.edu/lubin/

**Rochester Institute of
Technology***
College of Business
Bausch & Lomb Center
60 Lomb Memorial Drive
Rochester, NY 14623-5604
Phone: (716) 475-6631
Fax: (716) 475-7424
E-mail: admission@rit.edu
Web: www.cob.rit.edu

Saint John's University*
The Peter J. Tobin College of
Business
8000 Utopia Parkway
Bent Hall Room 111C, Grad
Division
Jamaica, NY 11439
Phone: (718) 990-6114,
(718) 990-6132
Fax: (718) 990-1677
Web: www.stjohns.edu/
academics/cba/

**State University of New York—
University at Albany**
School of Business
Office of Student Services, BA 361
Albany, NY 12222
Phone: (518) 442-4961
Fax: (518) 442-3944
E-mail: busapps@albany.edu
Web: www.albany.edu/business/

**State University of New York—
Binghamton***
School of Management
P.O. Box 6000
Binghamton, NY 13902-6000
Phone: (607) 777-2317
Web: som.binghamton.edu

**State University of New York—
Buffalo***
School of Management
Jacobs Management Center
Buffalo, NY 14260
Phone: (716) 645-3204,
(877) BFLO-MBA
Fax: (716) 645-2341
E-mail: sommba@acsu.buffalo.edu
Web: www.mgt.buffalo.edu/mba/

Syracuse University*
School of Management
Suite 100
Syracuse, NY 13244-2130
Phone: (315) 443-9214
Fax: (315) 443-9517
E-mail: MBAinfo@som.syr.edu
Web: www.som.syr.edu

University of Rochester*
William E. Simon Graduate School
of Business Administration
304 Schlegel Hall
P.O. Box 270107
Rochester, NY 14627-0107
Phone: (716) 275-3533
Fax: (716) 271-3907
E-mail: mbaadm@ssb.rochester.edu
Web: www.ssb.rochester.edu

NORTH CAROLINA

Appalachian State University
John A. Walker College of Business
Graduate Studies & External
Programs
P.O. Box 32037
Boone, NC 28608-2037
Phone: (828) 262-2922
Fax: (828) 262-2925
E-mail: mba@appstate.edu
Web: www.business.appstate.edu

Duke University†
The Fuqua School of Business
Towerview Road, Room 134W
Durham, NC 27708
Phone: (919) 660-7705
Fax: (919) 681-8026
E-mail: fuqua-admissions@mail.
duke.edu
Web: www.fuqua.duke.edu

East Carolina University*
School of Business
3203 General Classroom Building
Greenville, NC 27858-4353
Phone: (252) 328-6970
Fax: (252) 328-2106
E-mail: gradbus@mail.ecu.edu
Web: www.business.ecu.edu/grad/

University of North Carolina—Chapel Hill†
Kenan-Flagler Business School
CB 3490, McColl Building
Chapel Hill, NC 27599-3490
Phone: (919) 962-3236
Fax: (919) 962-0898
E-mail: mba_info@unc.edu
Web: www.bschool.unc.edu

University of North Carolina—Charlotte
The Belk College of Business Administration
Graduate Admissions
9201 University City Boulevard
Charlotte, NC 28223
Phone: (704) 547-3366
Fax: (704) 547-3279
E-mail: gradadm@email.uncc.edu
Web: www.uncc.edu/mba/

University of North Carolina—Greensboro
Joseph M. Bryan School of Business & Economics
1000 Spring Garden Street
220 Bryan Building
Greensboro, NC 27412
Phone: (336) 334-5390
Fax: (336) 334-4209
E-mail: mba@uncg.edu
Web: www.uncg.edu/bae/mba/

Wake Forest University*
Babcock Graduate School of Management
P.O. Box 7659
Winston-Salem, NC 27109
Phone: (336) 758-5422
Fax: (336) 758-5830
E-mail: admissions@mba.wfu.edu
Web: www.mba.wfu.edu

Western Carolina University
College of Business
Graduate Programs in Business
Forsyth Building
Cullowhee, NC 28723
Phone: (828) 227-7402
Fax: (828) 227-7414
E-mail: gwilliams@wcu.edu
Web: www.wcu.edu/cob/

NORTH DAKOTA

University of North Dakota
College of Business & Public Administration
The Graduate School
P.O. Box 8178
Grand Forks, ND 58202-8179
Phone: (701) 777-2945
Fax: (701) 777-3619
E-mail: UNDGRAD@mail.und.nodak.edu
Web: www.und.nodak.edu/dept/grad/mbahome.htm

OHIO

Bowling Green State University*
College of Business Administration
Graduate Studies in Business
369 College of Business Administration Building
Bowling Green, OH 43403
Phone: (419) 372-2488
Fax: (419) 372-2875
E-mail: mba-info@cba.bgsu.edu
Web: www.cba.bgsu.edu

Case Western Reserve University*
Weatherhead School of Management
10900 Euclid Avenue
Cleveland, OH 44106-7235
Phone: (216) 368-2030
Fax: (216) 368-5548
E-mail: questions@exchange.som.cwru.edu
Web: weatherhead.cwru.edu

Cleveland State University*
College of Business Administration
1860 East 18th Street BU 219
Cleveland, OH 44114
Phone: (216) 687-3730
Fax: (216) 687-5311
E-mail: cbacsu@csuohio.edu
Web: www.csuohio.edu/mba/

John Carroll University
Boler School of Business
20700 North Park Boulevard
University Heights, OH 44118
Phone: (216) 397-4524
Web: bsob.jcu.edu

Kent State University*

Graduate School of Management
P.O. Box 5190
Kent, OH 44242-0001
Phone: (330) 672-2282 ext. 235
Fax: (330) 672-7303
E-mail: gradbus@bsa3.kent.edu
Web: business.kent.edu/grad/

Miami University

Richard T. Farmer School of
Business
107 Laws Hall
Oxford, OH 45056
Phone: (513) 529-6643
Fax: (513) 529-2487
E-mail: miamiMBA@muohio.edu
Web: www.sba.muohio.edu/
mbaprogram/

Ohio State University*

Max M. Fisher College of Business
2108 Neil Avenue
100 Gerlach Hall
Columbus, OH 43210-1144
Phone: (614) 292-8511
Fax: (614) 292-9006
E-mail: cobgrd@cob.ohio-state.edu
Web: fisher.osu.edu/mba/

Ohio University†

College of Business
Copeland Hall 514
Athens, OH 45701
Phone: (740) 593-2007
Fax: (740) 593-4320
E-mail: rossj@ohiou.edu
Web: www.cob.ohiou.edu

University of Akron

College of Business Administration
259 South Broadway
Room 412
Akron, OH 44325-4805
Phone: (330) 972-7043
Fax: (330) 972-6588
E-mail: Gradcba@uakron.edu
Web: www.uakron.edu/cba/

University of Cincinnati

Graduate School of Business
103 Lindner Hall
Cincinnati, OH 45221-0020
Phone: (513) 556-7020
Fax: (513) 556-4891
E-mail: Julie.Dixon@uc.edu
Web: www.cba.uc.edu/mba/

University of Dayton

School of Business Administration
Miriam Hall 803
300 College Park
Dayton, OH 45469
Phone: (937) 229-3733
Fax: (937) 229-3301
E-mail: mba@udayton.edu
Web: www.sba.udayton.edu/mba/

University of Toledo*

College of Business Administration
2801 West Bancroft
Toledo, OH 43606
Phone: (419) 530-2774
Fax: (419) 530-4724
E-mail: Bruce.Kuhlman@
utoledo.edu
Web: www.utoledo.edu/mba/

Wright State University

College of Business
School of Graduate Studies
3640 Colonel Glenn Highway
Dayton, OH 45435
Phone: (937) 775-2975
Web: www.wright.edu/coba/

Xavier University*

Williams College of Business
3800 Victory Parkway
Cincinnati, OH 45207-3221
Phone: (513) 745-3525
Fax: (513) 745-2929
Web: www.xu.edu/colleges/cba/

OKLAHOMA

Oklahoma State University

College of Business Administration
M.B.A. Programs
102 Gundersen
Stillwater, OK 74078-0555
Phone: (405) 744-2951
Fax: (405) 744-7474
E-mail: rosenp@okstate.edu
Web: www.bus.okstate.edu

University of Oklahoma

Michael F. Price College of Business
307 West Brooks, Adams Hall
Room 105-K
Norman, OK 73019-4003
Phone: (405) 325-4107
Fax: (405) 325-1957
E-mail: awatkins@ou.edu
Web: www.ou.edu/business/

University of Tulsa
College of Business Administration
600 South College
BAH 308
Tulsa, OK 74104
Phone: (918) 631-2242
Fax: (918) 631-3672
E-mail: millsbm@centum.
utulsa.edu
Web: www.cba.utulsa.edu

OREGON

Oregon State University*
College of Business
Bexell Hall, Room 210
Corvallis, OR 97331
Phone: (541) 737-3150
E-mail: saveriano@bus.orst.edu
Web: www.bus.orst.edu

Portland State University*
School of Business Administration
P.O. Box 751
Portland, OR 97207
Phone: (503) 725-3712
E-mail: adm@pdx.edu
Web: www.sba.pdx.edu

University of Oregon†
Charles H. Lundquist College of
Business
1208 University of Oregon
Eugene, OR 97403
Phone: (541) 346-3306
Fax: (541) 346-3347
E-mail: mbainfo@lcb.uoregon.edu
Web: lcb.uoregon.edu

University of Portland
Dr. Robert B. Pamplin Jr. School of
Business Administration
5000 North Willamette Boulevard
Portland, OR 97203
Phone: (503) 943-7107
Fax: (503) 943-7178
E-mail: mba-up@up.edu
Web: www.up.edu

Willamette University*
Atkinson Graduate School of
Management
900 State Street
Salem, OR 97301
Phone: (503) 370-6167
Fax: (503) 370-3011
E-mail: agsm-admission@
willamette.edu
Web: www.willamette.edu/agsm/

PENNSYLVANIA

Carnegie Mellon University
Graduate School of Industrial
Administration
Schenley Park
Pittsburgh, PA 15213
Phone: (412) 268-2272
Fax: (412) 268-4209
E-mail: gsia-admissions@
andrew.cmu.edu
Web: www.gsia.cmu.edu

Drexel University*
Bennett S. LeBow College of
Business
32nd and Chestnut Streets
Philadelphia, PA 19104
Phone: (215) 895-6704
Fax: (215) 895-1012
E-mail: denise@drexel.edu
Web: www.lebow.drexel.edu

Duquesne University
A. J. Palumbo School of
Business Administration
John F. Donahue Graduate School
of Business
Room 704 Rockwell Hall
600 Forbes Avenue
Pittsburgh, PA 15282
Phone: (412) 396-6276
Fax: (412) 396-5304
E-mail: grad-bus@duq.edu
Web: www.bus.duq.edu

Lehigh University
College of Business & Economics
621 Taylor Street
Bethlehem, PA 18015
Phone: (610) 758-4450
Fax: (610) 758-5283
E-mail: incbe@lehigh.edu
Web: www.lehigh.edu

Saint Joseph's University*
Ervian K. Haub School of Business
5600 City Avenue
Philadelphia, PA 19131
Phone: (610) 660-1690
Fax: (610) 660-1599
E-mail: sjumba@sju.edu
Web: www.sju.edu/hsb/mba/

Temple University*
Fox School of Business &
Management
Speakman Hall
Philadelphia, PA 19122
Phone: (215) 204-7678
Fax: (215) 204-8300
E-mail: mcquillt@sbm.temple.edu
Web: www.sbm.temple.edu

University of Pennsylvania[†]
The Wharton School
102 Vance Hall
3733 Spruce Street
Philadelphia, PA 19104-6361
Phone: (215) 898-3430
Fax: (215) 898-0120
E-mail: mba.admissions@
wharton.upenn.edu
Web: www.wharton.upenn.edu

University of Pittsburgh*
Joseph M. Katz Graduate School of
Business
276 Mervis Hall
Roberto Clemente Drive
Pittsburgh, PA 15260
Phone: (412) 648-1700
Fax: (412) 648-1569
E-mail: mba-admissions@katz.
business.pitt.edu
Web: www.katz.pitt.edu

University of Scranton
Kania School of Management
Scranton, PA 18510
Phone: (570) 941-4387
Fax: (570) 941-4342
E-mail: wayne.cunningham@
scranton.edu
Web: www.sju.edu/hsb/mba/

Villanova University*
College of Commerce & Finance
800 East Lancaster Avenue
Villanova, PA 19085
Phone: (610) 519-4336
Fax: (610) 519-6273
E-mail: mba@email.vill.edu
Web: www.mba.villanova.edu

RHODE ISLAND

University of Rhode Island*
College of Business Administration
7 Lippitt Road
210 Ballentine Hall
Kingston, RI 02881-0802
Phone: (401) 874-5000
Fax: (401) 874-4312
E-mail: Hadz@etal.uri.edu
Web: www.cba.uri.edu/graduate/
mba.htm

SOUTH CAROLINA

Clemson University
College of Business & Public Affairs
124 Sirrine Hall
Clemson, SC 29634-1315
Phone: (864) 656-3196
Fax: (864) 656-0947
E-mail: MBA@Clemson.edu
Web: business.clemson.edu/MBA/

University of South Carolina
Darla Moore School of Business
H. William Close Building
Columbia, SC 29208
Phone: (803) 777-4346
Fax: (803) 777-0414
E-mail: gradadmit@darla.badm.
sc.edu
Web: www.business.sc.edu

Winthrop University*
College of Business Administration
213 Thurmond
Rock Hill, SC 29733
Phone: (803) 323-2204
Fax: (803) 323-2539
E-mail: hagerp@mail.winthrop.edu
Web: cba.winthrop.edu

SOUTH DAKOTA

University of South Dakota
School of Business
414 East Clark Street
Vermillion, SD 57069
Phone: (605) 677-5287
E-mail: mba@usd.edu
Web: www.usd.edu/mba/

TENNESSEE

East Tennessee State University
College of Business
P.O. Box 70699
Johnson City, TN 37614
Phone: (423) 439-5314
Fax: (423) 439-5274
Web: business.etsu.edu/grad/
mba.htm

**Middle Tennessee State
University**
College of Business
P.O. Box 115
Murfreesboro, TN 37132
Phone: (615) 898-2964
Fax: (615) 898-4736
E-mail: fester@frank.mtsu.edu
Web: www.mtsu.edu/~business/

**Tennessee Technological
University**
College of Business Administration
Box 5023
Cookeville, TN 38505
Phone: (931) 372-3600
Fax: (931) 372-6250
E-mail: g-admissions@tntech.edu
Web: www2.tntech.edu/mba/

University of Memphis*
Fogelman College of Business &
Economics
Graduate Admissions, AD 216
Memphis, TN 38152
Phone: (901) 678-2911
Fax: (901) 678-5023
E-mail: gradsch@memphis.edu
Web: fcbe.memphis.edu

University of Tennessee—
Chattanooga*
School of Business Administration
615 McCallie Avenue
Chattanooga, TN 37403
Phone: (423) 755-4169
Fax: (423) 755-5255
Web: www.utc.edu/gradstudies/
busadmin.html

University of Tennessee—
Knoxville*
Graduate School of Business
527 Stokely Management Center
Knoxville, TN 37996-0552
Phone: (423) 974-5033
Fax: (423) 974-3826
E-mail: mba@utk.edu
Web: bus.utk.edu/graduate.htm

Vanderbilt University†
Owen Graduate School of
Management
Director of Admissions
401 21st Avenue
Nashville, TN 37201
Phone: (615) 322-6469
Fax: (615) 343-1175
E-mail: admissions@owen.
vanderbilt.edu
Web: mba.vanderbilt.edu

TEXAS

Baylor University†
The Hankamer School of Business
Graduate Programs
P.O. Box 98013
Waco, TX 76798
Phone: (254) 710-3718
Fax: (254) 710-1066
E-mail: MBA@hsb.baylor.edu
Web: hsb.baylor.edu/mba/

Lamar University
College of Business
P.O. Box 10059
Beaumont, TX 77710
Phone: (409) 880-8604
Fax: (409) 880-8088
E-mail: swerdlowra@hal.lamar.edu
Web: www.lamar.edu

Rice University†
Jesse H. Jones Graduate School of
Management
Jones Graduate School—MS-531
P.O. Box 1892
Houston, TX 77251-1892
Phone: (713) 348-4918,
(888) 844-4773
Fax: (713) 737-6147
E-mail: enterjgs@rice.edu
Web: www.rice.edu/jgs/

Southern Methodist
University*
Edwin L. Cox School of Business
P.O. Box 750333
Dallas, TX 75275-0333
Phone: (214) 768-2630,
(800) 472-3622
Fax: (214) 768-3956
E-mail: mbainfo@mail.cox.
smu.edu
Web: www.cox.smu.edu

Stephen F. Austin State
University
College of Business
Graduate Office
P.O. Box 13004, SFA
Nacogdoches, TX 75962
Phone: (936) 468-3101
Fax: (936) 468-1560
E-mail: mba@sfasu.edu
Web: www.cob.sfasu.edu

Texas A&M University†
Lowry Mays College & Graduate
School of Business
212 Wehner Building
College Station, TX 77843-4117
Phone: (409) 845-0361
Fax: (409) 862-2393
E-mail: MaysMBA@tamu.edu
Web: business.tamu.edu

Texas A&M University—
Commerce
College of Business & Technology
Graduate School
Commerce, TX 75429
Phone: (903) 886-5190
Fax: (903) 886-5165
E-mail: MBA@tamu-
commerce.edu
Web: www.tamu-commerce.edu/
mba/

Texas Christian University*
M.J. Neeley School of Business
MBA Office
P.O. Box 298540
Fort Worth, TX 76129
Phone: (817) 257-7531
Fax: (817) 257-6431
E-mail: mbainfo@tcu.edu
Web: www.mba.tcu.edu

Texas Tech University
College of Business Administration
Box 42101
Lubbock, TX 79409-2101
Phone: (806) 742-3184
(800) 882-6220
Fax: (806) 742-3958
E-mail: bagrad@coba.ttu.edu
Web: grad.ba.ttu.edu

University of Houston*
Bauer College of Business
4800 Calhoun Boulevard
Houston, TX 77204-2161
Phone: (713) 743-1010
Fax: (713) 743-9633
E-mail: admissions@uh.edu
Web: www.cba.uh.edu

**University of Houston—
Clear Lake**
School of Business & Public
Administration
Enrollment Services
2700 Bay Area Boulevard, Ste. 1510
Houston, TX 77058
Phone: (281) 283-2520
Fax: (281) 283-2530
E-mail: admissions@cl.uh.edu
Web: www.cl.uh.edu/bpa/

University of North Texas
College of Business Administration
Toulouse School of Graduate
Studies
P.O. Box 5446
Denton, TX 76203
Phone: (940) 565-2110
Web: www.unt.edu/pais/grad/
cmba.htm

**University of Texas—
Arlington**
College of Business Administration
UTA Box 19376
Arlington, TX 76019
Phone: (817) 272-2681
Fax: (817) 272-2625
E-mail: graduate.school@uta.edu
Web: www2.uta.edu/gradbiz/

University of Texas—Austin*
The Texas Graduate School of
Business
P.O. Box 7999
Austin, TX 78713-7999
Phone: (512) 471-7612
Fax: (512) 471-4243
E-mail: texasmba@bus.utexas.edu
Web: texasmba.bus.utexas.edu

University of Texas—El Paso
College of Business Administration
500 West University Drive
El Paso, TX 79968
Phone: (915) 747-5174
Fax: (915) 747-5147
Web: www.utep.edu/coba/

**University of Texas—
Pan American**
College of Business Administration
Graduate Programs
1201 West University Drive
Edinburg, TX 78539
Phone: (956) 381-2206
Web: www.coba.panam.edu/mba/

**University of Texas—
San Antonio***
College of Business
6900 North Loop 1604 West
San Antonio, TX 78249-0631
Phone: (210) 458-4641
Fax: (210) 458-4332
E-mail: gradstudies@utsa.edu
Web: business.utsa.edu

UTAH

Brigham Young University†
Marriott School of Management
M.B.A. Program
640 Tanner Building (TNRB)
Provo, UT 84602-3013
Phone: (801) 378-7500
Fax: (801) 378-4808
E-mail: mba@byu.edu
Web: marriottschool.byu.edu/mba/

University of Utah*
David Eccles School of Business
1645 East Campus Center Drive
Room 101
Salt Lake City, UT 84112-9301
Phone: (801) 581-7785
Fax: (801) 581-3666
E-mail: masters@business.utah.edu
Web: www.business.utah.edu

Utah State University
College of Business
School of Graduate Studies
0900 Old Main Hill
Logan, UT 84322-0900
Phone: (435) 797-2360
Fax: (435) 797-1192
E-mail: ckeller@b202.usu.edu
Web: www.usu.edu/~mba/

VERMONT

University of Vermont

School of Business Administration
Kalkin Hall
University of Vermont
Burlington, VT 05405
Phone: (802) 656-0655
Fax: (822) 656-8279
E-mail: mba@bsadpo.emba.
uvm.edu
Web: www.bsad.emba.uvm.
edu/MBA/

VIRGINIA

College of William and Mary*

Graduate School of Business
P.O. Box 8795
Williamsburg, VA 23187-8795
Phone: (757) 221-2900
Fax: (757) 221-2958
E-mail: lois.fraley@business.wm.edu
Web: business.wm.edu

George Mason University*

School of Management
Mailstop 5A2
Fairfax, VA 22030
Phone: (703) 993-2136
Fax: (703) 993-1886
E-mail: gradadms@som.gmu.edu
Web: www.som.gmu.edu

James Madison University

College of Business
The Graduate School
MSC 1003
Harrisonburg, VA 22807
Phone: (540) 568-3253
E-mail: machda@jmu.edu
Web: cob.jmu.edu/mba/

Old Dominion University

Graduate School of Business &
Public Administration
Norfolk, VA 23529-0119
Phone: (757) 683-3638
E-mail: mbainfo@wdu.edu
Web: www.odu-cbpa.org/
graduate.htm

University of Richmond

The E. Claiborne Robins School of
Business
Richard S. Reynolds Graduate
School
University of Richmond, VA 23173
Phone: (804) 289-8553
Fax: (804) 287-6544
E-mail: mba@richmond.edu
Web: www.richmond.edu/business/

Virginia Commonwealth University*

School of Business
1015 Floyd Avenue
Box 844000
Richmond, VA 23298
Phone: (804) 828-1741
Fax: (804) 828-6949
Web: www.vcu.edu/busweb/gsib/

Virginia Polytechnic Institute and State University*

Pamplin College of Business
1044 Pamplin Hall (0209)
Blacksburg, VA 24061
Phone: (540) 231-6152
Fax: (540) 231-4487
E-mail: mba_info@vt.edu
Web: www.mba.vt.edu

WASHINGTON

Eastern Washington University

College of Business & Public
Administration
Riverpoint Phase I
668 North Riverpoint Suite A
Cheney, WA 99004
Phone: (509) 359-2803
E-mail: mbaprogram@ewu.edu
Web: www.cbpa.ewu.edu/~mba/

Gonzaga University

School of Business Administration
West 502 Boone
Spokane, WA 99258-0001
Phone: (509) 323-3403
Fax: (509) 323-5811
E-mail: lewis@gonzaga.edu
Web: www.jepson.gonzaga.edu

Pacific Lutheran University*

School of Business
Tacoma, WA 98447
Phone: (253) 535-7250
Fax: (253) 535-8723
E-mail: business@plu.edu
Web: www.plu.edu/~busa/mba/

Seattle University

Albers School of Business &
Economics
900 Broadway
Seattle, WA 98122
Phone: (206) 296-5900
Fax: (206) 296-5902
E-mail: grad-admissions@
seattleu.edu
Web: www.seattleu.edu/asbe/

University of Washington*
University of Washington Business
School
Mackenzie Hall Box 353200
Seattle, WA 98195-3200
Phone: (206) 543-4661
Fax: (206) 616-7351
E-mail: mba@u.washington.edu
Web: depts.washington.edu/
bschool/

Washington State University
College of Business & Economics
Todd Hall #473
Pullman, WA 99164-4744
Phone: (509) 335-7617
Fax: (509) 335-4735
E-mail: MBA@wsu.edu
Web: www.cbe.wsu.edu/
graduate/

**Western Washington
University**
College of Business & Economics
Bellingham, WA 98225-9072
Phone: (360) 650-3898
Fax: (360) 650-4844
Web: www.cbe.wwu.edu/mba/

WEST VIRGINIA

West Virginia University†
College of Business & Economics
P.O. Box 6025
Morgantown, WV 26506
Phone: (304) 293-5408
Fax: (304) 293-7061
Web: www.be.wvu.edu

WISCONSIN

Marquette University*
College of Business Administration
M.B.A. Program
P.O. Box 1881
Milwaukee, WI 53201-1881
Phone: (414) 288-7141
Fax: (414) 288-1660
E-mail: simmons@biz.mu.edu
Web: www.busadm.mu.edu/mba/

**University of Wisconsin—
La Crosse**
College of Business Administration
1725 State Street
La Crosse, WI 54601
Phone: (608) 785-8068
Fax: (608) 785-6700
E-mail: dittman@uwlax.edu
Web: perth.uwlax.edu/ba/

**University of Wisconsin—
Madison***
School of Business
2266 Grainger Hall
975 University Avenue
Madison, WI 53706-1323
Phone: (608) 262-1555
Fax: (608) 265-4192
E-mail: uwmadmba@bus.wisc.edu
Web: wiscinfo.doit.wisc.edu/
bschool/

**University of Wisconsin—
Milwaukee***
School of Business Administration
P.O. Box 742
Milwaukee, WI 53201
Phone: (414) 229-5403
Fax: (414) 229-2372
E-mail: sba@uwm.edu
Web: www.uwm.edu

**University of Wisconsin—
Oshkosh**
College of Business Administration
M.B.A. Program
Oshkosh, WI 54901
Phone: (902) 424-7425,
(800) 633-1430
Fax: (920) 424-7413
E-mail: mba@uwosh.edu
Web: www.uwosh.edu/coba/

**University of Wisconsin—
Whitewater**
College of Business & Economics
Roseman 2015
Whitewater, WI 53190-1797
Phone: (262) 472-1006
Fax: (262) 472-5210
E-mail: gradschl@mail.uww.edu
Web: www.uww.edu/gradstudies/
mba.htm

WYOMING

University of Wyoming
College of Business
P.O. Box 3275
Laramie, WY 82071
Phone: (307) 766-2449
Fax: (307) 766-4028
E-mail: MBA@uwyo.edu
Web: business.uwyo.edu/grad/mba/

Distance Learning M.B.A. Programs

Bellevue University
Phone: (800) 756-7920
E-mail: online-g@scholars.bellevue.edu
Web: www.bellevue.edu

California State University, Dominguez Hills
Phone: (310) 243-2162
E-mail: pputz@soma.csudh.edu
Web: www.csudh.edu/tvmba/

Capella University
Phone: (888) CAPELLA
E-mail: info@capella.com
Web: www.capellauniversity.edu

City University
Phone: (800) 426-5596
E-mail: info@cityu.edu
Web: www.cityu.edu

Colorado State University
Phone: (800) 491-4MBA, ext. 1
E-mail: bizdist@lamar.colostate.edu
Web: www2.biz.colostate.edu/mba/
distance.distance.htm

Florida Gulf Coast University
Phone: (941) 590-2315
E-mail: OAR@fgcu.edu
www.fgcu.edu/DL/

Golden Gate University
Phone: (800) 874-2923; (415) 442-6500
E-mail: biz@ggu.edu
Web: cybercampus.ggu.edu/mba.html

Henley Management College (United Kingdom)
Phone: 44 149 157 1454
E-mail: mba@henleymc.ac.uk
Web: www.henleymc.ac.uk

Heriot-Watt University
Phone: (800) 622-9661
E-mail: info@hwmba.edu
Web: www.hwmba.edu/prog/dlmba.htm

Indiana Wesleyan University
Phone: (800) 234-5327 (in state)
(800) 895-0036 (out of state)
Web: onlinemba.net

ISIM University (International School of Information Management)
Phone: (800) 441-4746
E-mail: admissions@isimu.edu
Web: www.isimu.edu/home/programs/mba.html

Jones International University
Phone: (800) 811-5663
E-mail: info@international.edu
Web: www.jonesinternational.edu

Keller Graduate School of Management
Phone: (630) 571-1818
E-mail: admissions@online.keller.edu
Web: online.keller.edu

Marist College
Phone: (845) 575-3800
E-mail: graduate@Marist.edu
Web: www.marist.edu/graduate/mba/emba.html

Marylhurst University
Phone: (800) 634-9982
www.marylhurst.edu

Morehead State University
Phone: (606) 783-2183
E-mail: k.moore@morehead-st.edu
Web: www.morehead-st.edu

New York Institute of Technology
Phone: (800) 345-NYIT
E-mail: admission@nyit.edyu
Web: www.nyit.edu

Nova Southeastern University
Phone: (800) 672-7223, ext. 5100
E-mail: eMBA@huizenga.nova.edu
Web: emba.sbe.nova.edu

Oklahoma State University
Phone: (405) 744-4048
E-mail: mba-osu@okway.okstate.edu
Web: www.okstate.edu/outreach/distance/

Old Dominion University
Phone: (757) 683-3163
E-mail: TTNET@odu.edu
Web: www.odu.edu/distlrn/

Regis University
Phone: (888) 622-7344
E-mail: mba@mbaregis.com
Web: www.mbaregis.com

Salve Regina University
Phone: (800) 637-0002
E-mail: mitcheld@salve.edu
Web: www.salve.edu/ges_mba.html

Stephens College
Phone: (800) 388-7579
E-mail: sce@wc.stephens.edu
Web: www.stephens.edu
(Note: Short residency required at the beginning and end of the program.)

Suffolk University
Phone: (617) 573-8372
E-mail: cmaher@suffolk.edu
Web: www.suffolkemba.org

Touro University International
Phone: (714) 816-0366
E-mail: info@tourou.edu
Web: www.tourouniversity.edu

University of Baltimore
Phone: (410) 837-4953
E-mail: rfrederick@ubmail.ubalt.edu
Web: www.ubonline.edu/webmbahome.nsf

University of Colorado—Colorado Springs
Phone: (800) 777-MIND
E-mail: busadvsr@mail.uccs.edu
Web: www.uccs.edu/~collbus/new/jecmain.htm

University of Maryland University College
Phone: (800) 283-6832
E-mail: gradschool@info.umuc.edu
Web: www.umuc.edu/mba/

University of Phoenix Online
Phone: (800) 747-4742
E-mail: online@apollo.uophx.edu
Web: www.phoenix.edu

University of Wisconsin—Whitewater
Phone: (414) 472-1945
E-mail: gradbus@uwwvax.uww.edu
Web: www.uww.edu/business/onlinemba/

West Texas A&M University
Phone: (806) 651-7909
E-mail: DEC@wtamu.edu
Web: wtonline.wtamu.edu/degree/mba.html
(Note: Some proctored tests.)

Worcester Polytechnic Institute
Phone: (508) 831-5220
E-mail: adln@wpi.edu
Web: www.wpi.edu/Academics/ADLN/

NOTES

NOTES

NOTES

NOTES

How Did We Do? Grade Us.

Thank you for choosing a Kaplan book. Your comments and suggestions are very useful to us. Please answer the following questions to assist us in our continued development of high-quality resources to meet your needs.

The title of the Kaplan book I read was: _____

My name is: _____

My address is: _____

_____

My e-mail address is: _____

What overall grade would you give this book?   Ⓐ   Ⓑ   Ⓒ   Ⓓ   Ⓕ

How relevant was the information to your goals?   Ⓐ   Ⓑ   Ⓒ   Ⓓ   Ⓕ

How comprehensive was the information in this book?   Ⓐ   Ⓑ   Ⓒ   Ⓓ   Ⓕ

How accurate was the information in this book?   Ⓐ   Ⓑ   Ⓒ   Ⓓ   Ⓕ

How easy was the book to use?   Ⓐ   Ⓑ   Ⓒ   Ⓓ   Ⓕ

How appealing was the book's design?   Ⓐ   Ⓑ   Ⓒ   Ⓓ   Ⓕ

What were the book's strong points? _____

How could this book be improved? _____

Is there anything that we left out that you wanted to know more about?

Would you recommend this book to others?   ☐ YES   ☐ NO

Other comments: _____

_____

_____

Do we have permission to quote you?   ☐ YES   ☐ NO

Thank you for your help.
Please tear out this page and mail it to:

Managing Editor
Kaplan, Inc.
888 Seventh Avenue
New York, NY 10106

KAPLAN®

Thanks!

Paying for graduate school just got easier...

The Kaplan/American Express Educational Loan Information Program.

Get free information on the financial aid process before you apply.

When you request your student loan applications through Kaplan/American Express, we'll send you our free Financial Aid Handbook. With the Kaplan/American Express Student Loan Information Program, you'll have access to some of the least expensive educational loans available.

- The Federal Stafford Loan—Eligible students may borrow up to $18,500 each year toward the cost of education.

- A Private Loan—If the federal Stafford Loan does not fully meet educational financing needs, additional funds may be available under a private loan program.

Make the most of your financial aid opportunities. Contact us today!

Educational
Loans

1-888-KAP-LOAN

*Kaplan is not a lender and does not participate in the determination of loan eligibility.
Telephone inquiries to 1-888-KAP-LOAN will be answered by a representative of a provider of federal and certain private educational loans.

About

KAPLAN

K aplan, Inc. is one of the nation's leading providers of education and career services. Kaplan is a wholly owned subsidiary of The Washington Post Company.

KAPLAN TEST PREPARATION & ADMISSIONS

Kaplan's nationally recognized test prep courses cover more than 20 standardized tests, including secondary school, college and graduate school entrance exams, as well as foreign language and professional licensing exams. In addition, Kaplan offers a college admissions course, private tutoring, and a variety of free information and services for students applying to college and graduate programs. Kaplan also provides information and guidance on the financial aid process. Students can enroll in online test prep courses and admissions consulting services at www.kaptest.com.

Kaplan K12 Learning Services partners with schools, universities, and teachers to help students succeed, providing customized assessment, education, and professional development programs.

SCORE! EDUCATIONAL CENTERS

SCORE! after-school learning centers help K–10 students build confidence along with academic skills in a motivating, sports-oriented environment.

SCORE! Prep provides in-home, one-on-one tutoring for high school academic subjects and standardized tests.

eSCORE.com is the first educational services Web site to offer parents and kids newborn to age 18 personalized child development and educational resources online.

KAPLANCOLLEGE.COM

KaplanCollege.com, Kaplan's distance learning platform, offers an array of online educational programs for working professionals who want to advance their careers. Learners will find nearly 500 professional development, continuing education, certification, and degree courses and programs in Nursing, Education, Criminal Justice, Real Estate, Legal Professions, Law, Management, General Business, and Computing/Information Technology.

KAPLAN PUBLISHING

Kaplan Publishing produces retail books and software. Kaplan Books, published by Simon & Schuster, include titles in test preparation, admissions, education, career development, and life skills; Kaplan and Newsweek jointly publish guides on getting into college, finding the right career, and helping children succeed in school.

KAPLAN PROFESSIONAL

Kaplan Professional provides assessment, training, and certification services for corporate clients and individuals seeking to advance their careers. Member units include:

- Dearborn, a leading supplier of licensing training and continuing education for securities, real estate, and insurance professionals

- Perfect Access/CRN, which delivers software education and consultation for law firms and businesses

- Kaplan Professional Call Center Services, a total provider of services for the call center industry

- Self Test Software, a world leader in exam simulation software and preparation for technical certifications

- Schweser's Study Program/AIAF, which provides preparation services for the CFA examination

KAPLAN INTERNATIONAL PROGRAMS

Kaplan assists international students and professionals in the United States through a series of intensive English language and test preparation programs. These programs are offered at campus-based centers across the United States. Specialized services include housing, placement at top American universities, fellowship management, academic monitoring and reporting, and financial administration.

COMMUNITY OUTREACH

Kaplan provides educational career resources to thousands of financially disadvantaged students annually, working closely with educational institutions, not-for-profit groups, government agencies and grass roots organizations on a variety of national and local support programs. These programs help students and professionals from a variety of backgrounds achieve their educational and career goals.

BRASSRING

BrassRing Inc., the premier business-to-business hiring management and recruitment services company, offers employers a vertically integrated suite of online and offline solutions. BrassRing, created in September 1999, combined Kaplan Career Services, Terra-Starr, Crimson & Brown Associates, thepavement.com, and HireSystems. In March 2000, BrassRing acquired Career Service Inc./Westech. Kaplan is a shareholder in BrassRing, along with Tribune Company, Central Newspapers, and Accel Partners.

Want more information about our services, products, or the nearest Kaplan center?

 Call our nationwide toll-free numbers:

1-800-KAP-TEST for information on our courses, private tutoring and admissions consulting
1-800-KAP-ITEM for information on our books and software

 Connect with us in cyberspace:

On the World Wide Web, go to:
1. www.kaplan.com
2. www.kaptest.com
3. www.eSCORE.com
4. www.dearborn.com
5. www.BrassRing.com
6. www.concordlawschool.com
7. www.KaplanCollege.com
Via e-mail: info@kaplan.com

 Write to:

 Kaplan, Inc.
888 Seventh Avenue
New York, NY 10106